D0867105

The American Dream

The American *Dream*

A Cultural History

Lawrence R. Samuel

SYRACUSE UNIVERSITY PRESS

∞ The paper used in this publication meets the minimum requirements of the American National Standard for Information Sciences—Permanence of Paper for Printed Library Materials, ANSI Z39.48-1992.

For a listing of books published and distributed by Syracuse University Press, visit our website at SyracuseUniversityPress.syr.edu.

ISBN (cloth): 978-0-8156-1007-6

Library of Congress Cataloging-in-Publication Data
Samuel, Lawrence R.
    The American dream : a cultural history / Lawrence R. Samuel. — 1st ed.
        p. cm.
    Includes bibliographical references and index.
    ISBN 978-0-8156-1007-6 (cloth : alk. paper) 1. National characteristics, American.   2. United States—Civilization—1945–   3. Popular culture—United States—History.   4. American Dream. I. Title.
    E169.12.S235 2012
    973—dc23   2012022220

Manufactured in the United States of America

To Freya, my American Dream

Somewhere, over the rainbow, skies are blue.
And the Dreams that we dare to dream really do come true.
—E. Y. Harburg

Lawrence R. Samuel is the founder of Culture Planning LLC, a Miami- and New York–based resource offering cultural insight to Fortune 500 organizations. He is the author of a number of books, including *The End of the Innocence: The 1964–1965 New York World's Fair* (Syracuse University Press, 2007), *Future: A Recent History* (2009), *Rich: The Rise and Fall of American Wealth Culture* (2009), *Freud on Madison Avenue: Motivation Research and Subliminal Advertising in America* (2010), and *Supernatural America: A Cultural History* (2011).

Contents

The American Dream

Introduction

So then, to every man his chance . . . his shining golden opportunity
. . . to live, to work, to be himself. And to become whatever thing his
manhood and his vision can combine to make him. This, seeker, is
the promise of America.
—Thomas Wolfe, *You Can't Go Home Again*

WHAT DOES IT MEAN TO YOU? I've been asking anyone and everyone recently, joining a long line of others who have tried to get a better understanding of the American Dream. The usual answers—financial stability or, more specifically, making enough money to be able to retire (still often one million dollars, despite inflation), "the good life" (usually a nice house in the suburbs with all the consumer trappings), to work for oneself, to have (at least) fifteen minutes of fame, the "pursuit of happiness," or, once in a while, the Statue of Liberty—come back, an interesting but somewhat frustrating exercise, as all the others found in their own formal or informal surveys. Besides reaching no real consensus, the responses do not come close to capturing the undeniable power of the American Dream, making it seem more like a wish list than what I believe to be is the guiding mythology of the most powerful civilization in history. The problem, of course, is that it does not exist. The American Dream's not being real, however, ultimately turns out to be the most significant finding about it; the fact that many of us have assumed it to be entirely real makes the story even more compelling.

The American Dream tells this story, in the process shedding light on virtually every major dimension of American culture, past, present, and future. Surprisingly, no book has yet to trace the narrative of the American Dream as expressed through popular culture since the phrase was coined in 1931. My main goal is to fill that Grand Canyon–size chasm in our literary landscape. There is no better way to understand America than by understanding the cultural history of the American Dream, I argue, a proposition that is vividly demonstrated throughout this book. Unlike the two fine intellectual histories of the American Dream, Jim Cullen's 2003 *The American Dream: A Short History of an Idea That Shaped a Nation* and Cal Jillson's *Pursuing the American Dream: Opportunity and Exclusion over Four Centuries* of the following year, this book is intended for both general readers and scholars interested in a research-intensive yet accessible approach to the subject. Anyone interested in American history will learn a lot by reading *The American Dream*, I firmly believe, the book serving as nothing less than a field guide to the evolution of our national identity over the past eighty years.

Much of the appeal of the subject naturally has to do with how central the Dream has been and continues to be to the American idea and experience. Rather than just a powerful philosophy or ideology, the American Dream (the *D* is sometimes capitalized, sometimes not, my preference the former) is thoroughly woven into the fabric of everyday life. It plays a vital, active role in who we are, what we do, and why we do it. No other idea or mythology—even religion, I believe—has as much influence on our individual and collective lives, with the Dream one of the precious few things in this country that we all share. You name it—economics, politics, law, work, business, education—and the American Dream is there, the nation at some level a marketplace of competing interpretations and visions of what it means and should mean. (A search of *American Dream* on Google in June 2012 turned up more than sixty-seven million hits, a crude but still impressive measure of its ubiquity.) Current debates on health insurance and Social Security, the role of government, and the personal loss that comes with a home foreclosure are certainly steeped in the dynamics of the Dream, proof of its amazing resiliency and enduring relevance. This is nothing new, of course, with the American Dream serving as the backbone of the great social movements of the twentieth century, including the New Deal and the Great Society. Even the counterculture and feminist and civil rights movements were much about the American Dream, one could reasonably argue, its grounding in the ideal of equal opportunity essentially guaranteeing it will play an important role in any major economic, political, or social conversation. As the world becomes increasingly flat and the nation becomes increasingly multicultural, the Dream will play an even more important role, I'm convinced, a key common denominator and unifying force.

While the "American Dream" did not exist until 1931, the roots of the phrase go back centuries, its origins to be found well before the nation was a nation. (Some trace its core ideas to the birth of civilization, in fact.) Other historians, including Cullen and Jillson, trace its evolution to the religious and political shackles of the Old World. The basic idea of the Dream arrived on our shores in the seventeenth century and, a century or so later, was formally articulated in the Declaration of Independence and Constitution.[1] That our station in life is earned rather than inherited is one of the founding principles of the American Dream, it is fair to say, and that we are a meritocracy versus an aristocracy something in which we have taken special pride. Most if not all of the key words and concepts we associate with who we are as a people (such as opportunistic, self-reliant, pragmatic, resourceful, aspirational, optimistic, entrepreneurial, inventive) are all present in the orbit of the American Dream. Its expansive and progressive undercurrent is rooted in our peripatetic orientation and frontier experience. (One of today's more popular expressions of the Dream, the recreational vehicle, or RV, is not all that different from one of the past, the covered wagon, if you think about it.) The desire to own a piece of land, to have a literal stake in the nation, is there, of course, as is our mandate to not be tread upon or fenced in (despite the iconic symbol of the white picket fence). The enduring desire to reinvent ourselves, to be whomever we want to be, is there as well, our famous restlessness very much part of the equation.

Although James Truslow Adams, a popular and populist historian (the David McCullough or Ken Burns of his day, it has been said), is credited with first using the phrase, he obviously borrowed ideas from a long line of great thinkers. Tocqueville, Whitman, Emerson, and Thoreau all addressed aspects of the Dream, notably, as did lesser-known but unquestionably brilliant minds such as James Bryce and James Muirhead. Historical figures, including Jefferson, Franklin, and Lincoln, famously espoused elements of the American Dream, while Dale Carnegie, Norman Vincent Peale, and, of course, Horatio Alger have served as some of its loudest spokespeople. A myriad of illustrious characters, including Babe Ruth, Elvis Presley, Frank Sinatra, Irving Berlin, Sam Walton, Ray Kroc, Mickey Mantle, the Jackson Five, Henry Ford, Walt Disney, Arnold Schwarzenegger, Hugh Hefner, Oprah Winfrey, Donald Trump, and Barack Obama have been considered the very embodiments of it (as has everyone's rich uncle who came over to this country with two dollars in his pocket). Iconic works ranging from *Death of a Salesman* to *The Sopranos* (not to mention the entire oeuvres of Frank Capra and Norman Rockwell) are deemed definitive manifestos of the mythology. The American Dream is, if it is not already clear, as American as Mom, apple pie, and Chevrolet, the purest, boldest expression of who we are as a people.

Despite being a constant presence, the American Dream has hardly been a straight line, this book clearly shows, its trajectory a roller-coaster ride of ups and downs and twists and turns. Frequently given its last rites, the Dream has always managed to bounce back to life, each miraculous recovery both shaping and reflecting a renewal of the American spirit. Suffering crisis after crisis (the most recent being the subprime-mortgage mess and ensuing financial meltdown), the mythology has proved its resiliency over and over, capable of surviving any traumatic event by what might be called adaptive behavior. The Dream has continually morphed yet somehow also remained much the same, this paradox a result of its profound ambiguity. Because it is a product of our collective imagination, it could mean whatever we want or need it to mean, after all, something as ethereal as the concept of "independence" or as material as a new Cadillac (or, these days, a good health insurance plan). Politically, the Dream has been equally likely to be claimed as the province of the Left and the Right (something that makes perfect sense given its reliance on both republican and democratic principles). The Dream is both radical and conservative, spiritual and secular, home to red state and blue state, and accommodating of virtually any preconception or agenda. Mutable and amorphous, the American Dream is the Zelig of mythologies, able to transform itself to fit virtually any situation or cause.

The breadth and scope of the American Dream are truly astounding, its history plainly reveals. Many of the familiar tropes of the American idea and experience—continually rising expectations (that tomorrow will be better than today), the entrepreneurial spirit, the sacredness of home, the seductiveness of wealth, the pressure to succeed, our perverse fascination with "hope" and "change," and the belief that "anything is possible"—are all embedded in the Dream. In her *Facing Up to the American Dream*, Jennifer L. Hochschild argues that success, or at least the opportunity to realize it, represents the core of the American Dream. The Dream is "the promise that all Americans have a reasonable chance to achieve success as they define it—material or otherwise—through their own efforts, and to attain virtue and fulfillment through success," she suggests, a brilliantly constructed ideology but one that is deeply flawed when put into actual practice. The American Dream can also be seen as a dominant theme in our civil religion or, perhaps, our civil religion itself. Any nation's civil religion "has its own seriousness and integrity and requires the same care in understanding that any other religion does," Robert Bellah states, something that certainly applies to the American Dream.[2]

Many other perfectly valid interpretations of the American Dream can be found in circulation, should one look for them. "The American Dream is a dream of consumption," Lee Artz and Bren Ortega Murphy flatly put it in their *Cultural Hegemony in the United States*, adding that the mythology operated as a powerful device of cultural hegemony. "The myth and its reality are closely tied to the ability of capitalism to deliver the goods, and the myth is defended by an ideology of individual merit that gently obscures collective subordinate conditions and experience," they hold. A plethora of alternative readings exist, I quickly discovered in my informal survey. The impetus for personal transformation, the fantasy of a perfect life, the desire to be someone one is not, the quest to achieve something just beyond reach, a society without poverty or crime, a good education for all, and our denial of class and conviction that we are "born equal" are only some of them. The Dream is, however, more coherent and cohesive than one might think, its popular history shows. Its various incarnations—equal opportunity, limitless possibilities, a better and happier future, a home of one's own, going from "rags to riches," to be one's own boss, to achieve more than one's parents—are really just variations on a theme, its progressive, utopian character at the heart of it all. For me, it is the devout belief that tomorrow can and will be better than today that best defines the American Dream and distinguishes it from other dimensions of public life such as the American Way of Life. "No phrase captures the distinctive character and promise of American life better than the phrase 'the American Dream,'" declares Jillson, this idea accounting for our legitimate claim of exceptionalism.[3]

Although the idea of perpetual progress (and, presumably, happiness) from one generation to another gives it a good run for its money, home ownership has to be the theme that most clearly symbolized the American Dream over the decades. "No American Dream has broader appeal, and no American Dream has been quite so widely realized," Cullen agrees, most of us determined to obtain a place we can call our own.[4] The possibility for anyone to own property was a big part of our breaking of the shackles of the Old World, of course, the Jeffersonian ideal of a house on a private piece of land one of our most cherished and iconic images. It was thus fitting and natural that the home became the bedrock of the Dream and the foundation for the consumerist lifestyle that revolves around it. That the government essentially subsidized the American Dream by making the interest on mortgage payments tax deductible further cemented the single-family home as something to strive for, lest an individual not be considered a full-fledged citizen. (For many, renting or even owning a co-op or condominium still affords one just secondary status in this country.) Strong passions consistently arose during those periods when it became difficult for the working class and even middle class to buy a home (or afford to keep one), the sentiment being that all Americans should have access to this major component of the Dream. The emotional maelstrom that surrounded the recent foreclosure fiasco was steeped in this idea, the seizing of a family's house by a bank a flagrant violation of our reverence of home ownership.

It is within the area of class, however, that the American Dream has proved to be most contentious, its history shows. Part and parcel of the framework of class is the notion of upward mobility, the idea that one can, through dedication and with a can-do spirit, climb the ladder of success and reach a higher social and economic position. For many in both the working class and the middle class, upward mobility has served as the heart and soul of the American Dream, the prospect of "betterment" and to "improve one's lot" for oneself and one's children much of what this country is all about. "Work hard, save a little, send the kids to college so they can do better than you did, and retire happily to a warmer climate" has been the script we have all been handed, with any major deviation from that script a cause for concern if not an outright assault to our national creed. Although in recent years study after study have shown upward mobility to be even a greater myth than the Dream itself, most Americans refuse to believe such a thing, the concept of class fluidity so ingrained in our national ethos. This feeling of entitlement, that if one plays by the rules one will in time reap his or her just rewards, had led many an American astray, this book makes clear, our mythology mistaken for a promise. The loss of faith in both their country and themselves that millions have no doubt experienced is the saddest part of the American Dream, every bit as tragic as the heroic stories of success that we love to celebrate. Besides having a happy ending, the latter remind us that we are a land of opportunity offering all citizens an even playing field and, on a grander level, that we are a chosen people assigned a unique and special purpose.

Not surprisingly, given its mythological power, the American Dream has been employed in a variety of ways by a variety of individuals and institutions. Because it is steeped in our special mission of democracy and experiment in pluralism, the Dream has often been used to challenge our idealistic principles, especially those ideals concerning the highly charged issues of immigration and race. (Gender and religion too have occasionally bumped into it over the years.) Well aware of the Dream's power, the government has employed it as a tool of propaganda, that is, a powerful ideological weapon of persuasion both here and abroad. The American Dream is, after all, the perfect brand, explaining in large part why the United States has retained such a popular image despite there being many flaws in the product itself. (The fact that the Dream is backed up by some important truths—studies show we work the longest, switch jobs the most, and will relocate for a better opportunity at the drop of a hat—makes our "unique selling proposition" that much more compelling.) As the foundation of our free-enterprise system, the American Dream has served as a convenient counterpoint to communism, the famous "Kitchen Debate" between Vice President Nixon and Soviet Premier Khrushchev in 1959 a good example of it in action. As well, critics of all persuasions have viewed the relative health of the Dream as a key social barometer, a way to determine if the country is moving forward or backward.

Because it is more about the journey than the destination, the getting there always more exciting than the arrival, the American Dream has not surprisingly been a staple within popular and consumer culture. The movies have shared an intimate relationship with the Dream, of course, the mythology used as a primary tool in Hollywood screenwriters' tool kit. "American movies presented American myths and American dreams," writes Robert Sklar in his *Movie-Made America*, believing that filmmakers like Walt Disney and Frank Capra served as important cultural mythmakers. The lyrics to the song "When You Wish upon a Star" from Disney's 1940 adaptation of *Pinocchio* ("If your heart is in your dream, no request is too extreme / When you wish upon a star, as dreamers do") were a prime example of how filmmakers integrated elements of the American Dream into story lines. The fact that the movies not only were what Sklar considers "the most popular and influential medium of culture in the United States" but also developed from the "bottom up" made them that much more of a powerful force in seeding the ideology of the American Dream.[5] Television too (and radio before it) has been a loud voice of the Dream, with every sitcom family from *The Goldbergs* to *The Jeffersons* to *The Simpsons* trying to climb the ladder of success while facing the trials and tribulations of modern life.

It hardly needs to be said that advertising is laden with the Dream, appropriated by corporate America as a principal marketing strategy. Political speechwriters have tapped the American Dream just as often and just as effectively, a hot button to be pushed in good times and in bad, much like that other ace in the hole, the proverbial "chicken in every pot." Many leisure activities such as board games (particularly Monopoly, which was invented just two years after the phrase, not coincidentally) have traded on its inherent competitiveness, and sports are often portrayed as metaphors of and for the Dream. As "America's game," baseball is the American Dream incarnate, its own mythic qualities (neatly exploited in the films *The Natural* and *Field of Dreams*) epic in scope. From Jay Gatsby to Jay-Z, the landscape of American popular culture has been strewn with fragments of the Dream, the desire to beat the odds by making full use of our God-given talents perhaps our most compelling story.

The American Dream has hardly been just an everything-is-coming-up-roses-and-daffodils fantasy there to cheer us on and up, however, having a dark side just as powerful as its positive side. For each and every American Dream, there is an American nightmare, this evil twin always lurking in the shadows when the country is going through interesting times, as the Chinese curse goes. In fact, the potential of an American nightmare was frequently conjured up since the very beginnings of the Dream, not too surprising given that the phrase was conceived in the darkest days of the Depression. Creative types often used the American Dream as sardonic fodder, casting it as the banal domain of the petty bourgeoisie and what was wrong with this country in general. It is easy to interpret the Dream as a distinctly negative concept, in fact. What is wrong with today and with what we already have? Why do we have to spend inordinate amounts of time and energy thinking about or trying to make real some imaginary future? Where does this chronic dissatisfaction come from, this belief that the grass is always greener somewhere else? Are we just a nation of malcontents or, maybe worse, Walter Mittys living in make-believe worlds of our own construction? The American Dream is certainly out of synch with today's present-focused, live-in-the-now therapeutic approach and contrary to pretty much everything to be found in au courant Buddhism, begging the question of if it is time we adopt a much different kind of guiding mythology.

Expectedly, the evolution of the American Dream has been heavily influenced by the rise of the self over these past eighty years. The shift from civic and communitarian interests to personal and private ones has swung the mythology toward individual concerns. It was during the

Reagan years that the Dream, already having strayed from Adams's original vision, swerved further away from "we" to "me," a number of social critics have reasonably suggested. "This latest recalibration saw the American Dream get decoupled from any concept of the common good . . . and, more portentously, from the concepts of working hard and managing one's expectations," wrote David Kamp for *Vanity Fair* in 2009, with escalating debt (both national and individual) through the 1980s a sign that our desires were exceeding our resources. Over the next couple of decades, Americans' dissatisfaction with what they had would continue to grow, even though life was typically better for them by any measure. By the early 2000s, "the American Dream was now almost by definition unattainable, a moving target that eluded people's grasp," Kamp argued, thinking that, for the average American, "nothing was ever enough."[6]

In his *The Progress Paradox: How Life Gets Better While People Feel Worse*, Gregg Easterbrook says much the same thing, the common pursuit to do better than the Joneses rather than just keep up with them ultimately not a winnable game. After all, one's position in life is relative, not absolute, as Alain de Botton eloquently discusses in his book *Status Anxiety*, meaning a comparative, competitive mind-set is bound to lead to at least some level of unhappiness. Having an all (great success) or nothing (great failure) perspective is a terrible attitude toward life, the simple truth that it is and should be something in between. Similarly, having (too) great expectations, driven in part by our cult of celebrity, I believe, is a very disturbing trend, something not boding well for the future of America and the rest of the world. We have lost sight of the things that really matter, this narcissistic expression of the American Dream suggests, our values clearly out of whack. "The self-made man, archetypical embodiment of the American dream," wrote Christopher Lasch in his classic *The Culture of Narcissism*, "owed his advancement to habits of industry, sobriety, moderation, self-discipline, and avoidance of debt." Over time, however, the Dream's foundation in the Protestant work ethic and self-improvement eroded and was replaced by an ethic of self-preservation, social survival, and individualism. Acclaim, admiration, envy, and public recognition had become the markers that conveyed realization of one's American Dream, Lasch astutely observed way back in 1978, substance deemed less important than being seen as having "made it."[7] Finally, faith in perpetual upward mobility is surely misguided and unsustainable, wishful thinking that shows a complete disregard for the actual cycles of history.[8]

The American Dream tells its story chronologically, showing that there have been six major eras of the mythology since the phrase was coined in 1931. The book relies primarily on period magazines and newspapers as its source material and secondarily on previous books written about aspects of the topic, as I firmly believe that journalists serving on the front lines of the scene represent our most valuable resource to recover unfiltered stories of the Dream. From these hundreds of journalists' reports from the field, many of them obscure and largely forgotten but important firsthand accounts, we really do get the first draft of history. In short, using popular sources is the best way to tell a story so ingrained in the popular imagination. The first chapter, "The Epic of America," discusses the beginnings of the Dream during the Depression and war years when it ironically faced its biggest threats. Chapter 2, "The Status Seekers," takes readers through the American Dream of the postwar years, a period in which our core mythology grew in both volume and importance. The third chapter, "The Anti-Paradise," tracks the Dream through the counterculture years of the late 1960s and 1970s, when the nation's idealistic faith in itself was put to the greatest test since the phrase was coined. Chapter 4, "Born in the USA," explores the American Dream of the 1980s, when a revival of red-white-and-blue patriotism clashed with the realities of a widening divide between the haves and have-nots. Chapter 5, "The Anxious Society," examines the Dream of the 1990s, when fin de siècle prosperity and abundance should have made the mythology real for many but largely did not. The final chapter, "American Idol," follows the American Dream from 2000 up to today, showing that its power and relevance remain as strong as ever in the twenty-first century. All signs are that the Dream will continue to be a compelling part of the cultural landscape, I conclude, our core mythology to serve as a central guiding force for both Americans and others around the world in the years ahead.

The Epic of America

What is the next chapter in the epic of America? What . . . is the
prospect for the fulfillment of the American dream?

— James Truslow Adams, 1933

ANYONE STOPPING BY ROBERT MCLAUGHLIN'S home at 1038 West
Forty-Ninth Street in Los Angeles around Christmastime in the late 1930s
would no doubt be struck by what the *Los Angeles Times* called an "American Dream Village." Each year, McLaughlin would take the model village, which he called "Sunnyville," out of its box, spreading Yuletide cheer
with its depiction of what the newspaper considered a "typical quaint
dream hamlet of the American scene." The village, which McLaughlin
and his brother-in-law had made themselves with just a hacksaw and pen-
knife, included a church (with a steeple bell that rang), a schoolhouse
(with logs outside as firewood), and a depot with an adjoining coal chute
and water tank. Miniature people gathered at the general store, fed tiny
animals on a little farm, and sang carols in front of neighbors' log cab-
ins. Snow (bleached cornflakes) covered the scene, and if you looked up
you could see Santa Claus approaching from the sky over a gold mine in
the hills that surrounded the town. McLaughlin would occasionally add
pieces to the village, 1938's addition being a new service station on the
edge of town.[1]

Battered by the Depression and worried about events overseas, it was
not surprising that citizens like Robert McLaughlin literally built their
own American Dream from scratch. "Sunnyville" had none of the myriad
of social and economic problems of Los Angeles or any other big American

city, its miniature citizens enjoying the kind of happiness, prosperity, and tolerance that were associated with the Dream. The 1930s and early 1940s were years in which many longed for the sort of life that Sunnyville offered, a mythology articulated most compellingly as "the American Dream."

Although the Dream had dwelled in the minds of many Americans even before the nation was a nation, it was then that the actual phrase was coined, not at all a coincidence. The Depression and war years would prove to be a fruitful period for the American Dream as the country struggled to retain a sense of identity amid economic, social, and political turmoil. The Dream would not only survive these tough times but grow stronger, affirming our faith in our experiment in democracy and our special place as the proverbial "city on a hill."

A Better, Deeper, Richer Life

That the term "American Dream" was created in the darkest days of the Great Depression was all the more interesting given that many feared it no longer existed. In his 1931 book *The Epic of America* and in articles published in the *New York Times* the following few years, James Truslow Adams defined what he meant by the American Dream, an idea whose essence has remained largely consistent these past eighty years:

> The dream is a vision of a better, deeper, richer life for every individual, regardless of the position in society which he or she may occupy by the accident of birth. It has been a dream of a chance to rise in the economic scale, but quite as much, or more than that, of a chance to develop our capacities to the full, unhampered by unjust restrictions of caste or custom. With this has gone the hope of bettering the physical conditions of living, of lessening the toil and anxieties of daily life.[2]

However, in the late 1920s, much like previous periods of overexpansion and out-of-control speculation, Adams argued, the nation had lost its way, its guiding philosophy forgotten in the wild pursuit of money and the things it could buy. "The dream of a richer, better, fuller human life for all citizens instead of for a small class had been turned by our leaders and ourselves into a statistical table of standard of living," he wrote, the market crash and subsequent depression a natural result (and something

Adams had predicted). Now, the nation having survived its "mental disorder," Adams was hopeful that its vision would be restored. "Like the passing of the shadow in an eclipse, the light of reason appears to be steadily extending over the horizon," he believed, the American Dream beginning to reemerge.[3]

Adams, modestly describing himself as a "student of history and surveyor of the American scene" (he was perhaps the most popular historian of his day), was well aware that his dream was much more than just a noble idea. "That dream is not only our most precious national possession but our only unique contribution to the civilization of the world," he wrote after spending a few months abroad in 1933, noting that many other societies past and present matched or surpassed the United States in wealth, power, discoveries, inventions, science, crafts, and the arts. But "the American dream has been unique in the social annals of mankind," he observed, its "dynamic belief" the thing that separated it from the rest of the pack. More so than other fundamental ideals—equality before the law and every citizen's right to vote and to an education, notably—it was Americans' "opportunity of rising to full stature and living the fullest possible life" that was truly special. Importantly, the American Dream in its original incarnation was thus not about getting rich, owning a piece of property, working for oneself, or some other later interpretation but, in Adams's words, the "inherent right to be restricted by no barriers" outside those of one's own construction. That the dream was intangible made it all the more intriguing to Adams, despite the inescapable fact that it had yet to be fully realized (especially among women and people of color, most obviously).[4]

Adams's best-selling book, with its thesis that we are and always have been a nation of dreamers, quickly captured people's attention. H. S. Commager of *Books* considered it "a courageous attempt to put the quintessence of American experience and character into brief compass," seconded by Karl Schriftglesser of the *Boston Transcript*, who called it "a keen analysis of the American mind."[5] Although some critics thought Adams had perhaps overreached in his ambitious thesis, most felt he had deftly translated some very complex concepts into simple and understandable terms. "In a mass of current historical writing, much of which is ephemeral or discursive, here is a book vibrant with ideas that have a meaning for every reflective American," wrote Allen Sinclair Will in his review for the *New York Times,* thinking Adams's "audacious attempt" of capturing the epic of America had matched or perhaps even bettered Walt Whitman's. Rather than defining the epic as a heroic tale of a people with superior spirit and morality—a standard trope of many historians up to that point—Adams suggested that Americans had often taken the path of least resistance when times got tough, quite an assertion. Our greatest achievement was not that we were a shining beacon for all the world to see but that each generation had saved the American Dream from forces that threatened to destroy it, this the genuine epic of the nation. "Possibly the greatest of these struggles lies just ahead of us," Adams proposed in the book, a prophecy that would turn out to be true.[6]

Though not the title of his book as he wanted it to be (his publisher unwisely nixed the idea), Adams's "American dream" was soon appropriated by politicians, scholars, writers, artists, religious leaders, and many others, both in the States and abroad, to describe the nation's state of affairs. It "entered the public domain . . . and took on a life of its own," Anthony Brandt reflected on the fiftieth anniversary of the publishing of *The Epic of America,* noting that the governor of Massachusetts was quick to use it in a speech made in front of the monument on Bunker Hill. The governor, Joseph B. Ely, tweaked the meaning of the phrase to match the particular occasion, something that would to this day become more the rule than the exception. (Adams himself provided at least three slightly different definitions of the Dream in his book, and would continue to modify the phrase in his future writings.) As soon as the book's ink was dry, "the boundaries of the phrase were becoming increasingly vague, a development to be expected from the vagueness implicit in the very notion of a 'dream,' of a dimly perceived vision of possible futures," Brandt suggested. In an essay published a few years later, for example, sociologist Robert K. Merton took the phrase to mean success, especially in the financial sense, further arguing that prosperity was Americans' primary goal. But Merton himself recognized the infinite possibilities of the American Dream ("there is no final stopping point," he wrote), this notion perhaps its most salient aspect. "The Dream stretches endlessly and forever toward the horizon," Brandt agreed, "the lure of 'more' and 'better' pulling us on, no matter what we accomplish, individually or collectively."[7]

Adams's "American dream" continued to spread through intellectual, artistic, and political communities, quickly becoming shorthand for the nation's guiding mythology. Before an audience in Berlin, Germany, in November 1932, for example, George Norlin, president of the University of Colorado, gave a lecture whose theme was the American dream, the speech clearly inspired by (but not credited to) Adams. The Dream was about "self reliance, self respect, neighborly cooperation and [a] vision of a better and richer life, not for a privileged class, but for all," Norlin told colleagues at the University of Berlin, the fact that he gave the address in German making it all the more interesting. For Norlin, and soon many others, the American Dream was the best to way to describe our national character, especially for audiences who did not quite understand or were critical of our way of life. "Striking features, such as the skyscraper, the multimillionaire, Fordism, Hollywood, prohibition, Al Capone and the like, impinge themselves upon the eye and obscure the less picturesque and the more normal aspects of the American landscape," he told Berliners, but the truth was a lot more complicated. The United States was much more than "das Dollarland," as Germans sometimes called it, a familiarity with the aspirations, principles, and practices that constituted the American Dream very useful in moving beyond such gross generalizations.[8]

Distinguished European visitors to this country likewise used the new phrase as the centerpiece of their own lectures, the rhetorical power of the American Dream steadily gaining strength as it became a recognizable feature of public discourse. Teaching a few courses at Columbia University in the summer of 1933, Florian Znaniecki, a professor of sociology at the University of Posen in Poland, found the phrase handy to warn of a rising threat of economic tyranny in the United States. "We are really going backward from the 'American dream' with the best intentions," he said, the current trend toward central planning and control a worrisome one. "The supreme value of mankind is the human individual, and the human individual realizes himself only in free and creative cooperation with others," Znaniecki told students and guests, the direction of this country not conducive "to realize what James Truslow Adams called the 'American dream.'"[9]

For George O'Neil, a poet and novelist from Kansas, the American Dream was not just in danger but perhaps already kaput. Unlike Adams, who had unfortunately been talked out of using "American Dream" as the title of his book, O'Neil seized the chance to use the phrase as the name for his 1933 play (his first to be produced) to make his message that much clearer. The Broadway play's three acts chronicled three periods in the history of a New England family, their experience serving as a metaphor for the gradual loss of the nation's mythic idealism. Whereas the Daniel Pingree of 1650 in the first act of the play refuses to marry the governor's daughter to become wealthy and the Daniel Pingree of 1849 in the second act chooses to go west in search of freedom and fortune rather than work at the local factory, the Daniel Pingree of 1933 in the final act is merely an intellectual rebel, writing revolutionary pamphlets while living in comfortable affluence. (The contemporary Pingree, held in contempt even by the Communists he supports, shoots himself at the end of the play, as if O'Neil's point was not already as plain as day.) Although O'Neil's play was panned by some critics ("a series of ill-digested assertions," thought Brooks Atkinson of the *New York Times*), *American Dream* brought the phrase further into public discourse and probably made many wonder if modernity had indeed extinguished the Dream. "It presents a fighting idea," Atkinson admitted, concluding that the play "lingers in the mind because of the essential truth of Mr. O'Neil's thesis." Had the social problems of the day—greed, vulgarity, corruption, materialism, and a general feeling of emptiness—made American independence, rebellion, and risk taking things of the past?[10]

The Reverend Halford Luccock, a professor at Yale's Divinity School, certainly thought so. Like Adams, Luccock believed that the pursuit of money and what it could buy was a distortion of the American Dream, the nation's economic collapse a natural result. "The American dream as expressed by James Truslow Adams in his *The Epic of America* is being frustrated," Luccock told the graduating class of Mount Holyoke in 1932, our obsession with the material world taking us further away from what the country was really about.[11] People from all ends of the political spectrum felt similarly, with a shared sentiment that the chase for the Good Life was a perversion of our national creed. The original American Dream "was not of a country teeming with luxuries in the form of consumers' goods, but . . . of a country of free men," Dorothy Thompson told an interviewer a few years later. A more equitable distribution of wealth was in the nation's best interests, she strongly believed, a sentiment she shared with her famous husband, Sinclair Lewis.[12]

The Battle of America

An equitable distribution of wealth could definitely not be found in a new board game that was sweeping the nation. Created in 1933 by Charles B. Darrow, an unemployed salesman (who, in the true spirit of the American Dream, sketched out the design on his kitchen table), Monopoly reflected the fantasy of getting rich at a time when in reality it had become much more difficult. Based on an earlier board game (Landlord's Game, which had been introduced in 1900), Monopoly had players try to bankrupt others in the chase for Atlantic City real estate, an even more Darwinian interpretation of the Dream than that of real life. But all people started off equal in Monopoly, just as our mythology held, and players seemed to relish the to-the-winner-go-the-spoils ethos of the game. With four pages of rather complicated rules, requiring hours to play, and having players go 'round and 'round in what sometimes seemed to be an endless exercise in ruthless capitalism, Monopoly was an unlikely hit, particularly during the Great Depression. But a hit it was and continues to be (McDonald's' recent sweepstakes version of the game was hugely popular), the pastime then and now a vicarious and fun version of the American Dream.[13]

While Depression-era Americans wheeled and dealed in the make-believe universe of a board game, critics of the New Deal claimed it was the actions of the US government that were most responsible for "frustrating" the American Dream. Cal Tech president Robert A. Millikan considered President Roosevelt's emerging New Deal policies a direct threat to the Dream, thinking the federal government had no business getting involved with private enterprise except to regulate it. FDR's brand of "paternalism" and "statism" was a dangerous thing, Millikan, a Nobel Prize winner in physics, said in a 1934 radio address, with dictatorship often the result when government joined forces with industry. "What is the American dream?" he asked, answering his own question by arguing it was "that this country may always remain a land of freedom and of opportunity," a definition he believed 99 percent of Americans past and present would agree with. But "foreign influences have weakened our own faith in our American ideal," Millikan warned, with the country now in a period of "confused public thinking." He concluded, "Recent happenings in the United States are enough to make one begin to wonder, if not to shudder," the future of the American Dream uncertain at best as the government assumed greater power.[14]

Seeing the fracas that the phrase he had coined was now very much a part of, James Truslow Adams stepped into the fray in 1934 to try to set things straight. "Many of those who profess the greatest fear lest the New Deal may destroy our 'rugged individualism' might be hard put to define sharply either of the two things which they consider to be in dangerous conflict," he wrote in an essay for the *New York Times*, arguing that throughout their history, Americans had in fact been less than individualistic and even less rugged. "In social life we have been notoriously unindividual," he reminded those persons confusing mythology for reality, the self-reliance of the farmer and the frontiersman more the exception than the rule. Even farmers in the early nineteenth century were more than happy to have the government build roads and canals to make it easier for them to get their goods to market, Adams correctly pointed out, and the freewheeling capitalists of the latter part of the decade were very much in favor of protective tariffs to keep their own profits flowing. "We have talked of rugged individualism, but what we have too often meant was cash," he added, giving a history lesson to those individuals who used the phrase recklessly to argue that communism or fascism was destroying the American Dream.[15]

In fact, Charles Beard, the legendary American historian, had said much the same thing in a 1931 essay for *Harper's*, "The Myth of Rugged American Individualism." Although Jefferson's agrarian-based creed of individualism remained a treasured piece of American identity, there was no doubt that the government played a bigger role in our everyday lives than we perhaps liked to believe. In transportation (railroads, waterways, shipping, aviation, highways), through laws (antitrust acts and tariffs), and via regulatory agencies (the Department of Commerce, Bureau of Standards, and Federal Trade Commission), the government acted as both a close ally and a vigilant overseer of the "rugged individual."[16] Still, Adams felt, the two pillars of the America Dream embedded in Jeffersonian democracy—individualism and equality—had served the country well and remained essential guideposts for the future. "America would have been in the past and would be now a very different place if these doctrines had not been constantly preached and sunk into us," he made clear.[17]

Even the most vocal critic of the New Deal would be hard put to carp about the Social Security Act of 1935, which by all accounts seemed to nicely complement the American Dream. "It is as if a magic wand had passed over our gray haired heads guaranteeing peace and security for the ebbing years," observed Shelby Cullom Davis in *Current History* in 1939, the federal government now literally invested in having its citizens live happily ever after. Although we take it for granted (or at least used to), the idea of a government-subsidized nest egg waiting for us when we got old (clearly inspired by the 1930s surge in life insurance, not to mention Keynesian economics) was nothing short of revolutionary. "If a prophet in 1929 had predicted that in ten years the nation would be giving payments to those over sixty-five, he would have been hooted down," Davis suggested, the concept "un-American and contrary to our tradition of self-reliance." With his European-style paternalism, there is no doubt that FDR infused the Dream with communitarian values, necessarily sacrificing some of its independence for peace of mind. "People had been trying all their lives to achieve security only to find, like the gold at the end of the rainbow, it usually remained out of reach," Davis surmised, the fact that people were living longer than they used to another good reason for the government to get into the American Dream business during the Depression.[18]

As beneficent as they were, however, the social programs of the New Deal were still not in the true spirit of the American Dream, according to some. Critics of the administration continued to point to the shaky health of the Dream as a clear indication that FDR and his programs were not serving the country's best interests. The business community was, not surprisingly, among the loudest critics of the general belief that the government was impeding the recovery of the Dream instead of enabling it. In a 1938 editorial, for example, *Fortune* told readers that rather than being "liberal," the New Deal was a reactionary movement "falling like a shadow across the American dream," quite the bold assertion. Increasing government control of individuals' lives was dangerous to liberty and thus to the American Dream, the editorial argued, calling for a more balanced political agenda.[19] In his 1940 *Lest Freedom Fail*, Nathan Ayer Smyth also accused the government of encroaching on the freedom of the individual, going way back to the establishment of the Interstate Commerce Commission in 1887 as the "first short step along the authoritarian road." But Smyth believed ordinary Americans were also much to blame for the erosion of individualism, our laissez-faire ethos a victim of self-centeredness. It was up to individuals to save their freedom by taking social responsibility into their own hands, he posited, the lack of doing so inevitably leading to greater government interference, regulation, and control. "If we are to survive as an individualistic democracy, we must revise our American dream," Smyth warned, and now was the time to reclaim our unique brand of self-reliance and self-determination.[20]

In his 1940 campaign run for the presidency, Republican candidate Wendell Willkie not surprisingly referenced the Dream, part of his accusation that FDR's New Deal was both inefficient and corrupt. Speaking at the New York World's Fair in Queens in October of that year, Willkie (who had never held public office) had a great platform to make his points surrounded by the futuristic "World of Tomorrow." "How can any man," Willkie asked the crowd, "visit these great exhibits and arrive at the conclusion that America has reached the end of its achievement?"—the fair's presentation of a bright, big, beautiful tomorrow evidence that the American Dream was flourishing, even as dark clouds appeared on the horizon. "I call upon you people here to join in the great crusade to change the power of America to industrial strength, to industrial vivaciousness and vitality so that all of our people may find work in the great American dream," his ten-minute speech at the Court of Peace concluded, a powerful message of hope in troubled times.[21]

One notable backer of Willkie's, Herbert Hoover, also used the emotion-laden American Dream to try to woo voters for the Republican candidate. "America needs a man who is truly devoted to the American dream," the former president said in a coast-to-coast radio broadcast just a week after Willkie's speech at the World's Fair, defining it as "a nation of free men—a nation of peace." No friend of FDR's (Hoover was not only routed by the man in his reelection effort in 1932 but accused of personally bringing on the Depression), the dyed-in-the-wool Republican labeled the president as an enemy of the American Dream. "If we are to save democracy we must save the roots of democracy," he asserted, the New Deal's unapologetic mission of economic planning and propagandist efforts to sway public opinion having "a pronounced odor of totalitarian government." Politically manipulating the various components of the economy (currency, credit, wages, prices, and production) was throwing a monkey wrench into the works of free enterprise, Hoover argued, the stuff of Germany, Italy, or Russia but certainly not the United States. "This is the battle of America," he informed listeners thinking about whom to vote for, hoping they would decide that a third term for Roosevelt would be one too many.[22]

Gone with the Wind

With just about everyone in agreement that the future of the American Dream was, at the very least, unsure, many during the Depression understandably looked to the American Dream of the past. Two figures of the nineteenth century—Abraham Lincoln and Mark Twain—were considered especially prime symbols of the Dream, each man acknowledged as possessing many of its classic characteristics. With their self-reliance, practicality, and dislike of aristocracy, Lincoln and Twain served as vivid reminders of what the American Dream was and, more important, what it could be again. "Samuel Langhorne Clemens and the gaunt man who was born in a Kentucky cabin and cleared a cornfield in the Indiana wilderness had the common qualities of their restless, expanding, boisterous age," wrote an editor for the St. Louis Post-Dispatch in 1935, a powerful image in a period of contraction and retreat. That Twain's real life was as big as his stories—filled with financial ups and downs, journeys to exotic places, and encounters with other famous figures—made the mythology that much more compelling, the American Dream a real, living thing rather than just a collection of tall tales.[23]

Popular fiction of the day also tapped into nostalgia for yesterday's American Dream. Louise Redfield Peattie's *American Acres* of 1936 was one such book, set in the still undeveloped West where real freedom could be found. "Every one of its golden sentences is a tug at the heartstrings, calling up the image that forever stands in each man's mind for the house and the fields wherein his first happiness was cradled," wrote Paul Jordan-Smith of the *Los Angeles Times* in his review, thinking the novel "call[ed] to mind the old brave days when Americans carved out homes from the forests and hugged close to the land and knew peace." Life on the frontier was certainly difficult but also simpler and more genuine than modern times, sentimental novels like *American Acres* told readers, the kind of independence enjoyed by settlers of the West now just a fond memory.[24]

Michael Foster's best-selling novel, the aptly titled *American Dream*, also mined the past to confront the present confusion surrounding the nation's guiding philosophy. Musing over the nature of modern life and, more specifically, the meaning of the American Dream, the book's protagonist, Shelby Thrall, a disillusioned West Coast newspaperman, thinks back on the lives of three generations of his family while rummaging through old letters and mementos in his attic. "In them he is looking for the American dream—that spirit, that way of life which evolved out of a land originally peopled by the discontented spiritual and political exiles of the world," wrote Stanley Young of the *New York Times* in his review, Thrall's quest a metaphor for the country's own self-searching.[25] Foster transported readers back to the early eighteenth century, gradually (the book ran five hundred pages) making its way to current times. Along the way, readers learned that the Dream was about justice, fairness, freedom, honesty, and decency—all things that would still serve America and Americans well. Foster did not seem optimistic that readers would take his message seriously, however. With greed and corruption the order of the day, Thrall moves to an isolated shack in the country at the end of the book, the American Dream of his ancestors apparently a lost cause.[26]

Could Americans get back their American Dream and, if so, how? In his 1936 book *The American Ideal*, Arthur Bryant argued they could, but only if they followed in the big footsteps of those persons who best expressed it and lived it. As "a call to America to re-examine thoughtfully what has been the well-spring of her strength," as Percy Hutchison of the *New York Times* described the book, Bryant (an Englishman) first defined what he considered "the American ideal": "That man should be at liberty to create as he saw good; that work, courage and initiative should be rewarded; that every worker should enjoy the fruit of his own labor—such was the American dream."[27] Bryant next used short biographies of eight men—Thomas Jefferson, Abraham Lincoln, Ralph Waldo Emerson, Walt Whitman, Theodore Roosevelt, Walter Hines Page (the US ambassador to the United Kingdom during World War I), Alan Seeger (a poet who died at age twenty-eight in World War I), and poet Vachel Lindsay—to illustrate "the American ideal" in action, a sort of case-history approach for readers to follow. Americans could learn a lot from Jefferson's concept of social freedom, Emerson's recurring theme of self-reliance, Roosevelt's determination to fight for what was right, and the ideals of the five other men, Bryant suggested, the American Dream still entirely possible if we studied our own history.[28]

The *Times* of London also saw the American Dream as heavily steeped in the past, an eighteenth- and nineteenth-century idea that was being crushed by the twentieth-century forces of Big Business and Wall Street. Responding to FDR's attempt to save "the American dream" of farm ownership (tenancy went way up during the Depression), editors for the newspaper located the mythology squarely within Jefferson's and Lincoln's ideals. "'The American dream' has always been that of a nation consisting as largely as possible of free citizens, each owning and running his own farm or his own business, independent both economically and politically, able and ready to stand up for his own rights and his own views against any pressure from others," the 1937 editorial read, something that was becoming more and more unrealistic as corporate America grew ever bigger. Because of our agrarian roots, the president, like most ordinary Americans, held a special place for farmers, believing their individual ownership and economic security should be a national priority.[29]

By 1939 it was clear that the nation's interest in its past had become more or less of an obsession. For most, the Great Depression had made the present disconcerting, to say the least, and Hitler's rampage across

Europe made the future even more unsettling. There was little doubt that the country was at a major crossroads, the promise of a "better, deeper, richer life" for all more of a fantasy than when Adams wrote those words eight years earlier in defining the American Dream. "It is no accident that Americans today are showing more interest in their own history and its meaning than at any previous time within the memory of the living," R. L. Duffus of the *New York Times* wrote in February of that year, thinking, "We are asking ourselves, as our ancestors did three-quarters of a century ago, what is meant by the American kind of democracy." Revolutions abroad and economic troubles at home had made looking to what was known and familiar (or just imagined) more popular than ever, our cultural myths now serving a very important social function. "In our casting about for comfort and reassurance we inevitably look to the past, with a sort of homesickness," Duffus observed, with novels, plays, and movies all shaping and reflecting this clinging on to yesterday.[30]

Indeed, popular culture of the day, both high and low, trafficked heavily in a historical memory of the American Dream, although the phrase itself was rarely used. Aaron Copland's music recalled an expansive American landscape that had largely disappeared, for example, while Charles Ives's modernist compositions recycled hymnals, traditional songs, parade music, and parlor ballads. On the radio (and in movie serials), "the Lone Ranger" fought for justice on the western frontier, the masked man enjoying a kind of "loneness" (despite his trusty sidekick, Tonto) that would be hard to find in 1930s America. Art too, both in Works Progress Administration murals and in "regionalist" paintings by Thomas Hart Benton, Grant Wood, and John Steuart Curry, drew upon a rural America of the mythic past, that many of the scenes were mostly or purely imaginary not detracting from the comfort and stability they provided.

But it was movies where the Dream was at its dreamiest, the latter part of the decade offering a long cinematic walk through "the epic of America." The Old West was a frequent backdrop, a tableau offering the possibility of copious amounts of adventure, heroism, and free-spirited men on horses (often carrying guitars). As Roy Rogers and Gene Autry battled it out to be the number-one singing cowboy, for example, the two matinee idols assumed nearly legendary status, reviving the image of "the old homestead" (the name of a 1935 Rogers film) "under western stars" (one of his 1938 flicks) in the process. Feature films of the thirties were hotbeds of nostalgia for an American Dream of the past, even if they took place in contemporary times. Gangster films of the early thirties like *Little Caesar, The Public Enemy,* and *Angels with Dirty Faces* glorified the rebellious (and entrepreneurial) criminal for his no-holds-barred pursuit of the Dream, as dark as it was, mirroring the admiration many felt toward real-life outlaws as they risked all to beat the system. Iconoclastic comics like the Marx Brothers and the Three Stooges rambunctiously upset the social apple cart, elevating the outsider in status over the ones wearing tuxedos and expensive jewelry, while director Frank Capra's 1936 *Mr. Deeds Goes to Town* and 1939 *Mr. Smith Goes to Washington* were valentines to small-town values and democracy at its best as the ordinary man took on the greed and corruption of the politically powerful and wealthy elite. Whether riding through tumbleweed, shooting up a bank, throwing a pie in the face of a rich dowager, or making a speech in Congress, the movie maverick defied social norms to do whatever he thought was right, a vanishing breed of American whom many fondly remembered whether he had actually existed or not.

Without a doubt, cinematic longing for an American Dream that appeared to be endangered if not extinct climaxed in 1939, that year also happening to be (perhaps not coincidentally) very possibly Hollywood's best year ever. While Capra sent James Stewart to Washington to remind our nation's leaders what this country was really about, director George Marshall sent him in *Destry Rides Again* to Bottleneck, an out-of-control town in the Wild West, to restore order. Although he spoke softly (and drank milk), Tom Destry carried a big stick, a warning to enemies abroad that we would vigorously defend our Dream if need be. (Knowing that Marlene Dietrich could be found in the local saloon perhaps made the task a bit easier.) Courage and sacrifice in order to preserve our way of life could also be seen in theaters that year in *Drums along the Mohawk* and *Stagecoach*, each of these movies ironically having Indians stand in for the bad guys. The Dream's sacredness of home and of owning a piece of land coursed through *Gone with the Wind* and *The Wizard of Oz*, of course, each of these films masterfully capturing the mood of prewar America despite bounding through time and space. Finally, *Young Mr. Lincoln*, starring Henry Fonda, traced Honest Abe's early years, reinforcing the very American idea that greatness could and did sometimes spring from humble beginnings.

Playwright Robert E. Sherwood's *Abe Lincoln in Illinois* likewise used the gangly log splitter to symbolize the American Dream in the late thirties. "It carries some of the shine of the American dream," acknowledged poet extraordinaire Carl Sandburg, himself quite an expert on the subject, of Sherwood's play, which ran at the Plymouth Theatre on Broadway for 472 performances from October 1938 to December 1939. Starring Raymond Massey (who repeated the role in the 1940 film) as Lincoln, the play was partly historical, partly invented, magnifying the legend of the man and his embodiment of the Dream. Lincoln's journey from shy, less-than-handsome country boy to successful lawyer to president of the United States was a personal narrative of the American Dream, of course, while his struggle to make the Dream possible for those Americans without it served as even greater evidence that the idea could be made real. That the play debuted while the situation worsened in Europe made the story only that much more striking and convinced many isolationists that the Dream was worth fighting for at any cost.[31]

Marjorie Berstow Greenbie's 1939 *American Saga: The History and Literature of the American Dream of a Better Life* served as a sort of capstone for this wholesale looking back, the book a panoramic reassembling of the seminal events that turned the nation into what it was. From the European explorers' arrival on these shores to the expansion and settling of the West, and from the Revolutionary and Civil Wars to the contradiction of slavery, the roots of the American Dream were present, Greenbie proposed, the central story line of our national saga. "These States were settled by people with ideals," she wrote, the country "a land of buried dreams." Like others, however, Greenbie argued that a fundamental change occurred around the turn of the twentieth century when divisiveness and self-doubt crept into the national zeitgeist, the dream of a better life for all fading into a wisp of what it once had been.[32]

Roads to a New America

If there was any doubt that the American Dream still existed, however, all one had to do was cast one's eyes upon Texas, a state whose brief national history (for ten years it existed as an independent republic) somehow continued to linger in the air. "Here the early American dream of perpetual expansion still persists," thought Rose Lee Martin of the *New York Times* in 1936, reporting that many considered the state to be the "last economic frontier." The Lone Star State was celebrating its one hundredth anniversary that year, with the Texas Centennial Exposition in Dallas bringing national and international attention to a part of the country that indeed seemed to be quasi independent. One thing making Texas appear to be a nation unto itself was its sheer size and abundant resources, of course, its quarter-million square miles a diverse landscape of hills, prairies, forests, and swamps. Ranches were now equipped with the comforts of any modern home but were often separated by as much as fifty miles, a twentieth-century version of Jefferson's self-sustaining yeoman farmer. Herds of cattle may not have been truly wild anymore, and one's home on the range was now neatly fenced in, but real-life cowboys remained, adding to its reputation as one of the few remaining places where a man could still be a man. Even in the city, many men wore Stetson hats and carried revolvers, vestiges of the Wild West that lent a certain kind of freedom that one would not find on Park Avenue or Hollywood Boulevard. Stories of oilmen striking it rich from new wells abounded as another reminder that not everybody was simply a cog in a big corporate machine. "Their Democracy is still of the practical Jacksonian type, the double heritage of the pioneer-farmer and of the plainsman who knew that a Colt's .45 makes all white men equal," wrote Martin, thinking that "for all their national patriotism, they are Texans even before they are Americans."[33]

Also boding well for the American Dream was that some observers of the scene were more interested in its future, however uncertain, rather than its glorious past. "Neither the American dream nor the Christian ideal can be fully realized in our rich nation until abject poverty is abolished, organized crime is ended, widespread ignorance is dissipated, and our inexcusable deficit economy gives way to a surplus economy," wrote

Rockwell Hunt of the *Los Angeles Times* in 1937. Keeping the Dream alive was important, perhaps essential, in order to keep moving forward. "What we dream for America today we dream for all mankind tomorrow," Hunt preached, the opportunity to realize a better life a universal ideal.[34] Likewise, with his 1938 *Roads to a New America*, David Cushman Coyle picked up the trail of the Dream where Adams had left off, arguing that what this country needed was better, rather than bigger, hopes. More money for education and public health, tax breaks for small businesses, and "old-age pensions" were just a few of the ways that the elusive American Dream could actually be realized by a good many citizens, Coyle thought, the mythology capable of becoming a reality if we really wanted it to be.[35]

Although Louis Adamic's *From Many Lands* was not intended to be a treatise on how to reinvigorate the American Dream, the stories that filled it showed that it was still all around us, an integral part of the people who had immigrated to this country. "Somehow, through hard and challenging decades, the dream has been confused, buried under rubble, distorted and sometimes tarnished, all but lost," wrote Katherine Woods in her *New York Times* review of the 1940 book, the Depression clearly taking a toll on our ardent faith in the future. "Yet it is still here, to be recovered where it is buried, restored where it is bent or broken, to shine anew where it is dull or stained," she continued, inspired by Adamic's view that the Dream was part and parcel of "the greatest migration in history." Real people featured in the book like Helena Karas from Bohemia, Manda Evanich from Croatia, the Steinberger family of German Jewish origin, the Tasjians from Armenia, the Meliskis from Poland, and Tone Kmet from Slovenia were all somehow ordinary and remarkable at the same time, their everyday heroism the thing that had made their American Dreams come true. For these immigrants and millions of others, the Dream was not so much about the ability to support oneself and one's family, achieving success, or even enjoying freedom but that, in Woods's words, "they made their contribution and it was accepted."[36]

What made *From Many Lands* even more interesting was that it was largely a product of the people themselves. Adamic (himself an immigrant) toured the country in early 1940 to announce his goal to achieve greater understanding among Americans of different ethnicities, this just one project of an organization he had recently founded, the Common Council of American Unity. In addition to going on the road to spread his vision of what he called "courageous and co-operative living" through common citizenship and a shared belief in democracy, Adamic sent out questionnaires to and solicited case histories from America's "melting pot," trading heavily upon Walt Whitman's famous description of the country as "a teeming nation of nations." "The American dream is a lovely thing, but to keep it alive, to keep it from turning into a nightmare, every once in a while we've got to wake up," Adamic repeatedly said in lecture halls, his book the result of this ambitious exercise in self-discovery, self-appraisal, and self-criticism.[37] Published on the eve of another world war, *From Many Lands* no doubt helped to remind Americans of their grand mission in unity through diversity. "In a broken, terrified world, amid the devastation of the evil to which their very existence is defiance, they hold our challenge of destiny," Woods concluded, those persons newest to the nation the key to the future of the American Dream.[38]

As V. F. Calverton explained in his 1941 book *Where Angels Dared to Tread*, the dream of not just a better life but a perfect one had actually been put into practice by those individuals who had lived in utopian communities, an interesting and often overlooked part of the nation's history. The American Dream was a direct descendant of these experimental communities that flourished from the late seventeenth century to the present, Calverton argued, the fact that essentially all had failed not taking away from the legacy they left for the possibility of a truly happy world. Indeed, many of the ideas central to utopian communities—freedom from oppression, tolerance toward religion and social customs, a willingness to work hard, and the belief that a new kind of society could be created— were expressed in the Dream, making them perhaps not as crazy as they might seem. Leaders of these communities typically believed they were divinely inspired or had developed a perfect-as-possible economic system (or both), these qualities also bearing a strong resemblance to the Dream's precepts. Although most utopian communities were based on communistic principles (and the fact that many were celibate or practiced "free love," equally un-American notions), they had elements we could learn from,

Calverton proposed, the establishment of a genuine democracy blind to religion, race, or creed an ideal still very much worth pursuing.[39]

Inspired by an article poet and librarian of Congress Archibald MacLeish had written in the *Survey Graphic* in early 1941, First Lady Eleanor Roosevelt expressed her own thoughts about the American Dream in her "My Day" syndicated column that ran in many newspapers. "America is not a pile of goods, more luxury, more comforts, a better telephone system, a greater number of cars," she wrote in her January 7 column titled "How to Realize the American Dream," but rather "a dream of greater justice and opportunity for the average man." By defining the Dream in ideological terms rather than material ones, Mrs. Roosevelt was perhaps preparing Americans for the wartime sacrifices they would soon have to make. "Devotion to democracy, devotion to liberty . . . give us the opportunity and hope for future dreams," she made clear, thinking that without a belief in our country's ideals, "all our other achievements amount to nothing."[40]

Cast against escalating fascism and totalitarianism in Europe, the American Dream appeared to be emerging as the country's unofficial slogan, shorthand for our complex national identity. The very same day that the first lady used the words in her column, in fact, the Chicago Public Library issued a list of recommended books under the banner of "The American Dream," another sign that the phrase was becoming a kind of marketing tool. "American novels which portray our never-ending search for a better way of life" were included on the list, the library's endorsement a sort of literary Good Housekeeping Seal of Approval.[41]

Not surprisingly, the American Dream was increasingly conjured up through 1941 as the probability we would have to enter the war increased. One prominent voice speaking of the Dream was James Truslow Adams, his phrase taking on new resonance a decade after he first articulated it. Again using the *New York Times Sunday Magazine* as a platform, Adams now saw his Dream as an invaluable resource to bring citizens of all backgrounds together in a fight against foreign enemies:

Far more potent than the common past as a unifying force in our national life has been the conception of the future—the American

Dream. From the very beginning all our immigrants of all races and creeds and from every nation have come here to realize that dream. . . . The dream of liberty in the religious, social, political and economic sense is the chief characteristic of American ideology. The Americans are a chosen people, not as the Puritans or the Jews understood that phrase, but in the sense that they have all wanted the same thing—to have the freedom to be themselves and to reach the limit of their capacities. The American Dream is a spiritual bond.

It would be, thought Adams, the "free choice of a free people" that would unite Americans if or when they decided to enter the war, this same unique characteristic precisely which would ultimately play an important role in achieving victory.[42]

As prewar patriotism rose through 1941, our appreciation for a sense of place and, specifically, the cultural geography of the American Dream also escalated. Although any part of the country could of course rightfully claim it was home to the Dream (especially Texas), New England was considered special in this regard. In June 1941, for example, Hal Borland of the *New York Times* took a trip to New England, capturing the pure Americanness of the region in almost mythic terms. "It is a corner of America that somehow sums up this whole sweet land of farms and homes and villages and cities, of sweat and toil and harvest, of free-spoken minds and of men and women who live proudly as individuals yet all combine into a nation strong in its own freedoms," he poetically wrote, his article clearly designed to inspire readers to defend their country if necessary. New England was for Borland not only the "root-bed of Democracy in the rock-bed of the nation" but also the "workshop of the American Dream," its farms and factories the central source of the mythology we created and believed in. With its rolling hills, winding roads, quaint villages, and old churches, New England certainly looked the part, that it was the first place to be settled by Europeans adding to its image as the original wellspring of the Dream.[43]

But more than the region's picture-book beauty and relative antiquity, New Englanders' notorious frugality helped define the area as where the idea of striving to do the most with what one had—an important strain of the American Dream—was born and remained strongest. Yankee thrift and ingenuity—making what one needed and selling what one did not need—were a prime path to realizing the Dream, explaining why many Americans viewed New England as somehow different (for both better and worse). The area long a home to some of the country's best gunsmiths, New England's factories were now churning out the weapons of war "to preserve that American dream which sprouted in this soil and has never withered," Borland told readers, confirmation that the region's almost two-century-old motto of "Don't Tread on Me" (or "Live Free or Die," if you prefer) was still very much alive. "Here on this rocky soil is the whole of the American dream," he concluded, "the very essence of democracy as we have built it, stone by stone, like a New England wall."[44]

Wild Geese and How to Chase Them

Whether in New England or another part of the country, the entry of the United States into the war did not mean its citizens should put their Dream on hold. In fact, perhaps more than ever, Americans were fully expected to strive for their particular Dream, in the interests of both individuals and the nation as a whole. One wartime book, Jay Franklin's *Remaking America*, stressed how important the American Dream was as a demonstration of our democratic principles to the world. "We . . . are now engaged in a tremendous struggle to determine whether the original American dream itself shall survive in a world of totalitarian tyranny," the aptly named Franklin wrote, our ideal of "life, liberty and the pursuit of happiness" facing its greatest test. Unlike some other critics, however, Franklin, a New Dealer, was optimistic that the Dream would not just endure but thrive in the years ahead. Eight years of New Deal policies and projects "have helped the American people to remake their country along broad, imaginative and intensely practical lines," he wrote, a much different story from the argument that FDR's paternalistic administration was squeezing the individualism out of the country like water from a sponge. Great advances in social justice, financial security, and public health, not to mention the conservation and creation of public works, proved that the nation was resilient, inventive, and vigorous—precisely the elements that made up the American Dream. More important than the ambitious social programs, physical improvements to the nation's infrastructure, and massive defense effort, according to Franklin, the American people had experienced a "moral reconstruction" over this same period, reaffirming their belief in and commitment to these fundamental ideals. "The future will be as we make it and we have found the will and the power to make that future ours," he boldly proposed.[45]

However, many Americans seemed to have simply forgotten about the American Dream or at least how to pursue it, not the war but the pressures of modern life pushing most to take the path of least resistance in both work and play. Finding this trend disturbing, Charles Allen Smart, a novelist and farmer, felt the need to write a book called *Wild Geese and How to Chase Them*, a kind of field guide to how to hunt for one's American Dream. Rejecting "our present timid, flimsy and dangerous idea of security," with its emphasis on possessions and prestige, Smart argued that living should be approached as an art, something that was not just courageous but vital to society. Smart proposed a "profoundly revolutionary doctrine" that work should be "for fun or subsistence only," recommending that readers first ask themselves a series of tough questions. "Why am I alive?" "Who am I?" "Why am I working?" "What is going on between me and other people?" "What is society doing to me and what am I doing to society?" Through this existential, proto-self-help exercise, Smart believed, individuals would identify which wild geese they should chase and, ultimately, ensure that the American Dream would remain a key marker of our national identity.[46]

Still others felt that there were now precious few wild geese to chase. Writing in the *Atlantic Monthly* in 1943, James B. Conant, the president of Harvard University, argued that whatever the nation's politics were and had been for the past decade, they had little to do with the American Dream. The Dream was, he reminded Americans on the home front, rooted in American radicalism, drawing on the intellectualism and spiritualism of people such as Jefferson, Emerson, Lincoln, Thoreau, Veblen, Whitman, and Henry George. The key characteristics of the Dream— equal opportunity (that is, the absence of privilege), independent thought (that is, freedom from government-, party-, or church-imposed ideologies), privacy, and the right to acquire property exclusively via the economic arena—were all radical ideas difficult to locate within the current political climate, he charged. Now the country was being forced to choose between two very different alternatives to American radicalism—European radicalism (based on the theories of Marx, Engels, and other socialists advocating communal ownership, high moral standards, and a strong police presence) and reactionaries. Whether one leaned left or right, much of contemporary American life, with its governmental bureaucracy, corporate empires, and vast inequality in the distribution of wealth and in education, suggested we were pursuing something much different from our unique kind of radicalism. The simple fact that the people were commonly referred to as "the masses" was disturbing, Conant felt, this fact something completely incompatible with the concept of the American Dream.[47]

Again, right on cue, James Truslow Adams offered his thoughts on the current state of the American Dream, acting as a sort of mediator among those persons using his term to serve their particular agendas. A dozen years (and seven books) after he brought it to life, Adams returned to the idea in *The American: The Making of a New Man*, the war an opportunity to revisit the concept. Now, for Adams, America itself was the "the dream," more specifically "the dauntless struggle, the ultimate success or failure, but the glory of *Opportunity* and of one's chance to make the most of it." Undoubtedly magnified by the contrast between "us" and "them" during the war, the distinguishing characteristics of Americans were elevated by Adams to nearly biological proportions, the people of the country the "New Man" of the book's subtitle. While the differences in Americans' physical appearance and everyday behavior were certainly interesting and worth noting, it was again their ideals that most set them off from Europeans, according to Adams. Liberated from the constraints and limitations of the Old World, Americans had for the most part delivered on the promise that their Dream offered, living up to both the challenges and the opportunities afforded by the revolutionary idea of social equality.[48]

Just as films of the 1930s directly influenced the trajectory of the Dream, wartime movies reinforced the mythology in different ways. *Casablanca*, for example, showed that even a rough-and-tumble expatriate running a gin joint in Morocco had a soft spot for America's ideals, while

Meet Me in St. Louis sent the message that family and home were more important than a better-paying job in the big city. Pure patriotism could be found in films like *Yankee Doodle Dandy* starring Jimmy Cagney, while *Holiday Inn* with Bing Crosby nicely captured the pure, unadulterated Americanness of New England that Borland had recently written about. (Irving Berlin's "White Christmas," which debuted in that movie, is itself a paean to the American Dream.) Good old shoot-'em-ups, preferably starring John Wayne (like the 1942 *Fighting Tigers*), showed the degree to which the Dream was being defended, making home fronters more willing to do what they could to do the same. Low-budget movies without big stars also were narratives of the Dream, however, no matter how the story was packaged. In the 1943 B-movie *American Empire*, for example, a couple of adventurous buddies go west after the Civil War, happily raising cattle on their own piece of land. But all hell breaks loose when their prosperous, peaceful life is interrupted by rustlers, a nineteenth-century Wild West version of what was actually happening in Europe. The film was, according to a review in the *New York Times*, "a properly respectful tribute to the American dream," a morality tale as much as good entertainment.[49]

Europeans too were exposed to a larger-than-life version of the American Dream through movies that made it across the pond during the war. "The movies give an impression of ease, of a social fluidity that may be fake but is certainly seductive," thought D. W. Brogan, a professor of political science at Cambridge University, in 1943, your average trip to the local cinema offering a glimpse of America as having "a flexible, ingenious, materially minded, likeable way of life." It was true that many Europeans learned about Americans through film (and vice versa, of course), their experiences in the dark typically dispelling negative stereotypes (again, like all Yanks cared about was money). Hollywood films were in fact powerful propaganda directed to both our allies and our enemies, exactly why Hitler resisted having them shown in Berlin. "They are 'life, liberty and the pursuit of happiness' in images—and images speak more effectively than words," Brogan proposed, seeing movies as "the most revolutionary instrument from America since the Declaration of Independence."[50]

Whether it was the movies or the fact that the tides of war were swinging distinctly in our favor, a sea change in the American Dream was occurring. By mid-1943, with victory very likely, the Dream seemed to take a different direction, reversing the mostly negative, pessimistic course it had taken over the past dozen or so years. "We are getting back the Horatio Alger feeling about the American Dream," thought an editor for the *New York Times* in July of that year, suggesting that something in the yet-to-be-named mythology had snapped in 1929 with the onset of the Great Depression. Before the crash, this theory went, the Dream was steeped in the idea of "a free and prosperous people dedicated to equal opportunity," an aspiration that was never intended to be fully realized. Just approaching a state of bliss, getting measurably nearer to it, was considered enough, with complete happiness and security accepted to be impossible in this life. Exceptions to the Dream were to be expected (as in the case of women and people of color), the mythology not a failure because of the occasional anomaly. "The American Dream was a goal and a purpose, and the national task was to keep on narrowing the gap between goal and achievement," the editor explained, the analogy of a man climbing a hill (with occasional rest stops) a fitting one.[51]

The narrative changed dramatically with the economic collapse, however. "In the years of business depression the American Dream became a sneer and a tragedy," the newspaper's editor continued, the myth now still a dream only in the sense of being a "mirage and nightmare." "The story had shifted from that part of America which found Opportunity to those Americans who failed," this writer believed, the Dream invoked not to cheer us on but rather to admonish us for our faults. Instead of a man climbing a hill, the American Dream had become more like a man who had fallen overboard and was unable to make it back to shore, his strength having given out. But now, in the summer of 1943, there was a palpable sense that the nation was again trying to make it up a hill. "Today, it is a pleasure to report, we are well back in the pre-1930 mood," the editor beamed, the American Dream "once more a shining hope, and not a mirage."[52]

The American Dilemma

For some Americans, however, being "back in the pre-1930 mood" offered little comfort. The most obvious contradiction to the reality of the Dream was the looming issue of race, of course, the nation's "Negro problem" increasingly impossible to ignore during the war. (The wartime interment of Japanese Americans and attacks on Latinos, resulting in the "Zoot Suit Riots," were other flagrant examples of the country's discrimination toward people whose skin color was not white.) The Carnegie Study of the Negro in America Life, led by Gunnar Myrdal, the notable Swedish economist, tackled the issue head-on, issuing a series of publications in the early 1940s that examined different aspects of the subject. Myrdal's own 1944 An American Dilemma was the best-known volume in the series, but Melville J. Herskovits's Myth of the Negro Past, Otto Klineberg's Characteristics of the American Negro, Richard Sterner's work The Negro's Share, Charles S. Johnson's Patterns of Negro Segregation, Edwin R. Embree's Brown Americans, Roi Ottley's New World a-Coming, Howard W. Odum's Race and Rumors of Race, and John La Farge's book The Race Question and the Negro also exposed how blacks were excluded from sharing in the American Dream.[53]

It was An American Dilemma that most thoroughly and compellingly described how the nation was not living up to its democratic principles in its treatment of blacks, however, the disparity between our ethos of equality and reality magnified when viewed alongside the Nazis' brand of racism. The idea of the American Dream was a big part of Myrdal's dilemma, simply impossible to ignore the fact that our ideal of a "better, deeper, richer life for all" was something not being universally applied. "Tensions exist in the mind of every one who becomes conscious of the difference between the claims he makes for himself and his children under the American creed and the claims he is willing to grant the Negro," wrote Rupert B. Vance of the Virginia Quarterly Review in his review of the series of books, the nation as a whole suffering from a "split personality" and "divided conscience." Because whites "cannot afford to compromise the American Dream," Vance thought, the country would have to try to solve its dilemma, accurately predicting that it would be the legal system where much of the battle for civil rights would be fought.[54]

The country also had an equal-rights dilemma with women. Many women, having either served in the military or taken factory jobs on the home front, had every intention of working after the war, perhaps even grabbing their piece of the Dream by starting their own businesses. "Will the American dream of going in business for one's self influence returning service women as well as men?" asked Malvina Lindsay of the *Washington Post* in 1944, wondering, if so, "what opportunities await them?" With fears of a postwar depression and massive unemployment rampant, the government was already doing what it could to help returning servicemen find jobs and, for more entrepreneurial types, create their own businesses. At the US Army's request, for example, the Department of Commerce was preparing a series of books on how to run twenty different small businesses, the guides designed to make it easier for former GIs to transition back to civilian life. But only four of the twenty enterprises had a "definite women's appeal," in Lindsay's opinion, making her think that women might find their American Dream outside of operating a beauty shop, apparel store, restaurant, and bakery. Why couldn't women run a hardware store or drugstore or open up a real estate or insurance office? For that matter, why couldn't those women with newly acquired mechanical experience open an auto repair shop, a gas station, a heating and plumbing business, or even a sawmill? "What line women's initiative will take in postwar business can now only be guessed," Lindsay mused, convinced that her sex would finally get a piece of their own American Dream.[55]

Regardless of gender, the Dream of being one's own boss exploded as the war wound down, no doubt fueled by soldiers' experience of having to take orders from anyone with more stripes or bars than they. Author Leo Cherne reported in 1945 that at least one out of every seven servicemen wanted to start a business after the war, a sentiment shared by many civilians. Newspaper reporters were thinking of starting their own papers, salesgirls trying to figure out how they could open up their own boutiques, and radar experts planning on capitalizing on what would certainly be a big boom in the radio business. "This is as it should be," Cherne believed, "the impulse toward business independence . . . one of the most forceful drives in American life." Despite the fact that a good many new businesses (half, actually) failed in their first few years, other experts urged Americans thinking about their future to take the entrepreneurial plunge. William Benton, a vice president at the University of Chicago, had recently made a passionate plea to young men to go into business for themselves, citing success stories like those of Samuel Zemurray (who went from banana-cart pusher to head of the United Fruit Company) and the Goldblatt brothers (who rose from nothing to department-store kings). Benton himself was a poster child for the American Dream, partnering with Chester Bowles to start an ad agency on the eve of the Depression that turned out to be so successful he retired at age thirty-six to devote his life to education. That six hundred thousand businesses had closed down during the war made the notion of owning one's outfit that much more appealing, the wads of cash that many Americans had socked away while there was little to buy another juicy carrot dangling in front of entrepreneurs-to-be. The loan provision in the GI Bill was extra incentive, knowing that Uncle Sam would pay back half of the amount borrowed (up to two thousand dollars) if one's business failed making the leap an almost no-lose proposition.[56]

Another, even bigger, dimension of the American Dream—owning one's own home, a vestige of Jefferson's self-sustaining farm—also escalated in importance in the final years of the war. Many of the millions serving overseas were not exactly sure where they would live when they returned, their relatives on the home front (often crammed in crowded apartments near defense plants) equally concerned about housing when Johnny came marching home. New housing was sharply curtailed during the war as building supplies and manpower were diverted, and those persons who had met Mr. or Miss Right in a uniform and planned to get hitched were less than excited about moving in with Ma and Pa when the fighting was over. Until William Levitt and other developers seized the opportunity by building affordable housing in new suburbs for young couples after the war, "home sweet home" remained a fantasy for many, and a growing part of the American Dream. New scientific discoveries made during the war in metal, plastics, wood, glass, and many other materials promised that homes would soon be better and cheaper, the prefabricated house that rolled off an assembly line just like a car the most exciting possibility. "Whether all these plans come true or not, it is clear that we are on the threshold of many interesting developments in the field," observed Dorothy Rosenman of the *New York Times* in 1944, asking, "Will these provide the more comfortable, less costly home of which so many Americans dream?" With all kinds of issues (expensive land, high real estate taxes, tight mortgage money, restrictive building codes, feisty trade unions, and a highly mobile population, to name just a few) in play, the answer was uncertain, but one thing was sure: the single-unit family home would soon gain a central place in the narrative of the American Dream.[57]

Right alongside the promise of a home of one's own after the war was the load of time we would inevitably have to enjoy it. The postwar years were popularly imagined as a period in which we would have to work fewer hours, a function of the great strides in efficiency made during the war, in terms of both manpower and manufacturing. Rather than be a boon to the American Dream, however, an opportunity to pursue our personal ambitions, hours not spent on the job posed a distinct threat, with experts fretting about what would almost certainly be an excess amount of leisure time. "Unless we use wisely our new opportunities for leisure, our civilization will totter and fall and we will . . . lose the American dream," warned William F. Russell, a dean at Columbia University, urging future teachers to educate their students in how to productively use all the extra hours in the day they would surely have.[58]

Too much leisure time would of course not turn out to be the problem some feared during the war. Rather, it would be the rise of another superpower that threatened to cause our civilization to totter and fall, the American Way of Life hanging in the balance. But with victory over those countries that had threatened our special purpose, the foundation was laid for a new and improved American Dream and the nation given a new chance to turn our mythology into reality. As the postwar years beckoned, the nation looked to the future with both confidence and trepidation, ushering in a new era in the history of the American Dream.

2

The Status Seekers

The American Dream is losing some of its luster for a good many
citizens who would like to believe in it.
—Vance Packard, 1959

IN DECEMBER 1960, Webster Gault, the financial editor of the *Hartford Courant*, opined that the "constant American dream" was "getting
a new car." A few months later, Virginia Irwin, another writer for that
newspaper, made an equally dubious claim, proposing that the American Dream was "eternal youth." Brock Brower, a writer for the *New York
Times*, had another idea, suggesting that same year that "it might be said
that the American Dream today is to sleep," given the nation's rampant
insomnia. In the early 1960s, it seemed that Adams's "vision of a better,
deeper, richer life for every individual" could mean just about anything.
"The American dream used to be a chicken in every pot and a car in every
garage, then it was a swimming pool in the backyard, but now, apparently, it's a golf course viewed through the picture window," observed
another writer for the *Hartford Courant* in 1963, the phrase going from
the sublime to the ridiculous.[1]

The American Dream splintered and fragmented in the postwar years,
pushed and pulled in many different directions as the nation itself became
more complex and multifaceted. Born during the Depression, the phrase
adapted nicely to a much different social, economic, and political climate, proving it really was our core mythology, if there were any lingering
doubts. Flexible, accommodating, and seemingly infinitely expandable,
the American Dream blossomed in the two decades after the war, the idea

applied to virtually any situation involving aspiration or achievement. By the end of this era, however, the future of the Dream was uncertain, with a new generation of Americans thinking that a much different expression of the nation's ideals could better serve the country and its citizens.

A Calm and Ordered Existence

With victory achieved but the postwar future unsure, Americans in the late 1940s had the chance to reinvent their Dream, the mythology in a sense up for grabs as the nation decided which direction to take. George Gallup, the pollster, announced that the "traditional" American Dream was that "every man can become a millionaire," quite a revisionist interpretation of Adams's original idea. For Gallup and certainly many others, the Dream was now mostly about opportunity, success, and financial gain, payback perhaps for the thrift and sacrifice the American people had to endure the past decade and a half and, without a doubt, a way to distance ourselves from Soviet communism. In 1947 Gallup's American Institute of Public Opinion asked a cross-section of citizens in all forty-eight states, "Do you think it will ever be possible for another American to build up a fortune like Henry Ford?" The answers would reveal the relative health of the American Dream, Gallup presumed, the late carmaker being the personification of the mythology realized. Interestingly, almost half of those asked responded "No" to the question, thinking that the days of amassing great wealth were over, in part because of the government's "soak the rich" tax rates. As always, the American Dream was commonly believed to be on the ropes, crushed by either big government or big business.[2]

Even the dream of making a million dollars, a fraction of Henry Ford's fortune, was now viewed as highly unlikely if not impossible for the average American. "It always has been a great American dream to strike it rich," wrote Greer Williams in the *Saturday Evening Post* in 1949, "to invent a better mousetrap, to write a best seller, to manufacture a gadget—and make a million dollars." Williams herself once wanted to make a million dollars but no longer had that goal, advising her readers to give it up as well. High taxes were the reason to drop this classic version of the American Dream. That year a married person earning an income of more than $200,000 had to pay $156,820 plus 91 percent of the amount over

$200,000 in federal taxes, meaning more than three-fourths of a million-dollar windfall would go right to the IRS. For Williams, this was not just egregious but significant from a historical sense, suggesting that what she called "the Horatio Alger epoch" could be over. "It isn't the American way to dream about making $231,507.24," she remarked, thinking, "something important was lost from our lives."[3]

Those within big business also lamented the apparent loss of the American Dream as the nation tried to figure out its postwar future. James H. McGraw, head of McGraw-Hill, would have definitely answered "No" to Gallup's question, thinking that much of the incentive to even try to earn a fortune had been lost over the course of FDR's four terms. The idea of getting ahead through hard work would be something children would only read about in history books, he feared, the hope, opportunity, and individual liberty that had defined the nation's economic system now mostly a memory. Unless we reversed our course, the United States would become another Great Britain, McGraw warned, our high taxes and big government spending likely to lead not just to industrial stagnation but to millions of people dependent on handouts in their older years. For McGraw, the American Dream was less about earning a Ford-size fortune than the ability to retire comfortably, something that was increasingly in jeopardy as the cost of living rose and the inducement to make enough money to be in a high tax bracket fell. "We could restore the odds of getting ahead to what they were in 1929," the publisher proposed, seeing classic Republican trimming as the way to get the country back on the path of prosperity.[4]

Others shared the view that the government was getting in the way of personal freedoms and, as a result, ruining the American Dream. Dwight D. Eisenhower, president of Columbia University in 1949, was outspoken in his belief that it was every citizen's responsibility to scrutinize every government proposal that had the potential of taking away some individual responsibility. "Unless we understand the American dream, it may become the American nightmare," he told a forum organized by the New York Herald Tribune, the nightmare being a scenario in which people became "the serf of institutions" they created. The former general, probably with thoughts of running for public office in his mind, seemed to sense a shift in the national mood, with Americans getting weary of the government's looming presence in their lives.[5]

Regardless of who was to blame for putting a damper on the American Dream, it was true that many young people after the war were reining in their expectations and hopes for the future. Becoming some kind of professional would be just fine, high school students told anyone who inquired about their career aspirations, the Depression and war no doubt making them more conservative in their outlook. In 1949 Malvina Lindsay of the *Washington Post* described the changes in the Dream over the years as imagined by or ascribed to youth, their anything-is-possible attitude replaced by a more achievable one: "Th[e] dream in its original essence was that any mother's son might be President. Later it became more generally the idea that anybody—or rather everybody—could strike it rich. Now it is youth picturing itself as a $25,000-a-year lawyer, engineer, scientist, or business executive." A woman thinking about her future husband too wished he be a professional, studies showed, the white-collar worker already becoming something of an icon in postwar America. The trouble, as experts in such things pointed out at the time, was that only 3 percent of all jobs could be considered "professional," meaning that many were in for a rude surprise when they graduated from college. As well, millions of veterans currently in college on the GI Bill would soon be entering the workforce, grabbing up many of the few available professional spots. "If the American dream is to be salvaged it will . . . mean a general cultivation of new social attitudes," Lindsay wrote, suggesting that a "well-adjusted, socially useful life" be considered as an alternative measure for success. "Thus could the American dream become democratized," she offered as the silver lining in the cloud.[6]

Not everybody saw this silver lining, however. Working for someone else, a violation of the go-it-alone ethos of the Dream, would be just fine, the college class of 1949 told pollsters, perfectly content that their future be "a calm and ordered existence," as Lindsay described it. In interviews recent graduates were asking about retirement and pension plans, something employers had never seen before. Skittish from the economic tsunami of the past twenty years, young people had seemingly lowered the bar of the American Dream, a disturbing development for more traditional types, as Lindsay reported: "Are we, they ask, becoming a Nation of weaklings? What has become of the spirit of '49, of the Oklahoma Sooners, the Alaska gold rushers? Why . . . are once aggressive, daring Americans following the drab, dull, regimented goal of security? . . . Moreover, where is youth that has the gambling spirit of its forbears to rush for free gold, homesteads, oil wells, timber, cattle lands?" For a couple of centuries now, Lindsay felt, those individuals feeling cramped by modern life had the opportunity to "go west" to find who knows what, but even this staple of the American experience had mostly dried up. (Oil actually remained a way to make a fortune.) Good medical and dental care had become more of a priority than taking a chance to hit it big, polls suggested, the country perhaps a little worse for it.[7]

Any American Boy

Although the prospect of making a bundle of dough shrank in the postwar years, another dimension of the Dream expanded exponentially. The country had gained an irrevocable perception of itself as a multicultural nation during the war, something that carried over into the postwar years and reshaped the American Dream in the process. Confronted with the uncomfortable position of being part of a caste society based on skin color, Americans addressed the problems of race in a way that they did not before the war. In 1947, for example, a series of radio dramas designed to fight prejudice and discrimination aired on WNEW in New York City, something unlikely prior to Myrdal's landmark *An American Dilemma*. The series, *Lest We Forget—the American Dream*, was sponsored by the Institute for Democratic Education, which offered the shows free to stations around the country. Starring the likes of Helen Hayes, Fredric March, and Ralph Bellamy, the series depicted stories of everyday life to illustrate how pervasive prejudice was in America. In one show titled "Face to Face," for example, Helen Hayes plays a schoolteacher who has to decide what to do when her students overhear a parent make a racist comment. The American Dream was for everybody, the series told listeners, and it was now the time for the nation to live up to its democratic ideals.[8]

Pluralism and the American Dream became further entwined in the 1950s as the country struggled to come to terms with its grand mission of equal opportunity. In his 1952 book *The American Dream,* for example, Father John A. O'Brien, a Notre Dame priest, located pluralism at the very center of the mythology. "If our strength and greatness as a nation are to be preserved, we must rout out the virus of distrust and hatred wherever it occurs," he wrote in the book, echoing some of the rhetoric at the recent Republican and Democratic conventions in Chicago, where civil rights was a hot issue.[9] Fully aware of the power of the mythology, political candidates used—some would say exploited—the American Dream to win voters over. Not just blacks but those individuals part of any minority group who had faced discrimination seized the Dream as a campaign tactic. In 1954 Abraham Ribicoff, the Democratic nominee for governor of Connecticut, told a packed crowd of Italian Americans that the upcoming election would determine if the "American dream is still alive—that any boy, regardless of race, creed or color, has the right to aspire to public office." Aware that not many Jews had run for governor of any state, Ribicoff seemed to be using the Jewishness of his name to his advantage, tapping into the pluralistic streak of the Dream.[10]

Ribicoff's designating his election as the litmus test of whether the Dream was still alive was absurd but also quite clever, raising the stakes of the race to an examination of our national identity. "Equality and the right of any American boy to dream, knowing that his dreams could come true," were the stuff that made America great, Ribicoff declared, a campaign platform that would be difficult for his Republican rival, incumbent John Lodge, to challenge. Italian Americans were just as rare as Jews in higher public office in the 1950s, making Ribicoff's speech particularly compelling (despite the fact that Lodge had in a way trumped Ribicoff by giving a speech to this same group in Italian). "We've always known that anyone has a right to better himself," Ribicoff closed, the former paperboy and caddy living proof that the Dream appeared to be alive and well.[11] Although a few days later a spokesman for Lodge accused Ribicoff of injecting ethnic and religious issues into the campaign with his speech, the Democrat swept into office, living his Dream as governor of the state for the next six years.[12]

Not just Jewish politicians but also rabbis leveraged the inherent pluralism within the Dream to motivate their congregations to action. On

Independence Day of 1956, for example, Rabbi Edgar Magnin gave a sermon at his Wilshire Boulevard Temple in Los Angeles that drew upon
the tremendous power of the American Dream during the postwar years.
Rather than being just a quarter-century-old, uniquely American idea,
he held, the Dream was an ancient concept that had existed everywhere
around the world wherever people had been oppressed. "The American
dream is as old as civilized man," the rabbi told the congregation, something present in the minds of slaves who had built the hanging gardens of
Babylon, moved the giant boulders of the pyramids in Egypt, and rowed
heavy oars in the galleys of ships lest they be whipped. The prophets of
Israel had even foretold the Dream, Magnin believed, envisioning that
one day there would be a place where all individuals would be respected
for who they were or wanted to be. Not until the creation of the United
States would this Dream come to pass, however, the freedom to speak
our thoughts and ability to worship the God of our choice evidence that
this millennium-old wish had come true. Still, the American Dream was
something that should be cherished and not assumed, the danger of losing
it ever present. Only through "our moral attitudes and our intelligence"
could the American Dream be kept alive, Magnin warned, every day both
an opportunity and an obligation to rededicate ourselves to "our pride of
country and loyalty to its noblest traditions."[13]

With his declaration that "any American boy" had the right to dream
the American Dream, however, even Abraham Ribicoff did not seem to
understand that just half the population had the chance of having it come
true. With all the linking of pluralism to the Dream in the postwar years,
precious little of it had anything to do with women, the nation's dilemma
concerning race (and, by association, ethnicity and religion) almost completely obscuring bias along gender lines. William Henry, a professor of
psychology at the University of Chicago, was one of the few people to rec-
ognize this point, and he went further by suggesting people do something
about it. Speaking before the National Association of Deans of Women in
1955, Henry acknowledged that women had demanded that the country
live up to the Dream's key tenet of equal opportunity for all, but they were
still routinely discriminated against, especially in work. "Strong ideological blocks" and the persistence of traditional gender roles were the cause

of bias against women, Henry argued, despite the fact that "many women have made their mark and are performing with distinction in many professional and executive positions in education, business, industry and the military establishment." Henry, who was also chairman of the university's committee on human development, proposed a research study among women executives to determine how supposedly "passive, emotionalized being[s]" could succeed in an environment that required objectivity and assertiveness. Answering such questions could help broaden the parameters of the American Dream, he felt, something that the eight hundred women in attendance heartily endorsed.[14]

Despite the heavy infusion of pluralism into the idea of the American Dream during the postwar years, the country's persistent racial problem was a firm reminder that it remained a mythology. Equal rights for blacks remained elusive in the early 1960s, the gap between the nation's ideals and reality still a large one. African Americans like the Reverend James J. Reeb of All Souls Unitarian Church in Washington, DC, recognized that the country was at a key juncture in its history, with nothing short of the Dream's promise of a truly democratic society at stake in the matter. "It is absolutely certain that this dream cannot be saved unless the Negro continues to believe in its value," the minister preached in 1962, urging his flock not to give up hope that people of all races, creeds, and religions could one day live together in peace and harmony. Some, notably those individuals within the Black Muslim movement, were becoming discouraged and embittered about discrimination in housing, education, and employment, thinking a separate state was the only answer. The reverend thought this idea would be a big mistake not just for blacks but for the nation as a whole, believing that if many more joined this cause, "the American dream would disappear."[15]

As Jim Cullen noted in his *The American Dream: A Short History of an Idea That Shaped a Nation*, Martin Luther King frequently referenced the Dream as part of his overarching theme of equality. In 1961, for example, King used the phrase at Lincoln University's June graduation ceremony ("America is essentially a dream, a dream as yet unfulfilled"), the following month at the National Press Club ("We are simply seeking to bring into the full realization the American Dream"), that fall in a speech praising lunch-counter protesters ("They are in reality standing up for the best of the American Dream"), and in December at an AFL-CIO convention ("a dream of a land where men will not take necessities from the many to give luxuries to the few"). During the March on Washington at the Lincoln Memorial in August 1963, King delivered his famous "I Have a Dream" speech ("a dream deeply rooted in the American dream that one day this nation will rise up and live out the true meaning of its creed"), this occasion for Cullen the peak of the man's power and influence. Although King would suffer some defeats and considerable resistance over the next five years, he did mention the American Dream on the last night of his life, very fitting given how much his philosophy and contributions were informed by the idea.[16]

The Most Powerful Idea in the World

While the American Dream played an important role within domestic issues like civil rights, the nation's magnified presence on the global stage after the war made the mythology a critical part of our fight against communism. As the Cold War escalated in the early fifties, the American Dream was viewed as a kind of secret weapon, something that was stronger than any army even though it was just an idea. Other countries subscribed to democracy or at least had experimented with it, but we had a right that went beyond the already astounding freedoms of speech and religion and from political oppression. Chester Bowles, the former advertising man whose résumé now included head of the Office of Price Administration and governor of Connecticut, explained how the American Dream, "an idea which potentially is the most powerful idea in the world," served as a vital part of our defense against the Soviets and their ideological movement:

> From our earliest days we have been convinced that individual man not only had a right to speak his mind and to worship God in his own way but also to prosper in line with his ability, to rise to whatever heights he was capable, to develop his talents for farming, industry or trade, to own his own land, to enjoy the benefits earned during his lifetime and to pass those benefits on to his children. We have also believed that individual

man had the right to live in a society free of class lines and arbitrary restrictions; the right to secure a good education and to participate in the life and progress of his community regardless of his race, creed or color. This expanding concept of human rights, so peculiar in its early stages to America, became accepted as the American Dream.[17]

Bowles conceded that the original American Dream had faltered as a complex industrial society eclipsed our agriculture-based one, requiring the government to provide protections against economic forces with which a citizen was powerless to contend. But the essence of the Dream remained intact, he insisted, being even more important than the military in protecting the nation from the Soviet menace.

As Bowles's flag-waving suggested, it was clear that by midcentury the United States had recovered much of the swagger it had lost during the Depression and war years. This renewal of self-confidence, much of it driven by anticommunistic fervor, had a direct impact on the American Dream, making the 1950s one of its golden eras. Rather than the incessant lamenting about the loss of the Dream—a running theme in the 1930s and even the late 1940s—self-congratulatory praise of the American creed was fast becoming the order of the day. On Edward R. Murrow's syndicated radio show, for example, Newbold Morris, a New York City politician and lawyer, was invited to offer his upbeat thoughts on the American Dream, a far cry from those persons arguing that its best days were behind us. For Morris (a descendant of a prominent colonial-era family and a cousin of Edith Wharton), the underlying foundation of the Dream was "an inward and spiritual vitality," the thing that made us different (and, implicitly, better) than other countries throughout civilization. This "restless force we call 'human endeavor'" could be found not only in free enterprise but also in subsidized education, public health programs, workmen's compensation laws, unemployment insurance, and Social Security, Morris argued, believing that the government could and did play an active role in individuals' achieving their American Dream.[18]

Some aspect of the American Dream was often woven into the popular culture of the 1950s, reinforcing the mythology while affirming our national identity. For many years, the American Dream could be found on *Cavalcade of America,* a radio program that moved to television in 1953. Week in and week out, the lead character, almost always a man, would fight all odds to achieve something great and find a place in history. A brave and beautiful woman was inevitably at his side, convincing her driven but self-doubting man to keep at it just when he felt all hope was lost. Eventually, of course, the man would make his great discovery, invent some lifesaving drug, or become president, these weekly success stories serving as dramatic tutorials in the American Dream.[19] By endorsing traditional gender roles, popular television shows of the 1950s such as *I Love Lucy, Make Room for Daddy,* and *Father Knows Best* served as lessons in a somewhat different but equally powerful Dream, with happiness and success seemingly waiting for those Americans who conformed to what a postwar family should look and act like.

With laissez-faire capitalism thriving in the midfifties, it was easy for some to argue that one conception of the American Dream was becoming real. Near the end of his life, Alexander Hamilton envisioned that the United States would be by the midpoint of the twentieth century the greatest industrial power in the world, a bold leap of faith given the mostly rural state of the young country at the turn of the nineteenth century. But the founding father turned out to be prescient, with the nation producing more than half of the world's goods in 1954 despite accounting for just 8 percent of the global population. Some saw this triumph of the free-enterprise system as the fulfillment of the American Dream and, almost as important, the inefficiencies of socialism and utter failure of communism. Also elevated to nearly sainthood status was Adam Smith, whose 1776 *Wealth of Nations* was now generally considered to be the bible of capitalism. (Hamilton freely admitted lifting ideas from the book.) Through an "invisible hand," Smith famously wrote, "the private interests and passions of men" led directly to a state of affairs "which is most agreeable to the interest of the whole society," a view that obviously informed James Truslow Adams's definition of the Dream a century and a half before he laid it out. Smith's seemingly paradoxical notion that the clashing of self-interests ultimately benefits all was the perfect theoretical framework for the postwar era, the welfare of the nation dependent on individuals vigorously pursuing their particular Dream.[20]

Public displays of patriotism were not surprisingly ubiquitous in the mid-1950s now that the American Dream was in full bloom. The "American Dream" historical pageant was one of the more memorable celebrations of the mythology and, as a bonus, kept the wheels of commerce spinning. The pageant consisted of a thousand "national treasures" that were taken by four trucks on a fifty-city tour in 1956, all of it exhibited for free at local department stores like Broadway in Los Angeles, Brown Thomson's in Hartford, and Woodward & Lothrop in Washington, DC. The exhibit was obviously inspired by the "Freedom Train" that between 1947 and 1949 took original versions of the Constitution, Declaration of Independence, and Bill of Rights to more than three hundred cities in all forty-eight states to remind Americans of their hard-fought liberties. Thousands of people, many of them schoolchildren with their teachers in tow, came out to see things like Thomas Jefferson's razor, a silver tankard made by Paul Revere, Babe Ruth's uniform, and W. C. Handy's trumpet at each stop on the "American Dream" cross-country tour that was sponsored by local businesses. (So many kids went for an imaginary ride in the US Air Force's model jet plane that it broke down and failed to make it across the country.) The "presidential exhibit" was a minipageant within the pageant, showing off things like a bottle of Lincoln's hair tonic and Teddy Roosevelt's pocket watch. Technological achievements like the first lightbulb (a replica), a solar battery, and a prototype of a space display were also on display, extending the Dream into the future. And if that were not enough, war trophies (including four original watercolors by Adolf Hitler dated 1917–19) were included in the pageant, a warning perhaps to Russia that the superpower had better not challenge the United States for world supremacy or some of their treasures would someday end up on display in a department store.[21]

The excitement of seeing Honest Abe's hair tonic (along with other items of his included in the "American Dream" historical pageant such as a portable writing desk, china honey dish, and even a dessert pan used by his wife, Mary Todd) was a fair reflection of the keen interest in all things related to the Civil War in the mid-1950s. As in the late 1930s, when the 1936 novel and 1939 film *Gone with the Wind* became cultural phenomena, the Civil War captured Americans' imagination like no other historical event, making observers wonder what it was all about. Ralph G.

Newman was one such observer, the coauthor of *The Civil War: The American Iliad* posing his theory in the *Chicago Tribune*:

> The present phenomenal interest in literature of the Civil war is more than an accident, and more than a matter of "escape" from the tensions of the present to a distant and therefore romantic past. It cannot be entirely accounted for by the approaching centennial of the conflict which convulsed a nation in a brother's war to prove whether the American dream was up for grabs, and whether, as Lincoln so succinctly put it, man is capable of governing himself. [Tho perhaps the fact that the question still hangs in a delicate balance has something to do with it.]

For Newman, the Civil War was "the drama that saved the American Dream," the reason the almost century-old event was such a subject of fascination. As the freer of the slaves, Lincoln was at the center of this attention, "the man who prepared the American dream for all men everywhere" the perfect protagonist to tell the nation's epic story.[22]

No one knew this fact better than Carl Sandburg, whose 1926 six-volume biography of Lincoln was, thirty years later, still considered a literary tour de force. In 1959 the sesquicentennial anniversary of Lincoln's birth, Sandburg took another look at the man in an essay for the *New York Times Magazine*, finding him as relevant as ever. "In the present international tumults, in the 600-mile-an-hour jet planes shrinking the globe, there are lines from Lincoln having companionship and counsel," he felt, the man's contribution as a figure of hope perhaps his most important legacy. As the quintessential struggler, Lincoln had something to offer everybody, this point being the reason Lincoln remained such a key part of our mythology almost a century after his death. "Mystery attaches to him—all that may lurk in 'Democracy' or 'The American Dream,'" the poet wrote, "a mystery that can be lived but never fully spoken in words."[23]

A much different larger-than-life figure—Babe Ruth—was also considered a classic example of the American Dream, the ten-year anniversary of his death in 1958 an opportunity to revisit the man's amazing journey. For one thing, no one had yet come along to dominate the game like Ruth had (sixty of the seventy-six records he set still stood), but it was more the legendary stories that surrounded him that elevated the Sultan of Swat to mythological status. Raised in an orphanage and having had little formal education, Ruth went on to become the world's most famous athlete, this fact alone credential enough to be considered the embodiment of the American Dream. But the man's sheer size and prodigious appetite for life's pleasures also helped make him seem as American as apple pie (or, in his case, fifteen hot dogs and sodas at a single sitting). The trajectory of some of his home runs, as well as his mighty swing itself, was nothing less than awe inspiring, turning him into a kind of superman among ordinary men. Ruth was also largely credited with making baseball a successful and profitable business, his huge salary (a whopping eighty thousand dollars a season in his prime) another reflection of the Dream's dimension of wealth and prosperity. Finally, the Babe's fondness for fast cars (and fast women) seemed to embody the nation's irresistible draw to risk and even recklessness, a sentiment very much in tune with the damn-the-torpedoes ethos of the American Dream.[24]

That same ethos had a lot to do with the canonization of Charles Lindbergh, another American who symbolized the Dream between the world wars. In his 1959 *The Hero: Charles A. Lindbergh and the American Dream*, Kenneth S. Davis showed how the man, with his May 1927 solo flight across the Atlantic to Paris, instantly became an icon of what in a few years would be called the American Dream. Coming from a less than loving family, spending much of his time alone in his teens, and dropping out of the University of Wisconsin shortly before he would have been expelled, Lindbergh embarked on his crusade of aviation that eventually led to his becoming one of the most famous people in the world. His fall from grace in the 1930s and war years and the subsequent restoration of his reputation (Congress appointed him a brigadier general in the US Air Force Reserve at President Eisenhower's request) were consistent with the classic mythological journey in which a hero rode a roller-coaster of highs and lows over the course of his or her life. As the definitive "Lone Eagle," Lindbergh captured the nation's spirit for solitary adventure like no man before (and arguably after), accounting for his place within the pantheon of American Dreamers.[25]

History in a sense repeated itself thirty-five years after Lindbergh's flight, however, as another opportunity rose to nominate an American pilot as the Dream incarnate. Lieutenant Colonel John H. Glenn's 1962 orbit around Earth in Friendship 7 was considered a perfect example of the American Dream in action, not just because it was a courageous achievement but for literally expanding the boundaries of the universe. For Henry J. Taylor of the *Los Angeles Times*, the flight "enlarged" the Dream, extending it into the unknown and into the future. Not since Lindbergh's feat had the nation's spirit been so uplifted, each event giving the country a much-needed boost in pride and self-confidence during periods of increasing cynicism and apprehension. (Each hero earned a ticker-tape parade after his safe return.) Coming less than a year after the Bay of Pigs disaster, Glenn's flight served as a timely confirmation of American know-how, reaffirming citizens' faith in their Dream. According to NASA, a few more orbits and setting up a space station were next and, after that, a trip to the moon, fulfilling the ambitious goal the president had set in a May 1961 speech before a joint session of Congress. Nothing short of the moon would be enough in these heady days, Earth no longer big enough to contain the American Dream.[26]

What Has Happened to the American Dream?

While heroic figures like John Glenn reached for the stars, ordinary Americans contented themselves with more earthly delights. As the central repository for what many considered "the good life," the suburban home became central to the American Dream during the postwar years. It was the Veterans Administration's home loan program, which had begun in 1944, that led to a boom in new housing after the war, especially in the burgeoning suburbs. Although well intended, the program created a mass exodus from big cities, leading in turn to what authorities felt was urban "decline." (Race obviously played an important role in this thinking and the decision to act.) With its Housing Act of 1949, Congress gave cities money to clear away "slums" and redevelop areas deemed unacceptable, literally paving the way for the wholesale demolition of older (and, many would say, perfectly fine) neighborhoods. The Housing Act of 1954 amended the 1949 act by providing funding for not just new construction but also the rehabilitation and conservation of "deteriorating" areas, another major step in the postwar urban renewal program.[27] Real estate

developers and those people involved in peripheral businesses were naturally delighted with the passage of each act, justifying their good fortune
by seeing the new laws as extending the American Dream. "The American dream of good homes for everyone is much closer to becoming a
reality," said Elliott Spratt of the Producers' Council, a trade organization
for building-materials manufacturers, after President Eisenhower signed
the 1954 bill. One key feature of the act was more affordable mortgage
terms to build a new home or to modernize an existing one, another way
the federal government essentially subsidized a domestic version of the
Dream in the postwar years.[28]

Some social critics were not happy to see the American Dream turned
into a ticky-tacky house filled with the latest appliances. Everybody seemed
to want to own the same things, they carped, this common desire for "the
good life" creating a more homogeneous, less individualistic society. "The
equality which is part of the American dream is equality of opportunity,
not equality of possessions," complained William Henry Chamberlin
of the *Wall Street Journal* in 1956, troubled by what he described as a
"universal leveling" within American culture. While keeping up with the
Joneses was indeed an avid pursuit in the fifties, it was, however, nothing
new. Tocqueville had observed the new nation's bourgeois leanings more
than a century earlier, taken aback by the profound materialism of early-
nineteenth-century Americans. "The first thing that strikes the observa-
tion is an innumerable multitude of men, all equal and alike, incessantly
endeavoring to procure the petty and paltry pleasures with which they glut
their lives," the Frenchman wrote in 1835, the seeds of mass consumption
already beginning to sprout.[29]

No one seemed more disturbed by this perversion of the American
Dream in the 1950s than Vance Packard. Packard, a journalist and author
who had had a major hit a couple years earlier with *The Hidden Persuad-
ers*, outdid himself in 1959 with *The Status Seekers*, an examination of the
nation's class system. Packard's principal argument was that since 1940,
upward mobility had become difficult for Americans, this rigidity in class
structure a source of deep frustration for persons wishing to climb the
social ladder. Socioeconomically, the country was as hierarchical as the
army, according to Packard, the Dream's promise of unlimited opportunity

largely a false one. Along with David Riesman's 1950 *The Lonely Crowd* and William H. Whyte's 1956 *The Organization Man*, Packard's best seller added to the belief that the American Dream had taken a wrong turn, its spiritual qualities reduced to a futile exercise in status seeking. In his review of the book for the *New York Times*, Orville Prescott acknowledged that the Dream had meant different things to different people, it being an amorphous idea since colonial times:

> The American Dream is a haunting phrase, but what it means has never been entirely clear. Some people think it was a vision of a classless society of equal opportunity where every boy could aspire to be President. Others, more cynical of mind, believe it was a dream of individual escape from an unsatisfactory present to a future of success, wealth and happiness in a land where the streets were said to be paved with gold. Wasn't Jefferson's ideal of a cultivated, agrarian society an American Dream? And Hamilton's belief in a nation where the rich and well-born could play their rightful role of leadership? And Jefferson Davis's goal of a plantation aristocracy based upon slavery?

Whatever the Dream was, it was clear that Packard believed most Americans had given up on it, having, in Prescott's words, "smugly settled for something else."[30]

Other critics believed that Packard was missing the point. The American Dream was not about acquiring and displaying signifiers of class and social status (going to an Ivy League college, living in a tony neighborhood, holding a prestigious job, driving an expensive car, or belonging to an exclusive club) but rather the ability to express one's individuality. The Horatio Alger "rags to riches" story had in recent years infused the Dream with outwardly defined measures of success, these critics claimed, twisting its original meaning. Such was the belief of John F. Bridge, another writer for the *Wall Street Journal*, who, despite his employer's financial orientation, understood that Packard may have had an interesting thesis, but it had little to do with the real American Dream. Instead, Bridge suggested, readers should look to another, much less popular, book just published, *The Delectable Mountains*, to understand what the mythology was about and how it was still very much alive. In his book, Berton Roueche told the stories of eight people or groups who were doing exactly what they wanted to do in life and thus living the American Dream. Long Island potato farmer George C. Strong (who grew the delectable Green Mountain variety of the book's title), Connecticut yoke-oxen breeder Percy Beck Beardsley, New York City glass cutter Louis Haft, and the Shakers religious colony were examples of the Dream in action, their pursuits having little or nothing to do with symbols of having "made it." Happiness and contentment, not class fluidity, were the heart and soul of the American Dream, Bridge concluded, Roueche's "little people" doing relatively little things much bigger in some ways than any of Packard's sociological types.[31]

One event in particular—Premier Khrushchev's planned visit to the United States in September 1959—became an opportunity to reevaluate what this country, and specifically the American Dream, was all about. The easy answer to each was obvious: it was the country's material wealth and how widely that wealth was distributed that best defined us, with our cars and supermarkets sure to impress the Russian and convince him that the American Way of Life was a very good one. But Khrushchev could just as easily point to the nation's many slums and fair number of unemployed, an effective counterattack to the premise that the United States was a superior society. A better answer was to look to America's freedoms, deeper thinkers such as an editor of the New York Times believed, as they existed long before the proverbial two-cars-in-every-garage. "From pioneer days the American dream has always been of a nation whose members decide their own fates and who are subject to no arbitrary power that stands higher than the law or public opinion," this editor wrote, the checks and balances guaranteed by the Constitution, antitrust laws, and limitations placed on unions the real essence of our society. "It's our freedom and democracy that make our way of life better than his, not our automobiles and our television sets," he made clear, not optimistic that Khrushchev would understand this point or want to believe it.[32]

Based on how often one particular question was being asked, it appeared that many Americans did not understand or want to believe that freedom and democracy were more valuable than automobiles or television sets. "What has happened to the American dream?" asked William Faulkner, he just one of many people posing this question as JFK's New

Frontier beckoned. "We dozed, slept, and it abandoned us," the great novelist believed, thinking that "there no longer sounds a unifying voice speaking our mutual hope and will."[33] Reverend John Bonnell of the Fifth Avenue Presbyterian Church in New York had the same question, asking his congregation, "What has happened to the American Dream?" in a 1960 sermon. Bonnell believed the Dream, or at least the way he interpreted it ("America as a free, enlightened and great nation, setting an example of greatness and benevolence for the world"), had become "clouded," our concept of liberty obscured by commercialism and self-interest. A century or half century earlier, our national purpose was clear, the reverend argued, but now we were not quite sure who we were or where we were going. With the rest of the world relying on us being a protector of the inalienable rights of everyone, we needed to reconsecrate ourselves to the original American Dream, Bonnell insisted, it being the only way to repair our "divided soul."[34]

Eleanor Roosevelt could not have agreed more. "What has happened to the American Dream?" she asked the following year in an article for the *Atlantic*, the former first lady believing the country had gotten "too concerned with ways of earning a living or impressing our neighbors or getting ahead." For Roosevelt, the Dream was now "a way of life, which we can come ever closer to attaining in its ideal form if we keep shining and unsullied our purpose and our belief in its essential value," a much different thing from the status seeking many Americans were pursuing. Daniel J. Boorstin went even further by using the question the next year in the title of his new book—*The Image; or, What Happened to the American Dream?*—and blasting Americans for being more interested in appearances than reality. As the United States became a nation of status seekers, the true, authentic American Dream had been lost, a disparate group of astute observers was saying, a disturbing notion if it were true. Although he did not ask the same question, the popular columnist Walter Lippmann might as well have. "The critical weakness of our society is that for the first time being our people do not have great purposes which they are united in wanting to achieve," he wrote in a 1960 column, claiming that "the public mood of the country is defensive, to hold on and to conserve, not to push forward and to create."[35] Was the Dream gone for good?

Some of American popular culture would suggest so. Since the end of the war, in fact, the dark side of the American Dream was a running theme in movies and theater, an important reminder that our central mythology was often elusive and occasionally went terribly wrong. (Even the holiday favorite *It's a Wonderful Life* of 1946 is in one sense a tragic telling of the Dream, with George Bailey never making it out of Bedford Falls despite learning, by the end of the film, that he is "the richest man in town.") Movies such as *Sunset Boulevard* (1950), *On the Waterfront* (1954), and *Sweet Smell of Success* (1957) were about as far away from Doris Day and Rock Hudson trifles as one could get, exposing the Dream's underbelly of self-delusion, missed opportunity, and unbridled ambition. And although we typically remember these years as the golden age of musical theater, plays such as *A Streetcar Named Desire* (1947), *Death of a Salesman* (1949), and *Cat on a Hot Tin Roof* (1955) were epiclike discourses in dashed hopes and decline of every stripe imaginable.

No one pierced the postwar Dream's bubble more than Edward Albee, however. Coming off his hit *The Zoo Story* (which was still running), Albee brought his aptly titled new play, *The American Dream*, to off-Broadway in 1961. Much like how George O'Neil used the term satirically in his play *American Dream* almost three decades earlier, Albee turned the mythology upside down as a critique of bourgeois values and domestic life. A good deal of the play involved Mommy and Daddy, a well-to-do couple sitting in identical armchairs in as innocuous a living room as could be imagined, engaged in small talk that, in typical Albee style, was loaded with irony and cynicism. The "American Dream" of the play's title most literally referred to the couple's Adonis-like son who, though beautiful, was soulless and intellectually vacant, the metaphor all too clear. "He is able to poke his finger in your eye and make you like it," thought reviewer Walter Kerr of Albee, finding his latest play "brittle" and "malicious" but often quite funny. Paired with *Bartleby*, a one-act opera based on the Herman Melville story in which the lead character consistently "would prefer not to," Albee's *American Dream* gave theatergoers a one-two punch in the banality of upward mobility.[36]

The barrage of criticism directed to the state of the American Dream by leading intellectuals, notable figures, and artists soon reached critical

mass. Sensing something going on in the cultural zeitgeist, and something not very good, the New York Times in conjunction with Life decided
to ask some leading minds of the day to weigh in on what they called
the "national purpose." The American Dream was a frequent theme in
contributors' articles, expectantly, directly tied to the even more nebulous
concept of our "national purpose." Everyone agreed that the Dream was in
trouble, confirming what some Life correspondents had found in a recent
survey of average Americans. "We have the mood and stance of a people
who have 'arrived' and have nowhere else to go," stated the Reverend Billy
Graham in his article for the series, going so far as to say that "a form of
moral and spiritual cancer" was plaguing the country. "That something
has gone wrong in America most of us know," wrote Archibald MacLeish
in his piece, despite the fact that we were richer than any other nation
past or present and had achieved many great things. "We feel that we've
lost our way in the woods, that we don't know where we are going—if anywhere," he thought, our national purpose as stated by Jefferson in the Declaration of Independence—life, liberty and the pursuit of happiness for all
men—no longer clear. Part of this purpose was aspiration, potentiality,
and hope, that is, the American Dream, something that MacLeish feared
had possibly become "out of date" with broad prosperity and abundance.
"Are we simply too thick through the middle to dream?" the librarian of
Congress asked, suggesting that our loss of identity could be the result of
overfeeding, both figuratively and literally.[37]

Junior Achievement

Ironically, individuals looking to personal prosperity as the main road
to their American Dream were in the wrong place at the wrong time.
Despite the generally good times, it was becoming ever more difficult to
get rich in the 1950s, a reflection of the political and economic impetus to
create a large middle class. Only 148 Americans made $1 million or more
in 1955 (annual income was frequently used as the measure of a millionaire), down from 219 in 1950 and a whopping 513 in 1929. The numbers
proved what many had sensed since the end of the war, that it was harder
to make a killing than before the Depression put a damper on the creation
of great fortunes. Higher tax rates and a higher cost of living were making

the purely monetary version of the American Dream almost impossible to attain, an unfortunate turn of events for people viewing wealth as the primary barometer of success. Getting rich from a salary alone assuredly was not going to get one to East Street, the lucky few making most of their loot from stock dividends or by selling real estate at a profit. "In the old days you were allowed to feel it, see it, even to use it," said comedian Bob Hope, even one of the richest people in America feeling the pinch of the IRS and inflation.[38]

The difficulty of creating a large nest egg during one's working years had much to do with why retirement became a significantly bigger chunk of the American Dream in the postwar years. An aging and more well-off population also brought more attention to the issue; the average life span of a baby born in 1900 was forty-eight, but by the late 1940s it had passed the sixty-five mark, changing the very nature of what an individual should do with the final couple of decades of his or her life. Although retirement dovetailed nicely with the American Dream of being able to stop working at a particular age to live happily ever after in a little cottage somewhere, it also contradicted the Dream's ethos of productivity and achievement. "It is our national creed (which conflicts with the American Dream) that hard work and its rewards are man's justification for being," wrote George Lawton for the New York Times, finding Americans "not prepared for a steady diet of recreation and relaxation."[39]

That retirement was turning out to be a mixed bag for many was rather surprising given the tremendous effort that had gone into making it possible for ordinary Americans. For the past couple of decades, the federal government had been effectively subsidizing the American Dream through "old-age" payments under the Social Security Act of 1935, a remarkable achievement from a historical sense. "Twenty-four years ago an alluring vision was added to the American Dream," John L. Springer observed in the New York Times in 1959, "the vision of happy, carefree retirement for the working masses" a nearly universal one, knowing that most of those sixty-five years and older now had little or no financial worries. Along with corporate pension plans, retirees were supposedly living the good life during their "golden years" by traveling, pursuing their hobbies, or just sitting in the Florida sun. New research was showing something much different, however, throwing a major curve into this aspect of the Dream. Retirement was not the happiest time of life, many social scientists, doctors, business executives, and retirees themselves were beginning to think, and for a lot of old folks it may not have been a happy one at all. Compulsory retirement (or "enforced leisure") at age sixty-five was leading to feelings of boredom, uselessness, and loneliness among some, with rapid physical decline often a result. Even worse, gerontologists were finding cases of "retirement shock"—a psychological condition often leading to depression, illness, and premature death. A productive life was the best life, more experts were coming around to believe, shifting the tectonic plates of the American Dream.[40]

There were, of course, exceptions. In what an editor for the *Wall Street Journal* described as "a strange twist [to] the old American dream," twenty-two Wisconsin farmers promptly and happily retired in 1959 when their land became part of the government's soil-bank conservation-reserve program. Getting paid for not growing anything on their land as the program stipulated was a literal Dream come true for these farmers (average age fifty-eight), the prospect of steady, guaranteed money something entirely alien and wonderful. "It won't ever freeze, a drought won't hurt it, and you don't have to work to get it," said one of the lucky growers, eager to take the money and run. The *Journal*'s editor found the program rather outrageous, however, thinking the founding fathers would never have supported the idea of taxpayer money going toward persons able to work. "There are lots of other people who would like to have the Government pursue their happiness for them so that they don't 'have to work to get it,'" he grumbled, seeing the farm program as part of a disturbing national trend of giving money away to people who did not earn it.[41]

Perhaps because it was so hard to do at the time, making a lot of money quickly seemed to be on many Americans' minds in the late 1950s. Besides getting lucky at that new oasis in the desert, Las Vegas (lotteries were a decade or two away), a television quiz show was probably the fastest way to make a quick buck or acquire something that the Joneses next door would really covet. Saul Pett of the *Hartford Courant* considered the great American Dream to now be "the pot of gold at the end of the quiz show rainbow," with shows like *Twenty-One, The $64,000 Question,* and *The Price*

Is Right doling out big money and prizes to the winners. Some of the winners were getting a little help from producers, it would soon be learned, but there were other problems besides the fixing. Pett warned future contestants with dollar signs in their eyes that the quiz-show pot frequently turned out to be filled not with gold but with a lump of coal, not the fast track to the American Dream they imagined. More often than not, mink coats would not fit, new cars were too big for the garage, and that modern piece of furniture did not match what one already had in the living room, with trying to sell the white elephant a losing proposition. Worst of all, the IRS was waiting in the wings to take its share, with the quoted retail value of a prize typically much higher than what it was actually worth. There were no shortcuts to the American Dream, it appeared, meaning people in search of it would have to find a more traditional path.[42]

One traditional path was, of course, starting one's own business. For would-be entrepreneurs not quite sure of their calling, there was the Start-Your-Own-Business Exposition, a five-day show at the New York Coliseum in its third year in 1961. "The American dream to be one's own boss was put on display at the New York Coliseum yesterday with details, blue-prints, specifications and price tags," reported William M. Freeman that year for the *New York Times*, with several hundred people strolling through the exhibits to see if opportunity knocked. One of the more interesting exhibits was a "jumping and tumbling net," something that both kids and adults on the West Coast were finding to be quite fun. For people who thought what would soon be called the trampoline may not be the Next Big Thing, there was the Washmobile car-washing venture, this once-in-a-lifetime opportunity requiring an investment of just $3,990.[43]

Given the celebration of entrepreneurialism and upward mobility in general during the postwar years, it was not surprising that not just one but two new biographies of Horatio Alger soon appeared in bookstores: John Tebbel's *From Rags to Riches: Horatio Alger Jr. and the American Dream* and Ralph D. Gardner's *Horatio Alger; or, The American Hero Era*. Each book revealed that Alger's actual life belied the fact that his name had become, as Hal Borland put it, "a synonym for implausible rise from poverty to wealth as a reward for virtue and industry." Given that by the end of his life in 1899 Horatio Alger had squandered the fortune he had earned from writing more than a hundred wildly popular books (each one a morality tale involving honesty, integrity, and hard work), it was indeed ironic that his name would forever be equated with the American Dream of success.[44]

Despite the fact that his real story was more tragedy than morality tale, the Horatio Alger mythology was a powerful one that provided a solid endorsement of America's free-enterprise system. Adults were not just interested in following the principles of free enterprise but also committed to teaching them to young people during the postwar years, considered an ideal way to train the next generation to be good citizens (and consumers). Thousands of teenagers across the country received a tutorial in free enterprise via Junior Achievement, an organization offering actual experience in business. In 1960 more than a thousand boys and girls were involved in Junior Achievement on the North Side of Chicago alone, the budding entrepreneurs running more than a hundred small businesses. "Junior Achievers Realize American Dream" went the headline of an article in the *Chicago Daily Tribune,* as the kids learned the basics of production, sales, and accounting via once-a-week "JA Nights" held throughout the school year. Groups of fifteen to twenty chose a product to manufacture and market, elected a board of directors, and sold stock to build capital, their goal of making a profit more often than not achieved. Big companies sponsored the organization and offered advice to Junior Achievers, no doubt happy to know that the next generation was being schooled in the ways and means of capitalism.[45]

All students were considered junior achievers, however, as the same newspaper made clear at graduation time that year. "Put the American free enterprise system to work for you!" exclaimed George Lill, those ten words in his opinion "the most inclusive counsel that can be given to June graduates." On the thresholds of their careers, high school and college graduates were considered the future of the American Dream, a weighty responsibility assigned to them whether they liked it or not. For Lill, and certainly many other figures of authority, getting young people to buy into the concept of free enterprise was critical to keeping the Dream alive: "Here is the American dream in terms of reality. In this phrase, the American free enterprise system, lies the key to the American way of life. In its fullest realization, it is a life of self-determination, opportunity, initiative, success, and happiness. The life-long dividends are available to everyone *in direct proportion* to how well the free enterprise system is applied in each case." As long as one chose a suitable career, got enough education to succeed in it, and approached every day at work with enthusiasm and pride, the possibilities were limitless. "If you're wide awake, you can put the American Dream to work," Lill told young readers, anyone and everyone capable of getting whatever they wanted out of life if they really wanted to. And, needless to say, to the victor would go the spoils. "The American dream is to move up to a better job, a nicer house, higher social position," wrote Kittie Turmell in her "Teenagers" column in the *Los Angeles Times* in 1960, advising her young readers to get the best schooling possible and enter a profession if they intended to climb the ladder of success.[46]

Like the research studies from 1949 showed, however, it was unlikely that there would be enough professional jobs around in the years ahead for teens to grab their piece of the Dream. A new poll from Purdue University in 1961 along with government data revealed that about 35 percent of teenagers intended to be some kind of professional—three and a half times the 10 percent of American workers who actually were professionals that year. "Lulled by a new version of the American dream, which runs, 'If you study real hard . . . you'll get the jobs you want,' today's teenagers may wake up to receive a rude shock," wrote Barbara Schulz in the *Chicago Daily Tribune,* the shock being that those jobs were not going to be there. If all the young people who wanted to become a professional did indeed become one, in fact, the American economy would essentially shut down, there being not nearly enough secretaries, factory workers, truck drivers, and other folks who did not wear a suit to work. It appeared that many teens were setting their goals too high or would end up with jobs they did not really want. Postwar pressure for a class-based measure of success, and specifically to go to college and perhaps graduate school, was perhaps putting the American Dream out of reach for a large part of an entire generation.[47]

Regardless, with far more students than ever before in the nation's history, the American Dream inevitably tilted toward education during the postwar years. "Today the overwhelming majority of Americans, regardless of political party, believe the American dream means every young American should have the opportunity of the kind and amount of education which will enable each to develop his fullest potential," wrote Ralph McGill of the *Hartford Courant* in 1963, believing the nation was falling well short in that regard. Geography, class, and race all played an important role in how good of an education a child received, of course, a direct contradiction to the democratic ideals of the Dream. As well, defense spending had risen dramatically since the end of the war, but education budgets had not, relatively speaking, which was a little ironic given that national security depended heavily on producing well-educated engineers and scientists. For McGill, unequal education was not just unfair but dangerous. Germany was a perfect example of how a school system based on classifications and rank could lead to totalitarianism, he thought, meaning free, popular education was the best recipe for free, popular government. Was America really the land of opportunity, or was the Dream the exclusive province of an elite few?[48]

Something New and Better

With people like Richard and Pat Nixon to look up to in 1960, teens and everybody else could plainly see that the American Dream could really come true. The fact that her husband was in the running for president of the United States was the "American dream coming true," said Pat Nixon in July of that year, defining the phrase as "where people of humble circumstance can go up the ladder through sheer hard work and obtain what they work for." Richard Nixon had served as vice president for the past eight years but was champing at the bit to realize what many considered the Dream of Dreams—to be the most powerful man in the country and probably the world. Just like his wife, Nixon referenced the American Dream during the campaign, a way to set himself off from the Democratic candidate, Senator John F. Kennedy. "If anybody had any doubts about the American dream, they ought to look at us," he said just two days after Pat met with the press, describing their struggle for success as a much different story than that of his rival, whose father was one of the country's richest men and whose wife came from money. Typically reluctant to discuss anything related to his private life, Nixon told reporters how his wife had been born in a mining camp and, after her mother died of cancer, took care of her father and four brothers. Nixon's own upbringing was just as tough, he continued, his family having scratched out a meager living on a ranch in California. "Ours was not one of the great American families," he emphasized, the implication being that he and his wife, rather than the Kennedys, represented the real American Dream.[49]

Although he narrowly lost the election, Richard Nixon's story of how he and his wife realized their American Dream was genuinely moving (and probably planted the seeds for the man's next, more successful, run). One person clearly impressed by his journey was Glen Bower, a fifteen-year-old freshman at Beecher City High School in Illinois. Bower, an honor student and member of the Illinois and United States Historical Societies, wrote an essay titled "The American Dream" that was published by the *Chicago Tribune* in 1964, part of the newspaper's "Voice of Youth" series. (The teen, who planned to be a lawyer, got paid five dollars for his submission.) For Bower, Nixon's declaration that his American Dream had come true (a theme he revisited in his acceptance speech at the Republican National Convention) was proof that the idea was real and that this country was the only place in the world where it could happen. Because of Nixon's "determination to fight until the job was done," as Bower put it, the teenager believed Nixon's best days lay ahead. "Only in America could he run again for a great office and win, as very well might happen," the young Republican accurately predicted, convinced that "this is the American dream."[50]

Like Richard Nixon, President Lyndon Johnson was known to reference the American Dream in speeches, he too going from humble beginnings to one of the most powerful people in the world. In May 1964 in Atlantic City, where the Democratic National Convention was going to be held that August, for example, LBJ used the Dream as the conceit of a joke, knowing it would get big laughs given that he had not yet announced his incumbent candidacy for president: "We meet in a historic hall tonight. In this very spot will be chosen an American leader for 1965, a person who symbolizes the American dream. I am sad that it becomes my duty to announce tonight that that person will not be me." Waiting a beat to give the audience enough time for a collective gasp, President Johnson then quipped, "It will be Miss America of 1965." Everyone quickly realized that the beauty contest was going to be held in that very same hall a month after the convention, relieved that the president was just having a little fun at their expense.[51]

Just a couple of weeks later, LBJ was a lot more serious in using the American Dream as the focal point of a speech. Johnson had returned to the site of the Johnson City, Texas, high school where he graduated forty years earlier (as the president of a class of six), an occasion to look back on his past and imagine the nation's future. "I have come back tonight from . . . a journey that providence of the Almighty has led from the friendly hills of our county to the first house of our country," the president said to the graduating class of seniors (now up to thirty), his story an amazing one but also one that any American could potentially repeat. "Something new and better is waiting for all of us," he told the class of 1964 (and a few teachers who remembered him as an average student), the country to be a place where "every child will grow up knowing that success in life depends only on ability and not on the color of skin or the circumstances of birth."[52]

A much different story could be heard at another graduation ceremony just a few days later, however. Able to see which way the winds were blowing in a way that LBJ could not, Grayson Kirk, president of Columbia University, informed some six thousand degree recipients wearing caps and gowns and ready to hear the usual "the world is your oyster" speech that "in one sense the American dream is over." The class of 1964 was inheriting a set of problems that no previous generation had, Kirk glumly reported, with racial inequality, labor unrest, and even some actions of the government things that had done irreparable damage to the American Dream. "The future once seemed to be so sure, so certain and so alluring," Kirk concluded, but "now we appear to be unsure of ourselves, sometimes of our course, frequently of our prospects."[53]

Although no doubt shocking to hear, Kirk's words would turn out to be prophetic. The American Dream, pulled apart in a myriad of directions and more than a little battered, would become increasingly scrutinized in the years ahead, its very meaning questioned and considered suspect by exactly the people Kirk was talking to. Many of the challenges that faced the Dream in the two decades after World War II—persistent racism, excessive consumerism, and the inescapable feeling that the country had lost its way—were about to become crises, making the future of our guiding mythology all the more uncertain.

3

The Anti-Paradise

America seems an Anti-Paradise to me, but it has so much space and
so many possibilities and ultimately one does come to belong there.

—Sigmund Freud, 1939

IN APRIL 1975, four residents of Mansfield, Connecticut, gathered
to discuss if and how the American Dream was different than during
Revolutionary times. The makeup of the gathering, the first in a series
of panel discussions commemorating the upcoming bicentennial, was
intended to reflect the diversity of the community. In the group were
R. Kent Newmyer, a history professor at the University of Connecticut;
James Barnett, sociology professor emeritus at that university; Ethel Larkin, a lifelong resident of the area; and Douglas Cohen, a junior at a local
high school. Newmyer spoke first, arguing that it had been possible to
make one's mark in the Revolutionary period by using one's talents, but
contemporary culture no longer allowed that option. Barnett was equally
convinced that things had changed for the worse, the Dream's "pursuit
of happiness" now dependent on getting some kind of assistance from
the government. Larkin made the point that families and neighbors in
Revolutionary times worked together to make their farms prosperous, but
people were now more independent, the American Dream currently, and
rather sadly, a solitary affair. Cohen, the teenager, was the most critical
about the changes to the Dream over the past two centuries, however.
The American Dream was now virtually extinct, he believed, with not
just drive and talent needed to make it happen but also a lot of luck and
good connections. "The future is not as certain for our children," said

Robert Norris, the moderator of the discussion and professor of education at the University of Connecticut, quite the understatement given the bleak outlook each of the four panelists laid out.[1]

Although the news was not good, the nation's two-hundredth birthday was a perfect opportunity to examine the state of the American Dream. The past decade had proved to be a particularly rocky ride for the Dream as the postwar vision of a "better, deeper, richer life" for all citizens crumbled into dust. Inflation was making owning a single-family house impossible for most Americans, and the recent energy crisis had dashed our hopes for limitless (and free, many believed) amounts of fuel and electricity to run our big cars, array of appliances, and heated swimming pools. A lower standard of living, combined with the social and political chaos of the past few years, was a clear sign that the American Dream was in decline. Would the Dream recover, many wondered as the tall ships sailed into New York Harbor, and, if so, how and when?

A Great Society

Few people in 1965 would or could have imagined that the next ten years would take such a toll on the American Dream. President Johnson's proposal to create a "Great Society" was especially exciting because it dovetailed so thoroughly with the democratic foundation of the Dream. "The most persistent American dream, originating with the Founding Fathers and periodically recurring for 200 years, has been that of creating on this continent a Great Society resting upon a people made politically free, economically secure, universally literate, culturally sophisticated, politically wise, morally right and naturally good," wrote J. R. Wiggins, editor of the *Washington Post*, just two weeks after LBJ's 1965 State of the Union message. Now, after a series of wars, depressions, and other crises, it appeared the country was ready to return to the original Dream, a more perfect society inspired by the ideals of the Enlightenment waiting in the wings. The best thing about LBJ's proposed "Great Society" was that it was grounded in aspiration, true to the reach-for-the-stars nature of the American Dream. Although the mere concept of a "Great Society" was indeed ambitious, the "gap between reality and expectation may be less than it ever has been any place on earth," thought Wiggins, the best of Henry

Luce's "American Century" likely still to come. Nothing short of a promised land could very well lay ahead, he and certainly many others believed
as the second half of the 1960s beckoned, the practicality of Johnson's plan
making it different from other grand and noble visions of the past.[2]

Not everybody had faith in an emerging Great Society, much less the
American Dream. Although it was a novel, Norman Mailer's *American
Dream* published that spring offered a much different view of the nation's
past, present, and future. Written in the first person, the book told the story
of Stephen Rojack, a successful man by any measure living the good life
with his beautiful, rich wife. When Rojack falls, he falls hard, however,
the crashing and burning of his American Dream a warning perhaps for
those individuals desperately trying to achieve it. (The book was a sequel
to Theodore Dreiser's *American Tragedy*, according to Conrad Knickerbocker of the *New York Times*.) For some critics, like Robert R. Kirsch of
the *Los Angeles Times*, the comparisons between Rojack and Mailer were
painfully (quite literally) clear, the larger-than-life social critic and occasional novelist filled with the same kind of destructive streak and self-hate
as his protagonist. Still, "when Mailer talks you have to listen," as another
reviewer, Paul R. Jackson of the *Chicago Tribune*, wrote. The book was
banned in Australia (along with Hubert Selby's *Last Exit to Brooklyn* and
Whyland Young's *Eros Denied*) but a best seller in Germany, a fair reflection of the extreme response anything by Mailer typically received.[3]

Two other intellectual heavyweights of the day, William F. Buckley
Jr. and James Baldwin, had the American Dream on their minds in 1965,
their divergent views indicative that the country was a long way from being
one big happy family. The editor of the *National Review* and the novelist
and essayist were invited by Cambridge University to debate the notion
that "the American Dream is at the expense of the American Negro," with
Baldwin taking the "for" position and Buckley the "against." More than
700 students packed into the room to hear the two go at it, with another
500 jammed into other rooms of the university's Union Society watching
the brainy brawl on closed-circuit television. Baldwin delivered the first
rhetorical blows, talking about what it was like to be black in America
and how the realization of the Dream relied on racial equality. "There
is scarcely any hope for the American dream" until whites accepted the

fact that blacks were an integral part of the nation's history and identity, he argued, the latter's mere presence something that would prevent the mythology from becoming real. "Unless we can establish some kind of dialog between those people who enjoy the American dream and those other people who have not achieved it," he added, "we will be in terrible trouble." Buckley responded at length, but it was clear that he had been overmatched; 544 students voted for the motion and 164 against, a convincing decision for Baldwin.[4]

The ideological divide between Baldwin and Buckley reflected the very different perspectives held by the Left and the Right regarding the American Dream in the midsixties. As in the 1930s, when FDR's New Deal sharply split liberals and conservatives on the subject, the Left and the Right disagreed about the impact LBJ's "Great Society" was having on the Dream. People of a conservative bent, like Richard C. Cornuelle and M. Stanton Evans, believed the president's grand plan was damaging the American Dream by limiting individual freedom, a story that sounded awfully familiar. "Unlimited government needlessly compromises the American dream because there is a better way to do most of its work," Cornuelle wrote in his new book, *Reclaiming the American Dream*, arguing that things worked out a lot better and smoother when citizens took it upon themselves to do them. Evans agreed, the last line of his new book, *The Liberal Establishment*, saying it all. "Liberalism is a creed profoundly hostile to American freedom," he posited, the writer for the *National Review* very concerned about the left turn the federal government had taken over the past few years.[5]

Those on the Left disagreed, of course, seeing liberalism as completely in the spirit of the American Dream, just as backers of the New Deal had. Americans on the extreme Left did as well, wholeheartedly believing radicalism was perfectly consistent with the Dream's tenets of independence and self-sufficiency. Staughton Lynd, an assistant professor of history at Yale, made the case that the "New Left" (the liberal and sometimes radical political movement focused on social activism) was a legitimate descendant of the American Revolution and the United States Constitution, something conservatives would dispute. "It is precisely the distinctly American dream that all movements should be subordinated to human rights," Lynd told the Yale Socialist Symposium in 1966, seeing the escalating Vietnam War as much more "un-American" than his brand of politics. Many nonradicals were, of course, beginning to think the same thing as the war heated up in the mid-1960s. The nation's youth was "waking to [the] demands of [the] American Dream," reported Lynn Lilliston of the *Los Angeles Times*, questioning how our presence in Southeast Asia was going to lead to the Dream's larger goal of greater international brotherhood and world peace.[6]

Like the Vietnam War, the battle for civil rights went to the heart of what the American Dream was about and who could share in it. In 1966, for example, two neighborhoods in Chicago, Gage Park and Belmont-Cragin, were the sites of racially motivated violence as white mobs attacked civil rights demonstrators protesting against segregation in housing. Many blacks from the inner city could afford to live in these neighborhoods (which were among twenty selected by Martin Luther King's Southern Christian Leadership Conference and local organizations for such demonstrations), but the locals, most of them immigrants or children of immigrants from Europe, made it vividly clear they were not wanted. The conflict was, essentially, a fight over and for the American Dream, one group trying to preserve theirs while the other tried to achieve it.[7] Over the next couple of years, blacks would themselves use violence in cities across America to protest their exclusion from the American Dream, a source of confusion for many whites. "The major outbreak of Negro violence is such a profoundly disturbing event because it calls into question so many optimistic assumptions about American society," observed William V. Shannon of the *New York Times* in 1967, the experience and outlook of most white people typically a world apart from the perspective of blacks. With real progress being made—blacks' income was rising, more blacks were graduating from college, and court decisions and civil rights laws were increasingly creating legal equality—why were blacks burning down their own neighborhoods?[8]

At least one man, Robert T. Pickett, a twenty-year-old prelaw student at Kent State, seemed to know and took advantage of the opportunity to share the information with Vice President Hubert Humphrey when he visited the university in 1968 (two years before the Kent State massacre).

Humphrey, a candidate for the Democratic presidential nomination along with Senators Robert F. Kennedy (NY) and Eugene McCarthy (MN), referenced the American Dream in his speech before eight thousand students, during which about thirty black "militants" and one hundred Vietnam War and draft protesters walked out. Pickett, vice president of the university's student body and a member of a "Black Power" group, stuck around, however, getting the chance to put Humphrey on the spot: "You say you believe in the American dream. I do not believe in the American dream simply because the American dream does not believe in me. If it did believe in me we wouldn't have had any riots in Newark or Watts. . . . The American dream to me is the American nightmare. . . . What will you do to restore my faith and my people's faith in America and the American Dream if you are elected?" Not rattled a bit, Humphrey responded by discussing his liberal stances on civil rights and social welfare and his substantial work in each area, with the vice president going so far as to describe himself as "a soul brother." With this revelation, the crowd— including Pickett—gave Humphrey a standing ovation, the two shaking hands after the event. When asked by a reporter whom he planned to vote for, Pickett revealed he had already compared the three Democratic candidates' positions on civil rights and was backing Humphrey all the way.[9]

For conservative political leaders, however, racial unrest and violent war protests were clear signs that the country was out of control, its guiding mythology a source of conflict rather than unity. "We are facing today nothing less than a crisis in the American dream at home and the American mission in the world," said George Romney in early 1968, the governor of Michigan and Republican presidential candidate adopting what he saw as "rampant lawlessness" as a campaign tactic. The Johnson administration was out of touch with the people, Romney charged, with many dissenters "giving up hope in America and taking up hatchets." The other major Republican candidate for president, Richard Nixon, also used an endangered American Dream as part of his campaign strategy, quite a different theme from the self-referential Dream of his 1960 run for the office. If the administration took steps to "move with both compassion and conviction to bring the American dream to the ghetto," the former vice president said in a radio speech just a month after Romney's, the summer of 1968 would be a "cooler" one in the nation's troubled cities. When "private enterprise gets into the ghetto and when the people of the ghetto get into private enterprise," Nixon predicted, the country's urban problems would be solved. In the short term, however, Nixon was not opposed to meeting force with force to stop the violence. "If progress is to be made, the first essential now is order," he added, no doubt appeasing more reactionary voters.[10]

Less than a month later, however, Martin Luther King would be killed, ensuring that the upcoming summer would not be a "cool" one in some of the nation's cities. "I see the Promised Land," King preached in Memphis the night before his death, sure that his people would realize the American Dream even if he himself did not live to see it. With the murder of Robert Kennedy two months later, the nation's woes went from bad to worse, he like King a leading voice of and symbol for the American Dream.

"Robert Kennedy believed so deeply in the American dream and acted so consistently on that faith," wrote Shannon of the *Times* a day after the assassination, both the senator and his brother John committed to the Dream's principles of "individualism, self-reliance, self-discipline and unending self-improvement." In churches and synagogues across the country the following weekend, Robert Kennedy was frequently eulogized as a man who represented the American Dream, his loss a severe blow to making it come true. The nation "face[d] the threatening death of the American Dream" with the assassination of Robert Kennedy, Reverend J. Alan McLean told an interdenominational crowd of six hundred at the South Congregational Church in New Britain, Connecticut, many of whom had attended an ecumenical service for King in the same church just six weeks earlier. The Great Society was off to a decidedly ungreat start.[11]

The Nouveau Avant

Although the American Dream did not die in the late 1960s, as many thought it would, the cultural chaos of the times did have a profound impact on what it looked and felt like. "Something funny has happened to the American Dream," wrote Frederic Morton for the *New York Times* in 1967, concluding that most of the people he knew had, much to their surprise, not succeeded in achieving the standard Dream's goal to "get there" and enjoy the good life. More important, perhaps, affluence had not brought happiness even for those people who had "gotten there," leading to a sea change in the American Dream. "Instead of dreaming rich, we've begun to dream hip," Morton suggested, the mainstream adopting the counterculture's mantras to "find yourself" and "do your thing" rather than define oneself by the things one owned. The bearded hippie was now the quintessential American Dreamer, he felt, the realization that one was a member of the bourgeoisie a major bummer. "Now we want to liberate our wild, free *avant-garde* persona from sodden prosperity," Morton thought, the nouveau-riche generation having given birth to the nouveau-avant generation.[12]

Ironically, however, individuals wanting to go from nouveau riche to nouveau avant were finding it a lot more difficult than they thought it would be. The aspiring avant's "pursuit of persona, like the pursuit of wealth, is just another American dream—only more frustrating," Morton continued, some people walking the straight and narrow not quite sure how to become flower children. "There is only one Allen Ginsberg for every ten Horatio Algers," he argued, finding the ability to write good poetry or just live a poetic life more of a challenge than going from rags to riches. But many of the nouveau riche were giving it a go, swapping out their *Vogue* magazines and English hunting prints for the *East Village Other* (an alternative New York City newspaper) and psychedelic posters. Young well-to-do couples from the suburbs were not that long ago driving big cars to their country clubs to have drinks with their equally well-to-do friends. Now, however, "they split for the Electric Circus in their (American Motors) Rebel to freak out with fellow swingers," Morton observed, the Manhattan discotheque *the* place to tune in and turn on. For at least a segment of the adult population and a good many young people, the upwardly mobile, materialistic American Dream was decidedly out, replaced by a more hedonistic and spiritual version.[13]

Morton's wry observations foreshadowed Charles A. Reich's landmark *The Greening of America: How the Youth Revolution Is Trying to Make America Livable* by a full three years. Like Morton, Reich believed that young couples who by all accounts had realized the American Dream were, underneath the bright and shiny surface, unhappy people, filled with resentment, boredom, and hatred of their everyday lives. Such couples were "the victim of a cruel deception," Reich wrote, having "been persuaded that the richness, the satisfactions, the joy of life are to be found in power, success, acceptance, popularity, achievements, rewards, excellence and the rational competent mind." Because it deprived individuals of a search for self, "Consciousness II," as Reich labeled this paradigm, had produced an alienated and impoverished society, the basis for the emergence of what he called "Consciousness III." A long excerpt of the book appeared in the New Yorker, and sales of the issue flew off newsstands, putting the article in the same league as other iconic ones the magazine had published such as John Hersey's "Hiroshima," Rachel Carson's "Silent Spring," and James Baldwin's "Letters from a Region in My Mind."[14]

What made The Greening of America such a sensation was not just that it was a critique of bourgeois values and the traditional American Dream as Packard's The Status Seekers was a decade earlier, but that it laid out a vision of the future. The coming of "Consciousness III" represented nothing less than a revolution in the works, Reich argued, a dramatic shift in awareness and way of looking at the world. Grounded in New Deal liberalism and reform and the Great Society's worship of logic, reason, and technology, "Consciousness II" was fast becoming obsolete, its priorities of efficiency, growth, and progress no longer relevant. What was causing the machine to break down? For Reich, it was clearly the Vietnam War, describing the conflict as "the Corporate State's one unsalable product." Young people were "the wrong market" to try to sell the war to, he believed, their refusal to buy it opening up the floodgates to the wholesale rejection of the "Corporate State" and its rigid, narrow version of the American Dream. It was, as the song from the popular Broadway show Hair went, the dawning of the Age of Aquarius, and the people embarking on this exciting journey would see the world as one family to which everyone belonged.[15]

It was highly unlikely that peace would guide the planets and love steer the stars, but a 1971 report based on Gallup interviews suggested that Reich's "Consciousness II" and its version of the American Dream may indeed have run their course. According to Albert H. Cantril and Charles W. Roll Jr.'s "Hopes and Fears of the American People," that paradigm's primary prescription for success (upward mobility) was in decline, with concerns about the health of the nation now the priority for most citizens. Americans were sick and tired of demonstrations, crime, drugs, and, most of all, the Vietnam War, the study showed, so much so that these problems had eclipsed personal objectives in importance. "The public faces continuing frustration and anxiety, bombarded as it is in our information-saturated society with details of problems at home and abroad about which the individual can do little," wrote the authors, which was posing great danger to the country should a major crisis arise. In short, the American Dream was fading, Cantril and Roll were basically saying, the loss of individually defined goals something the mythology could not withstand.[16]

As the loss of faith in the American Dream spread like a virus, one of its most avid spokespersons, Richard Nixon, was blamed for the apparent demise of our guiding mythology. "President Nixon has raised the curtain on what may be the last act of a play entitled, 'The Great American Dream,'" wrote James J. Kilpatrick for the Los Angeles Times in 1971. "No article of faith has been clutched more fiercely over these past 200 years than the doctrine of risk capitalism in a competitive marketplace," Kilpatrick continued, obviously surprised that it was a Republican president who was squashing our free economy. But by imposing a ninety-day freeze on prices, wages, and rents, levying a surcharge on dutiable imports, and suspending the conversion of dollars to gold (all efforts to try to stabilize the wobbly economy), Nixon was doing just that. "It was never a part of the great American dream that the play should turn out this way," Kilpatrick lamented, the marketplace itself supposed to keep things in proper balance. While the government's deliberate insertion of itself into the workings of the Dream was particularly unfortunate, it was just the latest step in the century-old decline of free enterprise and ascent of what Kilpatrick called "corporate socialism." In most businesses, private decision making had been reduced to a trickle, while international agreements in commodities had made those markets more cooperative than competitive. "Like good Christians invoking the Trinity, we may still hymn the free enterprise system, but we will not understand what it means," Kilpatrick stated, seeing its loss as a eulogy for the American Dream.[17]

Not just Americans but foreigners were disturbed about seeing the Dream become so torn and tattered. Writing for the New York Times from

Bonn, Germany, in 1972, Peter Petersen was admittedly worried about the litany of problems the nation was having (unemployment, violence, drugs, the busing issue), thinking the country was shrinking from its international responsibilities because it had its hands full back home. "There was a time twenty years ago when Americans often got on our nerves because they were so sure of themselves," Petersen explained, "but now we get nervous because Americans seem to be losing faith in their own destiny." Petersen had met Americans who apologized for being Americans and was angry at them for not recognizing they represented the hope of much of the world. "I know from many conversations in Communist countries that the people there understand that basically freedom is indivisible, and they dream the American Dream—not of Coca-Cola or two cars in every garage but of freedom as conceived in this country in 1776." If the United States failed, the world would fail, Petersen believed, which was his greatest concern.[18]

The twenty-five European contributors to a book called *Broken Image: Foreign Critiques of America* arguably made the strongest case that the American Dream was no more and, perhaps, may never have been. "Once upon a time America evoked nearly as many hopeful images as Heaven or Paradise," wrote Cecil Eby in his review of the book for the *Chicago Tribune*, the American Dream being one of various "quasi-mystical superlatives" the word itself brought to mind. But recently all those images—Land of Promise, Garden of the World, Last Asylum, Edenic Innocence, and, yes, American Dream—had faded, a result of the nation's social, economic, and political decline. *Broken Image* "peel[ed] off horny layers of national smugness like the action of hot lye on dead varnish," as Eby poetically put it, each essay knocking the country off its high horse. Hardly the heaven on earth many around the world believed it to be, America was a "hypocritical, thieving, snobbish, violent, boorish, and downright ugly" place, the book argued, very much the "Anti-Paradise" Freud had called it thirty years after his visit to the country in 1909. (Getting food poisoning was a fitting conclusion to his single, regrettable, trip to the United States.)[19]

America was definitely more dystopia than utopia in another book published that year, Hunter S. Thompson's *Fear and Loathing in Las Vegas: A*

Savage Journey to the Heart of the American Dream. Thompson (as "Raoul Duke") goes to Las Vegas with his Samoan lawyer, "Dr. Gonzo," to cover a motorcycle race for *Sports Illustrated* but is not exactly clear what the story is supposed to be. "Nobody had bothered to say," Thompson, who actually had gone there on assignment for the magazine, wrote. "So we would have to drum it up on our own. Free Enterprise. The American Dream. Horatio Alger gone mad on drugs in Las Vegas." That becomes the story, of course, as Thompson ("a monster reincarnation of Horatio Alger," the narrator calls himself) and his partner embark on a series of drug- and alcohol-fueled adventures. Thompson's American Dream was "a fanfare of baroque fantasy," as Crawford Woods described it in his review for the *New York Times*, the author himself not exactly clear what really happened and what he made up.[20]

Less Gonzo journalists saw things similarly if a lot more rationally. "What the United States seems to lack today is any one large, vocal and powerful group whose self-interest also coincides with the principles that once kept the American dream alive," thought Fred M. Hechinger of the same newspaper a few months later, believing the country was experiencing a mass "paralysis of the spirit." Creature comforts had turned us into a self-satisfied, "smugly docile" nation, Hechinger suggested, with "looking out for Number One" our primary concern. (President Nixon often referred to the country as "Number One," perhaps not coincidentally.) Playing the game to get one's piece of the pie was the order of the day, as Hechinger saw it, with few willing to challenge the system despite big problems like political corruption, a severe teacher shortage, and the continuing Vietnam War. "The dynamic optimism of the American experiment" was in jeopardy, the member of the newspaper's editorial board warned, replaced by pervasive disillusionment and a loss of idealism.[21]

Even the country's land appeared to be running out, a seemingly impossible scenario that also threatened the Dream. Real estate developers were indeed buying up large areas in existing suburbs to build new housing, creating a "land crisis" that limited further expansion. "As the land goes, so does the American dream of building and owning a new home," fretted the *Hartford Courant* in 1972, troubled that some would be excluded from one of our basic birthrights. Overcrowding in the suburbs, combined with the counterculture's back-to-nature movement, pushed some to look for an alternative lifestyle. Just as many a generation earlier fled the city to find their American Dream, more suburbanites were now heading out to the country to find a more peaceful and affordable way of life. "A place in the country, maybe a pond, certainly some trees," wrote Martha Patton for the *Chicago Tribune* that same year. "If this isn't the American dream, it comes darn close to it." A couple hundred years after he envisioned it, Jefferson's rural American Dream was back in vogue, a utopian paradise waiting for those individuals feeling fenced in.[22]

Besides a home on the range, about the only place one could find the American Dream in the early seventies seemed to be in advertising. "The American Dream has not vanished," noted Richard Christiansen in the *Los Angeles Times* in 1972, for "it flourishes on the television commercial." In a current Coca-Cola commercial, for example, friends and neighbors paint an old woman's house, while one for McDonald's had a cute little girl and her grandfather bonding over ordering cheeseburgers. The country was not complex and divisive but a simple, harmonious place, these commercials suggested, an ideal environment for the Dream to thrive. A spot for United Airlines topped them all. In the commercial, a young couple walked hand in hand in a field, pausing to rest under a beautiful tree. Enter Burgess Meredith, or at least his comforting voice, telling viewers they too could discover the United States through United Airlines. Then, rather incredibly, an image of the Statue of Liberty appeared while a chorus sang Woody Guthrie's "This Land Is Your Land," raising the idea of air travel to a patriotic act. "In an urbanized, crowded and often strife-torn country, these commercials tell us that we still long for the time and place of a happy, united and serene America," explained Christiansen, the Dream alive and well in the make-believe universe of advertising.[23]

American Dream No. 2

Some had not given up on a happy, united, and serene America, however, thinking it was going to be the next generation that was going to make it happen. A new and improved American Dream could very well be in the making, more open-minded adults believed, not letting young people's long hair and questionable grooming habits get in the way of what were actually some very ambitious aims. After all, was keeping up with the Joneses—and ideally keeping ahead of them by a bit—really what the Dream was about? The postwar years' obsession with outer-directed measures of success had warped the American Dream, many of those Americans born after (and some before) the war concluded, something that inevitably led to dissatisfaction among a good chunk of the people who would one day be called "the greatest generation." "The older generation may have attained the American dream but they are also likely to be repressed, discontented, unhappy, and lack any real sense of self-fulfillment," wrote Del Earisman for the *Hartford Courant* in 1972, the professor of English at Upsala College in New Jersey convinced that many young people were quite sensibly taking an alternative path that placed less emphasis on financial and material criteria. "Doing one's own thing" or trying to create a better world was a perfectly legitimate interpretation of the American Dream, one in fact that was arguably truer to Adams's original conception than upward mobility. A reasonable case could be made that striving for personal fulfillment and the social good was a lot closer to the essence of the Dream than the pursuit of income or status, something that seemed lost on the people griping that the younger generation lacked goals. Which was the more authentic American Dream, one could reasonably ask: working in a school in the ghetto after a stint with VISTA or becoming a highly paid lawyer trying to make really big money in the stock market?[24]

As parents and children battled that sort of question back and forth over the dinner table in many an American home, the contentious issue of affirmative action began to complicate matters even further. The rise of the affirmative action movement in the early 1970s directly intersected with the American Dream, its supporters firmly believing that the policy allowed groups who had been largely excluded from the Dream to achieve it. Others, however, saw it as an inhibitor of the Dream rather than an agent of it. "As I understood the meaning of the American Dream, it was, quite simply, the opportunity to achieve," wrote Marvin D. Rowen for the *Los Angeles Times* in 1972, the Beverly Hills attorney of the opinion that affirmative action was undermining the Dream's ideals. In order to remedy injustices of the past (and, many would say, the inequities of the present), two of the fundamental building blocks of the American Dream—equal opportunity and individual merit—were in some situations clearly taking a backseat to skin color or some other predetermined characteristic, something Rowen considered to be contrary to the nation's founding principles (and probably illegal). Though well intentioned, preferential quota systems were destructive to the American Dream, he argued, any kind of reduction in incentive and initiative bad for the country as a whole. "The making of the American Dream requires an honest approach to the social problems facing this country and an appreciation that all of its citizens have hopes, ambitions and goals," the lawyer closed, calling for policies that encouraged anyone to reach "unlimited levels of achievement in whatever area that individual chose to involve himself."[25]

Even the seemingly incontestable concept of equality, one of the cornerstones of the American Dream, was under attack in the contentious 1970s. There was no doubt that the "equalizing of America" was reshaping our values and institutions, this parallel movement affecting virtually all aspects of social and economic life. Quotas in business and education designed to boost the presence of women and minorities were commonplace, for example, with big changes going on in sports and the military as well. As with affirmative action, however, not everyone was happy about attempts to level the white, male-dominated playing field. "Many see the pursuit for equality as part and parcel of the American Dream [but] others see it as an oncoming nightmare of bureaucratic rule, deepening torpor, and—in time—national insolvency," explained George E. Jones of *U.S. News and World Report* in 1975, even the (retiring) secretary of health, education, and welfare concerned about "egalitarian tyranny." "We risk delivering our destinies over to the cold and lifeless grip of a distant egalitarian government whose sole purpose is to ensure an equally mediocre existence for everyone, achieved at the cost of personal liberty," Caspar Weinberger warned, our real (and unfinished) social agenda to "discover and reward excellence wherever we find it." What was sometimes called "the new equality" was raising the tension between two overlapping but quite different foundations of the American Dream—freedom and fairness—this historic battle reaching a new high in intensity.[26]

One way around the constraints of affirmative action and "the new equality" was good old American entrepreneurialism. Inventing something had always been a staple of the American Dream, of course, the desire to do so accelerating in the seventies as more traditional paths narrowed. For Judith Martin of the *Los Angeles Times*, "American Dream No. 2" was coming up with "a great idea for a gadget that nobody's ever thought of before," the sale of which would naturally result in millions of dollars. ("American Dream No. 1" was becoming a movie star after being discovered by a talent scout, but that scenario just did not happen anymore, according to Martin.) Many people were indeed trying to make "American Dream No. 2" come true. Seventy thousand patents were filed in the United States in 1971, each inventor perhaps thinking he or she could be the next Chester Carlson (Xerox machine) or Edwin Land (Polaroid camera). (Some of the founding fathers, notably Jefferson and Benjamin Franklin, were also impressive inventors, lending a patriotic spirit to coming up with a new device or process.) A sample of recent patent filings—a 360-degree insect swatter, a baby-bottle basket, dining furniture with built-in serving plates—appeared to be less promising than Carlson's or Land's breakthrough, but who knew? Many big companies had turned Carlson and his photocopier away, meaning the Next Big Thing could still be out there just waiting to happen.[27]

For those individuals not interested in tinkering in their basement or garage to try to become the next Thomas Edison, an entrepreneurial version of the American Dream could still be had by selling things right in people's homes. In 1975, 200,000 people around the world were doing just that for Amway, one of the biggest direct-sales companies, hawking 150 products ranging from vitamins to cleaning products to panty hose to friends and neighbors and their friends and neighbors. Moving up through the ranks was the key to success in direct-selling businesses like Amway, Avon, Tupperware, and Sarah Coventry, with big money awaiting anyone able to climb the ladder. True believers, many of them women, were not shy about expressing the enthusiasm they felt for their line of work. "For me the most beautiful opportunity for self-expression in the free enterprise system is owning your own business," said Bernice Hansen from Akron, Ohio, the sixty-three-year-old grandmother's millions of dollars in sales that year earning her big cheers at Amway's patriotic, revival-like annual meeting in Washington, DC. At the meeting, 18,500

Amway (a contraction of "*American Way*") distributors joined to sing "The Great American Dream," the company's own musical anthem. "We can all share" and "Thanks to Amway, it's really there" went some of the song's lyrics, "it" being the American Dream for people wanting to take their future into their own hands.[28]

Although certainly a good thing, the surge in entrepreneurialism during the 1970s could be interpreted as a sign that some of the tried-and-true ways of reaching one's goals had dried up. With the postwar American Dream gone, some felt it was time to take more drastic measures by forging a less grand but more credible one. "Whatever else all the dreary and demeaning events of the past decade . . . mean and may come to mean, they surely mean an end to the American dream as it was given to us," thought Leonard J. Fein, convinced that "that which we inherited we shall not be able to bequeath." The nation had experienced a break in its continuity over the past decade, the professor of politics and social policy at Brandeis University proposed in 1973, the urban riots, assassinations, violence at the 1968 Democratic National Convention, and, of course, Vietnam War proving we no longer could think of ourselves as the New Chosen People living in a New Jerusalem. Vietnam especially, which had been justified as preserving the Dream, had led to the nation's aimlessness and loss of faith in itself. "We are ill-served by those who yearn for the good old days and, presumably, the good old dream," Fein believed, "for the good old days led irrevocably to the bad times we have seen, and the good old dream bore bitter fruit." Wouldn't having just a good, decent society, Fein asked, be good and decent enough? Arrogant in its adolescence, its people thinking it could possibly achieve perfection, America now needed "a new, more modest, more mature faith that will bind us together."[29]

Nothing perhaps symbolized the advent of a smaller, more achievable American Dream than the downsizing of the Cadillac. Few material representations of the mythology crossed social boundaries with such reckless abandon as the Cadillac, the automobile almost universally recognized as the Dream on wheels. Of course, many wealthy corporate executives were partial to Cadillacs, some of them driven by chauffeurs, but so were good numbers of successful businesspeople of a different sort in inner cities.

Whether one was a Fortune 500 CEO or local pimp, arguably nothing else made in America said success more than a Caddy, the sheer size of the thing (at twenty feet, longer than some parking spaces) instantly conveying that one had made it. Since the end of World War II, in fact, the Cadillac had generally been considered the most prestigious automobile in America, but, by the early seventies, things were changing. Younger drivers on the way up or already there were increasingly opting for foreign luxury cars like Mercedes, not wanting to be associated with a status symbol revered by the previous generation. Others felt that what was sometimes called a "boat" was more quantity than quality, its gas mileage (eight miles per gallon) also a big drawback, especially during the energy crisis.[30]

Well aware that their top-of-the-line (and most profitable) brand was possibly becoming more white elephant than American Dream, GM executives decided to take action. Rather than talk about status, size, and luxury in its advertising, Cadillac began to emphasize performance and fuel economy, despite the fact that one could hardly feel the road while driving (more like steering) the five-thousand-pound behemoth. GM was also working on a new, smaller Caddy to better compete with the likes of Mercedes and other high-end cars that did not look like a house on wheels. For the moment at least, however, sales of the seventy-four-hundred-dollar Cadillac DeVille (half the price of Mercedes's biggest model) remained strong, meaning the stodgy gas guzzler was going to remain the automotive equivalent of the Dream for some time.[31]

While Cadillac may have been conceding that the American Dream was shrinking, another icon of the mythology, John Wayne, refused to budge an inch. In 1973 the "dean of patriotic action flicks" and "moviedom's conservative paternal superstar," as Jack Hiemenz of the New York Times called him, put out a record album called America, Why I Love Her, an unapologetic love letter to the red, white, and blue. Although many would suggest the LP came out a couple decades too late, the record was selling well, a sign perhaps that not everybody had lost faith in the country. The star of such films as True Grit, The Cowboys, and The Green Berets still appealed to a good number of people, it was clear, his unique take on the American experience perhaps a soothing tonic for the decadelong nightmare that was Vietnam. (Charles Champlin of the Los Angeles Times considered Wayne's 1969 *True Grit* to be "as straight-shootin' a western as ever was to celebrate all westerns and the West that was and the American dreams of self-reliance, resourcefulness, gumption, git-up-and-go . . . and grit.") Hiemenz was not a fan, however, thinking the Duke's answer to all of the nation's questionable actions—the defense of liberty—fell more than a little flat. "Perhaps no one can make the American dream seem deader than he who dreams it still," he wrote in his review of the album, considering Wayne to be this group's "biggest casualty."[32]

There was no doubt that some of the greatest films of the late 1960s and 1970s were a world apart from John Wayne's vision of the American Dream. Much like how gangster films of the 1930s turned the Dream upside down by featuring criminals as antiheroes, the Anti-Paradise of the counterculture years was an ideal climate for cinematic outlaws to pursue wealth and power. In *Bonnie and Clyde* (1967), *The Producers* (1968), *Butch Cassidy and the Sundance Kid* (1969), *The Sting* (1973), *Paper Moon* (1973), and *The Godfather* trilogy, the bad guys were the good guys, with empathetic audiences cheering on their bending or breaking of the rules to achieve the Dream. Films such as *The Graduate* (1967) and *Easy Rider* (1969) glorified characters brave enough to reject the norms of the "establishment," their freedom-at-any-cost approach to life actually quite true to the maverick ethos of the original American Dream. Other films like *Nashville* (1975) and *Network* (1976) depicted the Dream as out of control, a corrupt system encouraging individuals and institutions to do whatever it took in order to succeed. Martin Scorcese's *Mean Streets* (1973) and *Taxi Driver* (1976) pushed the envelope even further, their American Dreamers taking revenge on whomever they blamed for keeping them down. But one film—*Rocky* (1976)—perhaps redeemed them all, its hero fighting against all odds to reach the top and, along the way, endorsing the traditional values of the Dream.

In his essay "The Blue Collar Ethic in Bicentennial America: *Rocky* (1976)," Daniel J. Leab discussed how that movie served as a stabilizing force for a "severely shaken" American Dream. After the angst of the early seventies—Vietnam, Watergate, the Arab oil embargo, economic "stagflation," a fading but lingering countercultural movement, rise in crime and civil unrest, and demand for minorities to have their voices heard—Americans were more than ready for narratives that reaffirmed their faith in the nation's ideals. The timing thus could not have been better for the bicentennial celebration, which seemed to close an especially dark chapter in the country's history. *Rocky* was part of what Leab called "that bicentennial binge," the film serving as a reminder that the American Dream could still come true. "Even though dealing with the underside of contemporary America, *Rocky* is a celebration of the American Dream," Leab wrote, the hero's blue-collar, ethnic roots making his unlikely rise to the top of the boxing world that much more compelling.[33]

The cultural sensation that was *Rocky* (if not its five awful sequels) went further than its fortunate release just five months after the nation's bicentennial. Despite (or because of) the recent chinks in the country's armor, the uniquely American phenomenon of "Number Oneness" seemed to become more intense in the 1970s. The quest to be "No. 1" was the "All-American Dream," according to Steve Harvey of the *Los Angeles Times*, Henry Aaron's closing in on Babe Ruth's home run record in the fall of 1973 a perfect example of how this country still revered the "best" and the "most." In Aaron's case, unfortunately, that person remained the Babe for those individuals who did not want a black man to hold the record. In sports especially, coming in second was considered not just not winning but failure in the United States, something that was not true for Europeans. But the fascination with "No. 1" could be seen in everything from best-seller lists to the "Top 40" to Nielsen ratings to political polls, suggesting that superiority and victory remained binding threads in the national quilt. In fact, being the preeminent country in the world was a frequent theme in political campaigns and ordinary conversations, the notion that we were not "No. 1" in any measure that really mattered often considered anathema. The space race of the sixties and, most important, being first to land on the moon were not just about science, of course, with national security resting on an American's foot to be the first to touch the lunar soil. Historians suggested our pioneer legacy had a lot to do with all this "Number Oneism," the spirit of discovery and impulse to conquer the frontier responsible for our expectation to be first in everything. Psychology professor Bruce Ogilvie had another view, however. "We are in the same position now as a 16-year-old," he thought, our "schoolyard attitudes" responsible for wanting to be the best among one's peers. What-ever the reason, the pursuit to be "No. 1" in a particular field continued to be a primary goal for many, its realization proof that one had achieved the American Dream during some especially tough times.[34]

Keeping Up with the Plotkins

The persistence of our national obsession with being "Number 1" belied the obvious erosion of the American Dream in the 1970s. Compared with previous decades, the sheer volume of the Dream was lower, our bold proclamations of equal opportunity and "a better, deeper, richer life" for all reduced to a relative whisper. "One hears little about an American dream any more," observed Bob Walton of the *Chicago Tribune* in 1973, the rising cost of living, energy crisis, and deterioration of family life just some of the problems that were making being a US citizen more a matter of survival than dreaming of achieving great things. Margaret Mead, the famous anthropologist, was even more pessimistic about the nation's pros-pects, telling a Senate subcommittee that year that the American Dream had turned into a nightmare for millions of citizens. Bill Moyers, host of a public affairs show on PBS, was equally alarmed about the state of the American Dream. "When I graduated from college in 1956 it was fash-ionable for speakers on campuses across the country to talk about The Great American Dream," he said in a 1973 speech, the idea of a bountiful destiny, with the future there for the taking, popular if not assumed. That kind of optimism and sense of invincibility were gone, a "spiritual plague" now pervasive in the country. Ordinary Americans too felt the Dream was gone. A recent survey revealed that most Americans felt the country was in "serious trouble," with almost half believing we could be heading to a "real breakdown," even ordinarily upbeat college students discouraged about the nation's and their own future. Could the American Dream be restored, people wondered, and, if so, how?[35]

One way to revive the Dream, some believed, was to simply make it smaller. The idea of unlimited growth and prosperity was just not sus-tainable, many critics in the early seventies had concluded, meaning we should set limits on our hopes and expectations. Overpopulation and over-consumption were crashing the system, these experts (many of them of the "limits to growth" school) argued, with the pressures of everyday life demanding a fundamental change in the American lifestyle.[36] Vernon Jarrett, a writer for the *Chicago Tribune*, for example, held that the nation was "in the midst of a critical dream crisis," the manifest destiny of the American Dream no longer relevant or workable. "I believe that we need to seriously begin the conscious, deliberate task of creating for ourselves a new set of dreams, even if it means the elimination of precepts held sacred over years," he thought, the alternative possibly being "self-destruction." Art Buchwald, the droll syndicated columnist, was admittedly "fuming over the American Dream," peeved that keeping up with the Joneses was no longer the central driving force it had been. One of Buchwald's neighbors, a man named "Plotkin," had been for the past few years driving a Toyota, cause enough to be the target of scorn and butt of jokes. But Plotkin was getting twenty-five miles to the gallon in his little Japanese car, something quite enviable during the energy crisis. Now it was the Joneses in their big Cadillacs and Lincoln Continentals who were getting sneers as they pulled into their driveways. "Everybody in our neighborhood is now keeping up with the Plotkins," Buchwald confessed, "which is what we should have been doing all along."[37]

Paradoxically, the shrinking of the American Dream brought it into higher relief for some, the traumatic events of recent years cause to give more credence to the idea. George Elliott, professor of English at Syracuse University, noted that he had not thought much about the term until 1968, when the assassination of Martin Luther King seemed to make it a lot more relevant. If anything, Elliott had viewed the term as a pompous and self-conscious one, a sign of our bloated egos. "Whatever the people of Uganda and China are up to, they are doing it without benefit of 'The Ugandan Dream' or 'The Chinese Dream,'" he observed for the *Nation* in 1974, finding the three words, much like "100% American" and "the American Way of Life," cloying. Recently, however, intrigued by how the Dream could vary from such extremes as "the vulgarity of [Horatio] Alger's self-made, free-enterprise success" to "the nobility of King's vision of harmonious brotherhood," Elliott had decided to do a little investigative work among his friends to try to get a better understanding of what the phrase actually meant. "There was little agreement," he reported after his very unscientific survey, the meaning of the Dream amorphous and self-contradictory: "Some spoke of it in the past tense, most in the present; equality was mentioned, success, progress, the frontier, individualism, capitalism, the founding fathers. But on three things they agreed: none claimed to be very sure what it meant, they all touched on freedom of one sort or another, and they agreed that the Dream was important and affected the way lots of Americans behaved."[38]

Although it did not show up in Elliott's minipoll, everyone would probably have also agreed that it was the anemic economy that posed the greatest threat to the American Dream. High inflation (10 percent annually in 1974) was taking the wind out of the sails of both the middle class and the working class, much more so than your average recession. A recent Daniel Yankelovitch survey showed that patriotism and traditional values were down among young blue-collar Americans, as much so in fact as among college students in the 1960s. "Instead of a temporary albeit enormously unpopular war, many young Americans face what may be the end of 'The American Dream,'" wrote Kevin P. Phillips in the *Hartford Courant*, the likelihood of joining the middle class going in reverse. Most concerning to this group was the inability to afford a single-family house, which was "quite a blow for those conditioned by Dick-and-Jane readers and detergent ads to regard individual home ownership as a necessary badge of middle-class achievement." The cost of the average new suburban home was forty thousand dollars and climbing, with wage levels not keeping up with inflation. Extrapolating current trends was even more disturbing. If the 10 percent annual inflation rate continued for the next twenty-five years, a house selling for fifty thousand dollars in 1974 would cost more than a half million in 2000, making it seem as if only the wealthy would be able to afford an average home. (Wages typically rise with prices over the long term, lessening the real effect of inflation.) Still, inflation (actually "stagflation") was killing or had already killed the American Dream, many concluded in the 1970s, income just not keeping up with the cost of living.[39]

Other journalists chimed in about the disastrous effects inflation was having on the American Dream of owning a home. "An American Dream may be dying," wrote Ronald G. Shafer of the *Wall Street Journal* that same year, the Dream being "a detached house in the suburbs, with a big grassy yard and a white picket fence." The house was still there, Shafer noted; it was just that few people could move into it. The numbers pretty much said it all: assuming one was not going to purchase a house costing more than two-and-a-half times one's annual income, a commonly used rule, fewer than half of American families could afford to buy a home, either new or preowned. Unfortunately, things were getting worse, with the cost of land, labor, and materials rising fast, making some think that the single-family house was on the way to becoming exclusively a luxury for the affluent. Not helping matters were scarce mortgage money, high interest rates, and rising property taxes, although President Ford had recently signed a bill to lower minimum down payments and raise the ceiling on Federal Housing Administration loans. Many of those individuals lucky enough to already own homes found themselves stuck if they wanted to move, the cost of a new, bigger house or one in a nicer neighborhood just too much. Often making twice as much as their parents had, young couples wishing to own their American Dream were confused and frustrated, not exactly sure how things had gone so wrong.[40]

Seeing the writing on the wall, some developers decided to build more affordable homes, offering the nonaffluent what *Business Week* called in 1975 "the no-frills American Dream." By making homes smaller, eliminating garages, carports, and screened porches, and lowering ceilings by half a foot, developers were finding more buyers. Others were opting to not put in dishwashers, refrigerators, and other normally built-in appliances, some not even planting sod in the yard in order to lower the price. Using cheaper materials was another option, all these cutbacks palatably presented to consumers as a "back-to-basics" approach to home building. However it was termed, the economic realities of the 1970s were an "intruder on the American Dream," as *Psychology Today* put it, with money problems over how to spend, what to save, and where to skimp the source of considerable stress among many families.[41]

Those individuals belonging to the group for whom the American Dream arguably meant the most—the middle class—were especially confused and frustrated about not being able to afford a house or having to settle for something less than one they felt they deserved. "The great dream of most Americans has always been home ownership—the little cottage with a picket fence in a quiet neighborhood with good schools nearby," wrote Patricia Johnson in a letter to the Los Angeles Times in 1976, the middle-class Los Angeleno finding herself stuck between a rock and a hard place in her hunt for a house. After going through the real estate section of the newspaper and only seeing ads for that kind of home costing at least one hundred thousand dollars, Johnson was coming to believe that Los Angeles was becoming a city just for the rich and the poor. "Maybe we were born too late to have a part of the American dream," she thought, a sentiment many people in her demographic were feeling. Even people already owning what Johnson dreamed of found themselves "house poor" as inflation put the squeeze on upper-middle-class home owners. The cost of owning and running a nice home was taking a hefty chunk out of family income, leaving little money to enjoy the good things in life. In 1976, for example, Norman and Donna Kantor of Evanston, Illinois, opted not to send their daughter to summer music camp because of the cost of living in their eight-bedroom Victorian home. Travel and a new car every few years were also out of the question despite the fact that the Kantors earned more than 90 percent of all American families. Home ownership may be the American Dream, Mrs. Kantor concluded, "but I don't know if it's worth it."[42]

With the cost of the single-family home too dear for most Americans, a relatively new concept—condominiums and townhomes—began to become increasingly popular, especially among young singles and couples. Other kinds of living arrangements also were possible in the future, according to experts. One housing executive predicted in 1977 that "the American dream house of the future" would have two families living in it because neither could separately afford it. Each family would have its own bedroom wings but share common areas like the kitchen and bathrooms, thought Ken Agid, director of residential marketing for the Irvine Company, the cohabitation scenario drawing comparisons to the racy 1969 movie Bob & Carol & Ted & Alice. Was the Jeffersonian independent, self-sustaining household in jeopardy, and, just as important, was America about to become a nation of swingers?[43]

Much more wholesome, domestically speaking, were recreational vehicles, the homes on wheels considered "American dream machines" by Natalie Levy of the *Chicago Tribune*. There were seven million RVs rolling across America in 1977, some of them used just for vacations but others permanent homes for their owners. Besides being more affordable than one firmly planted in terra firma, RVs "combined freedom of exploration with America's addiction for mobility and comfort," as Levy described it, the very definition of the American Dream for anyone with a bad case of wanderlust. More mobile homes were also popping up across the country, much to the chagrin of local residents, who saw them as nothing more than dressed-up "trailers." People in the industry were naturally excited to see more Americans buying mobile homes, however, thinking the long-awaited era of the affordable "factory-built house" had finally arrived. "We are the only chance at the American dream of owning your own home that a lot of people will have," said Johnie Walkley, a salesman for Lawrence Welk Country Estates, a mobile-home development north of Escondido, California, owned by the popular television bandleader.[44]

America Dreams On

Confusion and frustration went well beyond the prospects of owning one's home in the 1970s, however. A 1975 survey commissioned by the *New York Times* revealed a significant decline in optimism about the future among Americans of all sorts, the nation's confidence, expectations, and aspirations having headed decidedly south. In fact, for the first time since 1959—when researchers began measuring such attitudes—Americans said their standard of living had fallen, a shocking revelation in a country taking it for granted that things would continually get better. "The assumed national birthright of rising expectations—some might call it the American Dream—has been replaced by a sense of falling expectations," reported Robert Lindsey, he just one of many wondering if it was just a temporary phenomenon or represented a historic shift in how we viewed things. Although Vietnam, Watergate, and the economy played significant roles in shaping Americans' attitudes, it was the idea that the rules had changed that was most responsible for the loss of hope. No longer would hard work and saving money lead to the primary symbol of the American Dream—a nice home in the suburbs—and no longer would a college education guarantee a good job, it appeared, these two new realities shattering the public's confidence about the future.[45]

It was no coincidence, then, that the self-help movement blossomed just as Americans' hopes for their future hit a wall in the seventies. Best sellers like *How to Be Your Own Best Friend* were in the right place at the right time, their authors capitalizing on the weakened self-esteem of the middle class. The "American Dream proves elusive but relax, it's not your fault," advised John Raines, an associate professor of religion at Temple University and author of *Illusion of Success*, he one of a considerable number of gurus advising people that they were probably not to blame for not having "made it." With the top 2 percent owning 44 percent of the nation's total wealth in 1975, it was easy to see how many felt like failures even though they were not. "The anguish of being told you live in an affluent society, where each year the deserving move up—while still experiencing your life as mostly running without much moving—explains much about our drive to find techniques of self-confidence building," Raines explained, the disappearance of the American Dream leading to a mass identity crisis.[46]

With all this gnashing of teeth, Robert Penn Warren, the Pulitzer Prize–winning novelist and poet, paused to consider the state of the nation as Americans approached the first centennial a century earlier, providing some valuable context in the process. In 1875, Penn noted in his contribution to a series of articles published in the *Hartford Courant* called "In Search of the American Dream," the country was facing a number of crises that rivaled if not surpassed the problems of 1975. The Civil War had ended just a decade earlier, for one thing, and Federal troops still occupied parts of the South to try to maintain law and order. The upcoming presidential election would turn out to be one of the most contested in American history, with disputed electoral votes in three states making it unclear whether Samuel J. Tilden or Rutherford B. Hayes was the actual winner (yes, Florida was one of the states). The robber barons of the Gilded Age were leaving just crumbs for the emerging middle class, and the bitter battle between labor and capital was beginning to really heat up. Political corruption of the day made Watergate look like a tea party, and city life was not exactly what one would consider particularly urbane (cities were "crowded with petty grotesques, malformations, phantoms, playing meaningless antics," wrote Walt Whitman at the time). "But somehow the mess got swept under the rug, the voice of the croaker and the carper was drowned by the brass band, and the big show went forward as scheduled," Warren reminded us, with classic American optimism soon returning to save the day. Good times were waiting around the corner in the twentieth century, history suggested, the American Dream to make another major comeback.[47]

There was also no doubt that the nation had improved significantly between 1875 and 1975 when it came to one important dimension of the American Dream: race. Although discrimination certainly still existed, of course, the country offered a much more equal playing field in terms of not just race but also gender, ethnicity, and religion, the civil rights movement of the past couple of decades in particular something Americans could be proud of. Despite the bad housing situation, more blacks were heading to the suburbs, a sign of progress that would not have been possible even just a decade earlier. Builders and neighbors were gradually (and sometimes reluctantly) accepting black families into previously all-white communities, with few problems reported. "The American Dream is to have your own house with a backyard, and we were no different," said Eddie Barney after he, his wife, Veronica, and their two sons moved to a subdivision of fifty-nine homes in South Sauk Village, a suburb of Chicago. While some real estate agents were still steering blacks from inner cities away from heavily white communities, the general trend was toward integration, moving the country closer to the popular image of a "melting pot."[48]

It was also clear that white ethic groups had successfully assimilated into the nation's dominant Anglo-Saxon Protestant culture. In order to try to determine "how the ethnics have done in their pursuit of the American dream," as Andrew Greeley described the objective, he and his colleagues at the National Opinion Research Center surveyed eighteen thousand people on two important measures: income and level of education. The results were quite surprising. White ethnic groups—Jews, Irish Catholics, Italians, Poles, and Germans—had higher incomes than the most "aristocratic" Protestant denomination, the Episcopalians. Irish Catholics were the best-educated group, this point too coming as a surprise for people assuming WASPs had the most schooling. "Whatever its defects, the American experiment has worked for the eastern and southern European Catholics—for whom by definition it was not supposed to work well," wrote Greeley, his overall conclusion that "the American Dream is true."[49]

Based on the results of a Gallup Poll done a few years later, Stanley Karnow of the *Hartford Courant* concurred, believing "the American dream is very much alive." The poll indicated that both racial and religious tolerance was on the rise in the United States, Karnow taking this fact to mean there was general support for the Dream's principle of equal opportunity. Thirty-six percent of Americans now approved of interracial marriage, compared to 20 percent a decade earlier, for example, suggesting that the nation's racial barrier was perhaps finally breaking down. Objections to interreligious marriage were also sharply down, another sign that Americans were accepting its inherent multiculturalism. "With all their difficulties," Karnow concluded, "Americans are evolving toward an attainment of their goals, and their evolution is testimony to the vitality of a democracy that, for all its faults, is nevertheless quite unusual."[50]

While the American melting pot may have been simmering, other studies suggested that the social division of class was an impenetrable barrier. As Vance Packard had argued twenty years earlier, the concept of upward mobility was pure fiction, new research revealed, an idea that again threatened to burst the bubble of the class-free American Dream. A child born in poverty had a slim chance of becoming a doctor, lawyer, or business executive, according to hard data, with most youngsters destined to achieve about the same level of education and financial success as their parents. Upward mobility was "the most illusory American Dream," wrote Richard H. deLone, the author of *Small Futures: Children, Inequality, and the Limits of Liberal Reform,* a depressing finding for anyone assuming that hard work or possibly a little push in the right direction would lead to real progress. Social and educational services had increased significantly over the past few decades, but breaking the "cycle of poverty" was proving to be a much tougher nut to crack than anticipated, these findings showed. Mistreatment in schools, a biased standardized test and grading system, and the simple fact of not being white and affluent (as well as male) were some of the things keeping children from low-income families down, despite all the emphasis on equal opportunity.[51]

All the research in the world would have done little to completely dispel the myth of the American Dream, however, as the *America Dreams On* exhibition at the California Museum of Science and Industry in downtown Los Angeles made clear. After viewing iconic images of the nation and hearing voices of the people who captured its essential spirit (including not only John Wayne but also the Beach Boys, Paul Simon, and the Beatles), visitors to the 1976–77 exhibition were invited to write down their own American Dream, specifically what kind of world they wanted to live in and what they wanted for themselves. Through this interactive exercise, museum organizers hypothesized, the Dream could perhaps be "updated and refined" based on Americans' common values and shared desires, quite an interesting project. In just the first two weeks, hundreds of different versions of the American Dream were submitted, with thousands more to come over the course of the six-month run of *America Dreams On*. After the exhibition closed, the museum planned to tabulate and analyze the results, optimistic that some general themes would eventually emerge. "My dream is that Kenny and I will get married and live in a blue and white house with a white picket fence," went one submission, the oldie but goodie suggesting that the more things changed, the more they remained the same.[52]

Traditional versions of the Dream appeared to be on the rise in postbicentennial America as it became evident that the nation had survived the cultural chaos of the past ten years. Television, which in conflict-oriented shows of the early seventies such as *All in the Family* and *Good Times* cast the Dream in disarray (the "moving on up" in *The Jeffersons* was a clear exception), was beginning to change its tune. In *Taxi*, for example, which debuted on ABC in the fall of 1978, a diverse collection of characters whose real passions resided somewhere else drove cabs for a living while hoping their big break would come. (The show was inspired by a real story published in *New York Magazine*.) Bobby (a struggling actor), Tony (a not very successful boxer), and Elaine (a receptionist at a gallery wanting to move up in the art world) each (vainly) tried to make their Dream come true, no doubt reflecting the uphill battle many viewers were facing in their own pursuits. "The show ultimately may be about failure, but it's also about hope and faith and living properly," wrote Gary Deeb of the *Chicago Tribune* in his glowing review of the season premiere, finding *Taxi* to be "a touching portrait of a tiny slice of life's underside."[53]

As the nation and the American Dream began to turn the corner, CBS News aired a two-part special that attempted to provide some closure on the chaotic decade. Aired over the very last couple of days of the 1970s, *American Dream, American Nightmare—the Seventies* looked back at the decade through the lens of three of its major events: the Vietnam War, Watergate, and the bicentennial celebration. The special was, according to Harry Reasoner, who narrated it, "a kind of reconnaissance into the national character, an unsentimental raid into the recent past." The crisis in confidence and erosion of faith in the American Dream were not surprisingly main themes of the program, by-products of the shaky economy, energy shortages, and the realization that we were not as invincible as we once were or at least believed we were. Disillusionment with our own government played the biggest role in our loss of idealism, however, the American Dream simply incompatible with a cynical view of the future. The bicentennial may have redeemed the decade, the show suggested, but the damage had been done, the Dream never to be the same again after the Me Decade.[54]

No one would have agreed with that assessment more than Michael Policastro, who taught a course called The American Dream at Ramapo College in New Jersey. His course was usually a popular one, but Policastro found himself with few registered students for the fall 1979 semester, a result of the college scheduling it at an inconvenient time (Friday at 4:15) in order to conserve energy. The American Dream had almost been canceled because of concerns about the cost of energy, which for Policastro was an "allegorical irony" that had much to say about the state of the nation. "One has to question the ability of the American Dream Machine to continue to churn out the traditional ingredients of opportunity and optimism when the raw materials of production are no longer available," he thought, the erosion of our natural resources going well beyond the need to turn the lights off when one left the room.[55]

Very soon, however, the American Dream Machine would again be churning out opportunity and optimism as new raw materials became available. As the nation's self-confidence hit rock bottom, so had the American Dream, the past decade and a half the most challenging years for the mythology since the Great Depression. The confluence of a bad economy, energy crisis, government scandal, racial tension, two assassinations, and an unpopular war did major damage to the ideals of both the Great Society and the counterculture and, correspondingly, the ideals of the Dream. The difficulty of buying a single-family home, which had been so easy to do a couple decades earlier, was the coup de grâce, convincing many Americans that, for the first time in history, we were moving backward rather than forward. But, as always, the cycles of history were about to spin in the opposite direction, the American Dream once again an idea to cling to for support and guidance.

4

Born in the USA

America's future rests in a thousand dreams inside your hearts . . . and helping you make those dreams come true is what this job of mine is all about.

—President Ronald Reagan, 1984

GEORGE WILL, the conservative columnist, found a visit to a car showroom in the early 1980s a deeply depressing event. By 1984 General Motors had made not only its Cadillac DeVille smaller but also the Buick Electra and the Oldsmobile 98, a decision designed to allow the company to better compete with the Japanese. Big-car lovers like Will were displeased to see what he called the "scrunching of the American Dream," refusing to use the industry's more friendly term, *downsized*. "What is the point of being an American now that General Motors has scrunched . . . what were its big cars?" he asked that year, viewing the trend as nothing less than a national disgrace. Lighter and two feet shorter than their massive predecessors and with front-wheel drive, the new models were more nimble and energy efficient, GM boasted in its advertising, but Will was unconvinced. "The miniaturization of what were the ocean liners of the automobile fleet" was one of the "most dreary aspects of contemporary society," he thought, considering the new Electra nothing more than an "Electrette."[1]

The "scrunching" of the American Dream in the early 1980s went far beyond the downsizing of Detroit's automobiles. Despite the election of a new president who had a grand vision of the Dream, many of the frustrations of the 1970s continued, the mythology as elusive as ever. Buying a house had become even tougher, most notably, the cost simply too much for most families. Inflation and unemployment continued to wreak havoc on the economy, with the middle class, as usual, taking it directly on the chin. The good times of the postwar years seemed like a distant memory, making many baby boomers feel like they had simply missed out on the American Dream. Would the Dream ever return, Americans wondered, and, if so, when?

Losing It

As 1970s malaise segued into early 1980s uncertainty, the nation received a much-needed jolt of inspiration and pride when the United States Olympic hockey team defeated the much more powerful Soviet team in Lake Placid. "An American Dream Comes True," declared the *Los Angeles Times*, the against-all-odds victory (the Soviets had not lost an Olympic hockey game in twelve years) transcending sport to become what reporter Ted Green called a "national catharsis." The underdog story reminded Americans that the traditional virtues of hard work, dedication, and team spirit had not been completely thrown into the dustbin of history and that dreams really could come true. (The "Miracle on Ice" squad would forever be known as the "Dream Team," not coincidentally.) As in the Revolutionary War, David had beaten Goliath, an event that not only gave Americans something to feel good about but proved to foreshadow the end of the Cold War at the end of the decade.[2]

While encouraging, a hockey game was not nearly enough to wake the American Dream from its coma. "What America needs today is fewer image-makers and more myth-makers," thought Herbert I. London and Albert L. Weeks of New York University and the authors of *Myths That Rule America*, blaming the nation's loss of faith and aimlessness on the disappearance of its myths. "At a time in which the American Dream, once the reigning myth of our country, has been interred, where our heroes are toppled like Humpty Dumpty and legends are dismissed as shams, how, it might be asked, can we resurrect or create beneficial myths to invigorate the nation?" London and Weeks believed the answer resided in looking to our past, our "myths of industry, achievement, and optimism about the future" the well from which we should once again draw. Until we reimagined ourselves as an Eden in the making, a land that was always becoming, a sense of powerlessness would remain our fate. "These United States still represent a place in which individual freedom can thrive, where problems affecting the globe may be solved and where enterprise and achievement are well awarded," the two insisted, remembering who we were the way to rediscover who we are.[3]

Studs Terkel also believed we should pay more attention to our myths, his new book *American Dreams: Lost and Found* an exploration of the idea of hope among one hundred Americans of all ages, races, and levels of success. "Terkel has gone in search of the little man with a big story of struggle," noted John Lahr in his review of the book for *Harper's*, thinking that within "these tales of frustration, demoralization and occasional success, a strong sense of the Dream *politik* emerges." A startling array of people, including businessmen, a professional football player, a former Ku Klux Klan member, a past Miss USA, and a lumberjack, told their stories to Terkel, each one shedding some light on the notion of aspiration and achievement in this country. As the book's title suggested, one myth in particular was of keen interest to the author. "Did you ever hear that phrase 'the American Dream'?" the sixty-eight-year-old Chicagoan asked everyone he interviewed (two hundred others did not make the cut), determined to find out what people thought it meant. The usual answers—"to be better off than you are," "to be famous," "owning a piece of land"— typically came back, although occasionally someone thought beyond financial success or being recognized on the street. "It's people having control over their lives," said one twenty-five-year-old man, this statement a lot closer to James Truslow Adams's original vision than the more status-oriented points of view that had developed over the years. For whatever it was worth, Terkel offered readers his own hopes and dreams that were, for a best-selling author and media celebrity, unexpectedly modest. "My goal is to survive the day, to survive it with a semblance of grace, curiosity and a sense I've done something pretty good," he told *Newsweek*, something perhaps not as easy as it sounded.[4]

Others were less sanguine about the prospects for reaching one's goals. Celeste MacCleod, author of *Horatio Alger, Farewell: The End of the American Dream*, was not at all optimistic, as the title of her 1980 book made clear. MacCleod believed that going from rags to riches through hard work and virtuous living—her definition of the Dream, inspired by the nineteenth-century writer—was over forever, there being simply not enough wealth or natural resources now to go around for everyone.[5] Marvin Harris, author of America Now: The Anthropology of a Changing Culture, which was published the following year, also felt the American Dream was in the nation's rearview mirror. Where did we go wrong? Harris, an anthropologist at the University of Florida, had no shortage of answers, but thought major changes in the American economy over the past couple of decades—a shift from a production-based model to one focused on services and information, the outsourcing of manufacturing overseas, and the increasing size and power of big business at the cost of small businesses—were the root of the problem. With many in the nation's workforce alienated or, worse, jobless, the American Dream had little chance of reemerging, Harris argued, the way people make a living the key to the relative health of any society.[6]

Even some of those people perfectly happy at their jobs were not happy about the way they were living, resentful that their American Dream had not come true. People making thirty thousand dollars a year—squarely middle class in the early eighties—just never had any money to spend, the cost of living making what was once believed to be a very nice salary seem more like peanuts. Going out to eat, seeing movies and plays, or even having a savings account was difficult if not impossible, the living paycheck to paycheck an economic vise from which millions could not break free. Getting sick could prove disastrous, a looming fear that the life one worked so hard to build could come crashing down at any time. Striving to "make it" but not really going anywhere was devastating to the American Dream, argued Robert C. Yeager in Losing It: The Economic Fall of the Middle Class, his book showing how nasty inflation could be on real people's lives. Gus Tyler, author of Scarcity: A Critique of the American Economy, agreed, the lifestyles of the current middle class nowhere near as comfortable as they were in the postwar years. "Although a major reduction was being made in the ranks of the nation's poor, the historic American dream of moving upward from one class into another frequently went unfilled," Yeager explained, the belief that one's ship would come in someday crushed by harsh economic realities.[7]

Popular culture, especially rock music, reflected the disillusionment many Americans were feeling in the early eighties as they saw their Dream disappear. "They still sing of love and sex, but some pop lyricists are now setting the grimmer facts of contemporary life—unemployment, poverty and loss of hope in the American dream—to music," observed Yardena Arar of the *Los Angeles Times* in 1982, thinking that "rock has caught up with the recession." Billy Joel's song "Allentown" was a perfect example of "recession rock," the titular city symbolic of the decline of the American Dream among the working class. The song was less about a specific place than "a metaphor for the American dilemma," Joel made clear, the dilemma being that there were "no guarantees anymore." Getting a job in a factory where one's father had worked was considered a birthright in Allentown and hundreds of other industrial towns across the country, the apparent end of this tradition proving to be a shock to the system of local communities. Joel had actually started writing the song in 1973, another rough patch for the nation, but it did not gel until he read of the recent problems of the steel industry in Pennsylvania's Lehigh Valley. "The great American blue-collar promise that the postwar kids were raised on isn't there," said Joel, still hopeful that things would turn around in what had been named in 1975 as an "All-America City."[8]

Also singing the blues for the American Dream among the working class was Bruce Springsteen. Although he had covered similar territory in *Darkness on the Edge of Town* and *The River,* Springsteen's 1982 *Nebraska* was his bleakest album yet, each of the ten songs illustrating the potential effects of forces beyond the control of individuals. "Instead of pointing a finger at causes the way '60s pop militants did, Springsteen concentrates on case studies to show the rips in the American Dream," Robert Hilburn of the *Los Angeles Times* thought, the album one-half John Steinbeck social realism and one-half Woody Guthrie folk commentary. (Springsteen also often sang Guthrie's "This Land Is Your Land" in concerts, the lyrics as relevant as ever a half century after they were written.) If one did not know better, one might have assumed that *Nebraska* was a product of the Depression, its characters living lives of quiet and not-so-quiet desperation in tough economic times. (Consisting mostly of guitar, harmonica, and vocals and recorded at home on a four-track cassette, the album even sounded like it was made during the middle of the Dust Bowl.)⁹ Although President Reagan's campaign managers mistakenly believed the title cut from Springsteen's *Born in the U.S.A.* of 1984 was a jingoistic jingle when they used it in their reelection advertising, both the song and the album were also about the economic wall the working class had hit. "*Born in the U.S.A.* is a sad and serious album about the American dream—of economic hope and security, and of community—for a dwindling segment of our society," wrote Stephen Holden in his rave review for the *New York Times*, he also seeing the Boss as a Woody Guthrie in rock and roller's clothing.¹⁰

Tough times could be found on television as well in the early eighties. In an age of fluffy fare like *Dallas*, *The Waltons*, and *Soap*, a new show called *The American Dream* was refreshingly realistic. The family drama that ran for just one season on ABC in 1981 was not afraid to address problems of contemporary life like money issues, unplanned babies, and sick relatives. What made the show most interesting, however, was its central conceit in which the Novaks moved from a new house in the Chicago suburbs to an older one in a rough, integrated neighborhood in the inner city, a turning upside down of the American Dream to which many viewers could no doubt relate.¹¹ Tired of commuting downtown, crunched for space, and sick of the bland, phony suburbs, Danny Novak led his family to find a new, more authentic American Dream on the urban frontier, something that predictably turned out to be a lot tougher than he envisioned.¹² Interestingly, the show made possible a real American Dream for at least one Chicago family, the Daggetts. The not-so-proud owners of a crumbling Victorian mansion near dicey Wicker Park, Ken and Sandy Daggett were quite pleased when location scouts chose their home for shooting because producers ended up spending more than $150,000 to renovate the house. (Scouts for *The Blues Brothers* considered the Daggetts' home to use as the orphanage in the movie but passed when they saw the dilapidated interior.) But this time the couple's dream came true, happy to put up with moving themselves and their two kids, eleven cats and dogs, and furniture out of the hulking wreck so that carpenters, paper hangers, painters, and plasterers could move in. Soon the house was restored to its original 1889 grandeur, a happy ending that the fictional Novaks could only wish for.¹³

If the Dream was difficult to find in pop music and television, movies occasionally came to its rescue. In the most popular and successful film of the decade, Steven Spielberg's 1982 *E.T.: The Extra-Terrestrial*, an alien tries to get home much like Dorothy in *The Wizard of Oz*, reinforcing the domestic orientation of the Dream. In *Scarface* of the following year, a Cuban immigrant realizes his American Dream but, much like in gangster films of the 1930s, comes to learn that crime does not pay. It was two movies about another one of our civil religions, baseball, however, that best expressed the nation's search for a lost American Dream. In *The Natural*, a 1984 movie based on Bernard Malamud's 1952 novel set in the 1930s, a not-quite-over-the-hill baseball player gets a second chance at his American Dream, a metaphor perhaps for what the country as a whole was hoping for. (With its thunderclaps and lightning bolts, slow-motion home runs, Coplandesque music by Randy Newman, and a magical bat, the film was almost as mythic as the Dream itself.)[14] And in the 1989 *Field of Dreams*, based on W. P. Kinsella's 1982 novel *Shoeless Joe*, Kevin Costner played Ray Kinsella, an Iowa farmer who hears a mysterious voice telling him to build a baseball field where his corn is currently growing. "If you build it, he will come," the voice says, with Kinsella deciding to heed the call despite everyone except his wife thinking him crazy. "He" turns out to be Shoeless Joe Jackson, the now quite dead left fielder involved in the 1919 "Black Sox" scandal, who leads Kinsella on a magical ride through the past. The movie is ultimately about the capacity to dream, something Kinsella along with the irascible Terrence Man (a J. D. Salinger doppelgänger played by James Earl Jones) did as activists back in the sixties. *Field of Dreams* "could have been made only in the U.S.A.," thought David Ansen of *Newsweek*, finding it "a lovely pipe dream about a country that exists only in our imaginations." The baseball field in the movie was and is very real, however, a popular destination for both the merely curious and those on a pilgrimage to rediscover their own Dream.[15]

These few movies of the 1980s were great examples of what Jerome Charyn appropriately called "Movieland," a sort of adolescent (or even infantile) state in which hope played the starring role. "We're a country of wishes and expectations, frozen into some idyll where all things are possible," Charyn, an English professor at the City University of New York, wrote in his book, with literally larger-than-life movie stars the people we longed to be. Something big was waiting just around the corner, the movies made us believe, further ingraining the American Dream in our individual and collective consciousness. Was it all just a dream, or was there a chance it could become real?[16]

My Blue Heaven

Although the answer to that question was unclear, there was little doubt that the domestic version of the Dream was not going to go away anytime soon. "Americans have always cherished an almost ideological longing for a house of their own," wrote Lance Morrow for *Time* in 1981, most of us still clinging to "the sweet fantasy of the dream house, the little fortress of home, My Blue Heaven," despite the hard economic realities. During the postwar years, what had once been just a hope became seen as an entitlement, which was the thing that was proving to be so difficult for Americans unable to afford a house because of inflation and high interest rates. "The baby-boom children of the broad middle class were especially seduced by the illusion," Morrow continued, fully believing that when they were good and ready, they would "find houses like the ones their parents owned—or much nicer, maybe—and therein comfortably get on with the American dream." A garden-apartment rental on an iffy side of town was not what the Me Generation had in mind as they literally bought into the ethos of consumer capitalism.[17]

Others agreed it was not so much the economy that was ruining the American Dream for baby boomers as it was their expectations. "The problem for young people is the old American dream," Arthur Anderson, a sociologist at Fairfield University, told *Forbes*, the bar their parents set a high one that was proving difficult to reach, much less jump over. A tough job market, devaluation of both undergraduate and graduate degrees, and an onerous housing situation were, at least for the moment, making seventy-six million baby boomers a pretty grumpy group of people. It was no wonder that Americans, once the most optimistic people anywhere, now ranked seventeenth among nations in the free world in that respect.[18]

Americans' deep longing for a house of one's own was, of course, a familiar trope within pop culture. At the end of *Swing Shift*, for example, a 1984 film about the home front during World War II, two soldiers talked excitedly about the future. The GIs, home from the war, passionately exchanged their mutual dream of having their own houses, a conversation that assuredly had taken place among real veterans. Ellen Goodman, the syndicated newspaper columnist, was quite struck by the scene. "These were the men and these were the motives that built the America we live in today," she wrote that year, their conversation the "psychic chemistry that transformed something as ephemeral as an America dream into something as solid as a house on a plot of land with a mortgage." Much had changed over the course of forty years, however, leading to a major misfit between the houses men like these bought and how Americans now lived. "The American Dream was shaped for men in civvies and women in aprons and a bumper crop of babies in back yards," Goodman believed, the Dream as powerful as ever but our homes no longer practical or affordable. Having to commute long distances between work, home, and day care and need-ing two jobs to pay one mortgage were two things conflicting with the Dream, she felt, the fact that houses got bigger while families got smaller also making things a lot more complicated than they were after the war.[19]

Like Goodman, Dolores Hayden, author of *Redesigning the American Dream*, believed the gap between the Dream and the way that American families now lived had become too great. Even though the private sub-urban house no longer suited the needs of many Americans, most still wanted one, this fact the real problem rather than its high cost. "For the first time in history, a civilization has created a utopian ideal based on the house rather than the city or the nation," Hayden wrote in her 1984 book, that ideal proving to be a persistent one despite the realities of every-day life. The American dream house was designed around the breadwin-ner and housewife model of the postwar years, she pointed out, a way of life that only 12 percent of households were now choosing. A cooperative residential neighborhood with offices and day care nearby would make a lot more sense, Hayden argued, but, given how entrenched the single-family suburban house was in our imagination, redesigning the American Dream would be a (very steep) uphill battle to climb.[20]

Given the cost of that house, however, redesigning the American Dream made even more sense. "The goal that has come to be known as the American dream has crossed a historic threshold," Peter T. Kilborn of the *New York Times* wrote in reporting the news that the average price of a new single-family home topped one hundred thousand dollars for the first time in 1984. As prices rose, fewer people were buying houses, a much different story than in the postwar years when more than half of American households were home owners (that number also historically significant). The rise of interest rates also had a lot to do with the increasing difficulty of buying a home. Interest rates on the popular fixed thirty-year conventional mortgage of the 1950s and 1960s were as low as 4 percent, but in the 1970s that number began to change when rates climbed to 10 percent. By 1976 the average family's monthly home payment was one-fourth of its income, but now, just eight years later, it was more than one-third and still rising, a disturbing trend.[21]

The fundamental urge for Americans to own a piece of property, whether to feel "settled" or as an investment, pushed many to look for alternatives as the single-family home increasingly became seen as unaffordable, impractical, or both. Although cooperative apartments and condominiums had gradually been making inroads in the American real estate market for the past decade or so, it was clear by the mid-1980s that they were well on the way to changing the literal landscape of the nation. "The 'American Dream' is in large part land," wrote Matthew L. Wald of the *New York Times* in 1984, thinking that the rise of shared housing could very well reshape society and perhaps even have a significant effect on our national identity. The number of co-ops and condominiums had more than tripled between 1973 and 1981, according to the Census Bureau, increasing from about 0.5 million to 1.7 million. While only 8 percent of current home buyers were opting for co-ops and condos, new buildings were springing up fast, and many apartments were converting from rental to ownership. Wald wondered about the social implications of shared housing eventually becoming as or more popular as the freestanding house. "For a society in which a man's home is his castle, and in which the American Dream is literal ownership of a private chunk of the landscape, the change is heavy with symbolism," he ventured, this relatively new form of habitation potentially altering the very nature of social interaction. Would they, for example, weaken community or encourage it? Would residents feel like it was just a temporary stop on the way to a house in the suburbs, making us a nation of transients? Would this kind of housing be mostly for single women wanting to avoid the maintenance of a house, making us more segregated by gender and marital status? No one knew for sure, the future of the American Dream perhaps hanging in the balance.[22]

Mobile-home dealers, already on a roll, so to speak, also went into high gear to position their product as an attractive alternative to the big, expensive suburban family house. Traditionally marketed much like used cars, with loud salesmen wearing equally loud sports jackets on late-night television commercials, mobile homes went upscale in the mideighties to claim their rightful place as home to the American Dream. "We've had an image of making homes for the newlywed and the newly dead," admitted one industry person, but now, according to another, "we're trying to get away from the image of a salesman in a green leisure suit and white belt." Some builders of "manufactured homes," as they now preferred to be called, were putting in fireplaces, French doors, and cathedral ceilings, others using sophisticated marketing techniques to reach higher-income, better-educated consumers. And at roughly half the price of a similarly sized conventional house, mobile homes would certainly appeal to some who were unable to afford the standard American Dream complete with a yard and white picket fence.[23]

The man who almost single-handedly created suburbia, however, was not about to let condos or mobile homes ruin his American Dream parade. William Levitt, seventy-seven years young in 1985, was acting like it was 1947, when he built and sold homes (all identical eight-hundred-square-foot Cape Cods for eight thousand dollars on sixty-by-one-hundred-foot plots complete with appliances, no cash down) to seventeen thousand families to create the first Levittown on Long Island. Levitt quickly became known as the "Father of Suburbia," his face appearing on the cover of *Time* in 1950 over the headline "For Sale: A New Way of Life." Now, three decades plus (and two hundred thousand houses) later, Levitt was launching a two-billion-dollar, seven-year project near Orlando for twenty-six thousand families spread over thirteen villages, each one having its own shopping and recreation centers, schools, and churches. (Times having changed, Levitt was now offering houses in eleven architectural styles costing forty to sixty thousand dollars, with 5 percent cash down.) Having sold his original company in 1968 for a reported ninety-two million dollars back in 1968, Levitt hardly needed the money, but it was clear he still loved the game. "[The] backlog of desire and need and want was so huge [in 1947] that we had people sleeping out on the ground for three days waiting for us to open up a model home," he remembered, the story confirming the reality behind the scene in *Swing Shift.* Fully aware that 75 percent of Americans now could not afford the average family home, Levitt was up to his old tricks, building houses for the masses and having no plans to retire.[24]

As with Dolores Hayden, Mark Baldassare would no doubt believe Levitt's attempt to re-create the suburban American Dream was less than a great idea (although probably a lucrative one). In his *Troubles in Paradise,* Baldassare, an urban sociologist at the University of California at Irvine, argued that suburbs were no longer the idyllic alternative to cities and centerpiece of the middle-class American Dream that they were (or were considered) in the postwar years. Baldassare pinpointed the transformation in 1970, when growth and industrialization in the suburbs accelerated. (Not coincidentally, 1970 also marked the year in which more Americans lived in the suburbs than anywhere else.) Many Americans were "holding out hope for the suburban dream and . . . ignoring the fact that suburbia was something that existed in the past and won't exist [in that way] again," he told the *Los Angeles Times* in 1986, the dream of paradise more powerful than the reality of something else.[25]

For some groups, however, the suburban American Dream was virtually brand-new. A new black middle class (most historians agreed it was the third such group since the end of slavery) emerged in the 1980s, many of them heading directly to the suburbs as whites had done for decades. Unlike in the postwar years, many companies now had suburban offices, the short commute also much of the draw for African Americans (and whites as well). Juliette and James McNeil, for example, each originally from Alabama, were living quite comfortably in a three-thousand-square-foot four-bedroom colonial in Lake Devereux, a mostly white subdivision in Fairfax County, outside Washington, DC. With great jobs, a Volvo, and a four-year-old daughter named Ashley, the couple's Dream had apparently been realized, something impossible as recently as ten years earlier. Similar things were happening in Los Angeles, Long Island, Atlanta, Chicago, and Detroit, as the black middle class made noticeable strides in income and education. While inequalities obviously still existed, the seeds of the civil rights movement of the past couple of decades appeared to be bearing fruit, with more African Americans sharing in the bounty of a traditional American Dream. "The members of this middle class are not simply a few skyrocketing superachievers," observed Joel Garreau of the *Washington Post* in reporting the story, concluding, "They are a large, church-going, home-owning, child-rearing, back-yard-barbecuing, traffic-jam-cursing group remarkable only for the very ordinariness with which they go about their classically American suburban affairs." For some African Americans, in other words, the suburbs in 1987 were a lot like they were for the white middle class in 1947.[26]

The Brass Ring

A house in the suburbs was not the only American Dream in play in the 1980s, however. For some, making big money represented the Dream, all the better if it arrived fast and did not require a nine-to-five job. As in the 1950s, when quiz shows were considered one of the few ways to get rich quick, the less patient were interested in any and all shortcuts to the American Dream. One of them was contests or sweepstakes, the holy grail being the much-sought-after grand prize. Professional "contesters," as they liked to be called, spent inordinate amounts of time hand-addressing and stamping envelopes filled with proofs of purchase and three-by-five-inch pieces of paper, their houses already filled with the fruits of their labor. Appliances, furniture, furs, vacations, cars, and cash were up for grabs in sweepstakes, and contesters were determined to win them through sheer persistence. Entering frequently and consistently to better the odds was the key to winning, experts advised, with many pros belonging to contest clubs and subscribing to a newsletter that detailed rules and prizes. As with quiz-show winnings, however, white elephants and taxes were big problems for contesters, even their accelerated American Dream no free lunch.[27]

For those individuals not willing to sit at their kitchen table for hours or days stamping envelopes, there were a lot of other ways to try to beat the odds and make a killing in the process. Gambling of all kinds was having a field day in the United States in the 1980s, with forty-six states declaring it legal if not encouraging its citizens to get in the game. "A new 'American Dream'—striking it rich by taking a chance on chance—is putting billions of dollars into state coffers and millions of dollars into bettors' pockets as the fever spreads from baccarat tables in Atlantic City to new lottery games in Washington state," wrote Scott Kraft of the Associated Press in 1984, the numbers speaking for themselves. Americans bet forty-four billion dollars the previous year in legal gambling (more than half of what was spent on automobiles), with seventeen state lotteries accounting for five billion of that figure. Interestingly, casinos' take was relative pocket change, with Las Vegas and Atlantic City each bringing in less than two billion dollars each. Although opposition to gambling remained strong in parts of the country for different reasons, state governments were delighted to convert their winnings into social services, and it was clear that Americans seemed willing to bet on anything if there was money to be made. Alaskans were betting on when the ice would break up in the Tanana and Chena Rivers in the spring, for instance, and Floridians were putting their money on horses, dogs, and jai alai players. Slot machines and table games were also more popular than ever, making some in other parts of the country try to figure out how they could get in on the action. Bingo too was big business, with some of the biggest games taking place on Indian reservations. Many of these games offered huge payoffs, the American Dream just waiting for the first person lucky enough to yell "BINGO!"[28]

Although certainly a much longer road to wealth than contests or gambling, franchising was another way more entrepreneurial types could fast-track their American Dream. Like direct-distribution organizations such as Amway, franchising gave the "little guy [a] chance to grab [the] brass ring," as Sally Saville Hodge of the *Chicago Tribune* put it, the field known by its proponents as the "great American dream machine." Anyone brave enough to strike out on his or her own received business training and advertising support in exchange for a specified level of investment, with franchise opportunities ranging from automobile repair shops to tanning salons to ice cream stores. The average McDonald's made one hundred thousand dollars a year in 1985, making that franchise the most desired, with Midas Mufflers another almost-sure bet.[29] Whereas 65 percent of all small businesses failed, just 4 percent of franchise outlets did, according to the Department of Commerce, more reason to sign up with a chain if one could afford it. Franchise operations had come a long way from the 1950s and 1960s, with required registration, government regulation, and a code of ethics now part of what had been a rather dubious field. (Despite Federal Trade Commission oversight, fraud was still not uncommon.) New kinds of franchise businesses like dental care centers and maid services were continually being formed, good news for anyone who wanted to be their own boss. (No fewer than 1,265 companies offering franchises were listed in the *Franchise Opportunities Handbook* published by the Department of Commerce.)[30] Women and minorities were especially attracted to franchises, understandably believing they had a better chance of grabbing their brass ring there than in white, male-dominated corporate America.[31]

With its own mythic story, McDonald's was much more than a moneymaking machine for a franchisee lucky enough to own one (or, even better, a handful). Like an Amway convention, a biennial McDonald's owner-operator get-together was a nearly spiritual experience designed to keep franchisees and affiliates motivated and, ultimately, highly profitable. It was no coincidence that the theme of the three-day event attended by seven thousand in 1987 in Washington, DC, was "Sharing the Dream," the narrative of the company (a revolutionary idea, humble beginnings, rapid expansion, and eventually an empire) paralleling the nation's. "Oh yes, he is the American dream," said one woman after her husband won the much-coveted Golden Arch Award during the ritualistic recognition ceremony. (Having automatic urinals in his store was one reason the owner-operator was so honored.) New people got "McDonaldized" and made "McFriends," the company, like any subculture, having its own (Mc)Language. Through big production numbers (for example, "It's a Mac World" and "See Those Arches"), skits, a film featuring Paul Newman, speeches from corporate executives, marching bands, and a lot more, the company communicated what was known as the "McDonald's Message," with the meeting taking on the tone of an evangelical rally. Especially exciting was the moment when hyperkinetic professional singers and dancers acted out the "Sharing the Dream" theme, the lyrics to the tune ("We're the real believers and we keep coming through! / We're sharing the dream!") no doubt making everyone eager to go out and sell burgers.[32]

While franchising was a good way for women and people of color to parlay a small nest egg into a pile of dough, other minorities were finding their Dream in more traditional ways. "The American Dream Is Alive and Well in Koreatown," declared a *Wall Street Journal* title in 1985, the once run-down area of Los Angeles now a thriving center of small businesses. With the largest concentration of Koreans in the United States, the five-square-mile district was a magnet for entrepreneurs wanting to climb the ladder of success, much as Jewish and Japanese immigrants in different parts of the country had done decades earlier. "The Koreans' success in the U.S. demonstrates that the nation's ladder of upward mobility still works," Earl C. Gottschalk Jr. of the *Journal* suggested, their accomplishments proof that "hard work, attention to detail and the entrepreneurial spirit can still pay off." In Los Angeles, Koreans tended to own liquor stores, small food markets, gasoline stations, dry cleaners, restaurants, and clothing stores, while in New York, which had the second-largest Korean community in the country, they had done well in the fruit and vegetable business. Part of Koreans' success in this country had to do with their natural inclination to be entrepreneurs, perhaps even more so than Americans. "Koreans know that a salaried man will never get rich," said Won H. Chung, president of Koreatown's Hanmi Bank, convinced that "a salary man is nothing here."[33]

Besides their contempt for salarymen, Koreans' approach to small business differed significantly from Americans' debt-heavy model. Allowed to take up to one hundred thousand dollars out of their country, Korean immigrants then typically worked for a number of years here to save yet more money before opening up their own business. Most would not go to a bank to take out a loan until they wanted to expand or buy a second business, thinking it best to prove themselves first. And not only did Koreans almost always pay off their loans, but they often did it before the loans were due, a function of the great shame that bankruptcy was considered in their community. (Bankruptcy was actually almost unheard of among

Koreans, with declaring oneself insolvent not a temporary shelter from debtors but, as Chung put it, "really the end.") Interestingly, despite their impressive record as small-business entrepreneurs, a full two-thirds of Korean immigrants had college degrees, with most having been middle-class professionals in their country. After arriving in the United States, however, many of them decided to go the small-business route, with either language issues or the desire to make more money faster the reason to put away their three-piece suits and pursue the great American Dream.[34]

The upward mobility of Koreans and other Asian immigrants was not lost on some marketers who viewed these groups as an attractive target market. Many companies were already making appeals to the nation's seventeen million Hispanics, but the Asian American market was "virgin ground," as Peter Kim, vice president of J. Walter Thompson USA, described it. Diverse dialects and cultural differences among the five million Asian Americans were challenges, everyone agreed, but their median family income was higher than the US population as a whole, the kind of stuff that made marketers lick their chops. That twice as many Asian Americans were college graduates than whites on a per capita basis was all the more reason to try to gain their brand loyalty. Metropolitan Life Insurance was one company blazing this trail, taking out a newspaper ad during the Chinese New Year to say it "would like to join the Chinese-American community in fulfilling the American dream." Metropolitan had also hired more than three hundred Asian Americans to sell its products, thinking the market's educational level and family orientation made them ideal candidates to invest in financial security. With the Population Reference Bureau predicting that the Asian community would double by the year 2000, more marketers, including AT&T, United Airlines, and McDonald's, were beginning to advertise to them, positioning their products as essential parts of the American Dream.[35]

Gaining Asian Americans' brand loyalty made even more sense given the academic performance among many young people in their community. Over the past decade, the success of young Asian Americans was nothing less than extraordinary as measured by their presence in the nation's best schools. At Harvard, for example, Asian Americans accounted for 14 percent of freshmen in the 1987–88 academic year despite representing just 1.5 percent of the country's population. Forty-one percent of the students at Stuyvesant, arguably the best high school in New York City, were Asian American, and 30 percent at Bronx Science, which was close behind. "The success of these immigrant youngsters is proof that, for all its troubles, New York City is still a place where it's possible to make the American dream work," Tony Schwartz of *New York Magazine* wrote in 1988, "to succeed despite disadvantages, merely by working hard and persevering." Working hard and persevering was the simple explanation for young Asian Americans' scholarly achievements, with most of the students accepting their parents' very high expectations for them without an ounce of hesitation. "My parents didn't seem to be asking for too much from me, and I was eager to please them," said one of them, Daisy Tsui, who had been accepted for early decision at Harvard for the upcoming fall. Much like Jewish Americans one and two generations earlier, Asian Americans were getting a jump start on the American Dream the old-fashioned way, benefiting from the high value placed on education in the home despite, quite often, economic hardship.[36]

Does America Still Exist?

Young Asian Americans' amazing academic success notwithstanding, many were understandably concerned about the future of the nation's children. Philip Moffitt, editor in chief of *Esquire*, wondered what lay in store for those individuals who had been born over the past few years, a group who would later be called Generation X. "What will be the dreams for themselves and for their country?" he asked, sure that their dreams would be much different from the aspirations of their baby boomer parents. The graying of America would certainly play an important part in their experience, he felt, as would major strides in the biological sciences and computer technology. Whatever their future would be, Moffitt felt the nation should start planning for it now. "There must be a rearticulation of the American Dream, a redefinition of the nation's priorities in the context of today's possibilities," he stated, the old Dream simply not viable for this generation when they became adults. "There has to be, as it were, a postmodern set of promises, embracing our traditional values but adjusted to our new self-image—a view of tomorrow that reflects the lessons of the last fifty years," Moffitt argued, proposing a new and improved American Dream for a new generation.[37]

Moffitt's call for a reinvention of the American Dream was a refreshing idea that challenged the usual proposals to try to get the old one back. It was clear that two decades of great economic challenge, political turmoil, and social change had left an indelible mark on the national zeitgeist, all of it perhaps making previous articulations of the Dream unviable for the future. It was unarguable that the postwar consensus, if there ever really was one, had by the 1980s shattered into a seemingly infinite number of pieces, this fragmentation having a direct effect on the American Dream. "The multiplication of so many purposes has led to a good deal of confusion as to what, if anything, the dreamers of so many American dreams hold in common," editors of *Harper's* observed in 1984, deciding it was due time to step back and ask a very important question: "Does America still exist?" "To a foreigner the question would seem to verge on the preposterous," the editors confessed, our money, products, and weapons difficult to miss everywhere around the world. At home, however, the question was not so absurd, as without "a constitutional contract under which every citizen remained free to invent his own god, life, fortune, and destiny," as they aptly described the American promise, what did we really have?[38]

Doing yeoman's duty, *Harper's* posed the pithy question to ten authorities (all men, notably), hoping that their responses would provide some clarity to the haze that was our national identity in the 1980s. (George Orwell's *1984* also seemed to have something to do with all the intense naval gazing of the time.) Harold Livesay, a history professor at Virginia Polytechnic Institute and author of *American Made: Men Who Shaped the American Economy*, went first, more than a bit surprised at the question. "You bet your ass it does," he spat out, citing the perennial candidate for president Harold Stassen, the Border Patrol, the Immigration and Naturalization Service, and the admissions officers at American universities as some people who would definitely agree with him. It was the country's space that underpinned our faith in infinite possibilities, Livesay believed, this space the difference between us and our crammed, hemmed-in European kin. Our eternal youth was another thing keeping the Dream alive, he maintained, taking issue with people who argued that the nation had reached middle age, its problems a result of that fact. "It seems to me that America is more like a spoiled child," Livesay wrote, "impatient, quick to resort to violence, insistent on being the center of attention, determined to be captain or not play at all, hungry for applause for modest achievements, arrogant and blustering, but prone to cry easily and riddled with self-doubt." Finally, Livesay listed a few of his favorite things (Ford's V-8 engines, cable TV, and twenty-four-hour supermarkets, among them) that not only proved America existed but also left him in a self-described state of "hog heaven."[39]

Philip Berrigan, a Catholic priest and antiwar activist, agreed that America definitely existed. But Berrigan's America was a lot different from Livesay's, arguing that it was more the military that defined it than powerful cars, great entertainment, and that you could go grocery shopping at three in the morning. "The United States was built on the Lockeian principles of liberty, democracy, equality, and peace," he wrote, "but after World War II, these gave way, with astonishing speed, to the military principles of authority, hierarchy, obedience, force, and war." Because the government believed war "worked," fighting communism in the name of national security became our main reason for being, as Berrigan saw it, and served as evidence that America still existed. Another America, consisting of people like himself who were raging against the machine, also existed, Berrigan believed, the two factions engaged in a kind of war all their own.[40]

Robert Nisbet, a professor at Columbia University and the author of a number of books, also did not doubt the existence of America but felt that our sense of national community had reached its lowest point since the Civil War. "We are like members of a church in which faith in dogma has waned," Nisbet believed, "a church whose structure has become badly weakened." Having peaked during World War I, a result in part of Woodrow Wilson's "100% Americanism" campaign, our civil religion began to break apart in the 1920s, he thought, with little hope of putting our disintegrated society back together again. Louis L'Amour, who had by 1984 written eighty-eight books (almost all of them about life on the American frontier), was as sure as Livesay that the nation still existed, as did the American Dream. Opportunities were all around us, L'Amour insisted, with talent recognized and rewarded here more than anywhere else. We had a better standard of living, better medical care, better educational system, better everything than ever before, and the fact that we were still growing was proof enough that we were still very much alive.[41]

Finally, for an immigrant to this country or even a child of immigrants, there was no question that America still existed, as Richard Rodriguez's essay in *Harper's* made clear. Himself a son of parents from Mexico, Rodriguez, a writer, found evidence of the nation's presence everywhere, on billboards, in the smell of french fries and popcorn, and through the mere pace of life here. Although we publicly celebrated diversity and differences, the process of assimilation was our driving force, he felt, the coming together of people from other places the thing that most and best defined us as a nation. "The American story is the story of immigrant children and of their children," he concluded, our revolving door a guarantee that this country would continue to survive.[42]

It was precisely the nation's usually open but increasingly closed door that Mario Cuomo, the governor of New York, addressed a couple years later in an article called "The American Dream and the Politics of Inclusion" for (oddly) *Psychology Today.* President Reagan was considering signing the Immigration Reform and Control Act that would make it illegal for employers to knowingly hire illegal aliens, which was probably the impetus for the governor to put pen to paper. Cuomo (a child of immigrants) believed the central theme in the nation's history to be "the struggle to include," that is, who was able to share in the equality, life, liberty, and pursuit of happiness promised in the Declaration of Independence. The politics of inclusion was "forever reminding those of us who already possess some share of the American dream that the dream is not yet fulfilled, the promise of our founding fathers not yet complete, until everyone has been included," Cuomo wrote, his experience (and success) as a first-generation American obviously shaping his view. "Our society must resist those who would close our doors to future immigrants," he demanded, seeing open and free borders as essential to keeping the Dream alive.[43]

It's Morning Again in America

If there remained any doubt that the America Dream existed, all one had to do was watch a little television. As in the early seventies, when TV commercials seemed to be the only place where a vibrant Dream could be found, advertising of the mid-1980s was replete with images of and references to the mythology. Although the 1984 Summer Olympics in Los Angeles certainly contributed to the renaissance of patriotic advertising, it was President Reagan's reelection campaign that pushed the red, white, and blue over the top. "It's morning again in America" went Reagan's syrupy-as-a-Vermont-maple-tree campaign theme, each commercial serving up hefty portions of hope and traditional values over images of purple mountain majesties and amber waves of grain. Advertisers immediately jumped on the flag-waving bandwagon, celebrating everything from entrepreneurship to protectionism to economic freedom to trade unionism. "Here's to you, America," viewers sitting in their Barcaloungers at home were told by Anheuser-Busch, with Miller beer informing them that their suds were "made the American way." The *Wall Street Journal* was now "the daily diary of the American dream," with Kodak's "America" series of commercials and Dodge's "American Revolution" campaign also tapping into an ethos of jingoistic nationalism. "Insuring the American Dream is a big job," a Crum and Forster insurance headline went, while Perry Ellis apparel was offering "looks you'll pledge allegiance to." Coca-Cola and Chrysler, meanwhile, were telling viewers about their efforts to restore that giant symbol of the American Dream, the Statue of Liberty, all of it making some in the advertising business cringe. Upon seeing an ice cream commercial from the National Daily Board set to the tune of "America the Beautiful," advertising consultant Larry Lowenthal ran into his bathroom and turned on the faucet, hoping the sound of the water would drown out the music. "The ad was a travesty," he said, with others in the industry agreeing that the country's sacred symbols were being abused by Madison Avenue.[44]

It may have been morning again in America, but many did not like what they were waking up to. "The American dream is dying," wrote Richard N. Goodwin in 1985, believing the nation's income gap was wreaking havoc on the middle class and democracy itself. Goodwin, who had worked for both President Kennedy and President Johnson, first defined what he meant by the Dream, a view very close to Adams's original idea: "A society in which all would have a chance to share in growing abundance;

a land without huge inequalities of wealth or fixed class divisions; a nation that promised each individual not a certain income but the opportunity to achieve for himself to the limits of his capacities." Now, however, a half century after Adams conceived it, the American Dream was in deep trouble, a victim of "trickle-up economics" and other national policies favoring the rich. Reducing taxes on large corporations while raising the taxes of poor and middle-class families and exporting jobs overseas were just a couple of ways the Reagan administration was enabling big fish to gobble up the small, he argued, this "sea change in American life . . . a retreat from the principle of universal opportunity."[45]

Whereas liberals like Goodwin had no trouble expressing what they thought of Ronald Reagan and his policies, the president was quite a puzzle to political scientists like Benjamin Barber. Barber, who taught at Rutgers University and was the author of *Strong Democracy: Participating Politics for a New Age*, considered Reagan to be an "optimistic conservative," a seemingly oxymoronic concept. "The true conservative resists dreams, knowing they are on a collision course with reality," Barber thought, but the president was a firm believer in dreams, even defining his job as an enabler of Americans' dreams. "We believed then and now that there are no limits to growth and human progress when men and women are free to follow their dreams," Reagan said in his second inaugural address, making Barber wonder where and how his peculiar politics was formed. It was not very hard to come up with the answer, of course, the Gipper's legacy as an actor and president of the Screen Actors Guild difficult to separate from his second career as a politician. Hollywood had laid the foundation for Reagan's unique brand of optimistic conservatism (or conservative optimism, perhaps), Barber posited, the aspirations and desires embedded in movies much like the dreams he imagined the American people having. The president's dreams were "celluloid vistas," he proposed, filled with solitary heroes using their God-given abilities to be victorious against something larger and more powerful—a perfect definition of the American Dream.[46]

Although some observers of the scene like Goodwin had a much different view, Barber thought Reagan was an ideal president for the times given that the nation had been founded on dreams. "The election of a

Hollywood dreamer to an office so badly tainted had been a balm to the troubled American spirit," he wrote, the renewal of hope and confidence as reflected in recent polls bearing out this claim. "Hope is a precious and necessary commodity in a democracy," Barber proposed, so "if it takes a Hollywood dreamer to revive it for us, so be it." Even he was concerned that President Reagan's American Dream was an entirely private one, however, cut out of the same cloth as that of iconic individualists like John Wayne and Horatio Alger. "In truth, the great American dream has always been a *public* dream," he pointed out, with equal opportunity for all just as important as the pursuit of private liberty and personal fortune. By focusing exclusively on individuals, progress, and prosperity, Reagan was ignoring half of the Dream, Barber felt, with citizenship and community the other half of the equation. "To be a land open to private dreams, America must itself be a public dream," he wrapped up, reminding readers that the Constitution begins, "We the people."[47]

Even more so than during his first term, Reagan used rhetoric steeped in the American Dream to propel the GOP agenda in his second term. Such was the case when Reagan made a concerted effort to save the Republican majority in the Senate in 1986, for example, swinging through thirteen states that fall with his wife, Nancy, occasionally at his side. Like his own campaign a couple years back, these rallies were typically unabashedly patriotic affairs, filled with emotional language in which the American Dream played a central part. In Costa Mesa, California, the last stop on his tour, Reagan went all out, toning down his usually partisan speech to elevate the event to a celebration of national pride. "Each generation must renew and win for itself the precious gift of liberty, the sacred heritage of freedom," he told a mostly teenage audience of eighty-five hundred in the conservative community, letting them know that it was up to them to preserve the American Dream (even though they could not vote, a little oddly). In addition to the obligatory sea of waving flags, the rally included fireworks, a skydiver, and, last but not least, a live elephant in all its GOP glory.[48]

Even a literal elephant in the room was no match for Reagan, however, as he used the event to call for the end of the Cold War. After putting in his plug for Representative Edwin Zschau, who was trying to unseat

Senator Alan Cranston, the Democratic candidate, Reagan addressed Mikhail Gorbachev, whom he had met with in Iceland during the "Reykjavik Summit" just a few weeks earlier. "It's no threat, Mr. Gorbachev," the president declared, speaking of Americans' wish that the whole world would enjoy "the blessings of liberty," something the Soviet leader confessed he found intimidating. "It's just a dream we call the American dream," Reagan continued, "the oldest dream of humanity, the dream of peace and freedom, a dream that someday must belong to every man, woman and child on earth." Cheers of "U.S.A., U.S.A.," filled the air, the young people in the crowd excited to take on Reagan's challenge.[49] Fittingly, the American Dream was the capstone to Reagan's final State of the Union address, which he made before a joint session of Congress (and a national television audience) a little more than a year later. His administration had, "at a critical moment in world history, reclaimed and restored the American dream," the president proudly announced, revisiting his familiar tune that the nation remained "a shining city on a hill."[50]

A shining city on a hill was not what Studs Terkel found in his latest series of conversations with ordinary Americans, however. At seventy-six, the Pulitzer Prize winner was covering much of the same terrain he had written about for decades, his oral histories important slices of life documenting the times. In his 1988 *The Great Divide: Second Thoughts on the American Dream*, Terkel explored "the deepening chasm between the haves and the have-somewhats and the have-nots," this gap the source of the book's title. Echoing Goodwin, Reaganomics and big business were most to blame for the divide, Terkel believed, with regular folks fighting back to save the Dream the real heroes of the day. "Something is happening out there, across the Divide, often in unexpected quarters," he wrote, praising leaders of grassroots movements who were trying to level the playing field.[51]

If You Are Capable, You May

Given how hard it was for many to find the American Dream in the 1980s, in fact, a few people decided to hit the road to go look for it. Charles Kuralt had been going "on the road" on *The CBS Evening News* since 1967, his occasional segments exploring the nooks and crannies of the country beloved by many viewers. In 1985 the peripatetic journalist put some of his stories in a book, *On the Road with Charles Kuralt*, a good many of them touching upon some aspect of ordinary Americans' pursuit of the Dream. Another book published that year, Bob Dotson's . . . *In Pursuit of the American Dream*, was more direct, the longtime NBC News correspondent thinking the American Dream could be found by looking for the extraordinary in everyday life. Another person trying to track down the Dream was Jay Leno, documenting his effort in a one-hour special for Showtime. In *Jay Leno and the American Dream*, the comedian (he had yet to take over *The Tonight Show*) drove around Chicago in a 1955 Buick Roadmaster, his stops including a school, bingo parlor, French restaurant, Mr. Beef (locally famous for their Italian beef sandwiches), and the state's immigration and naturalization department. Between segments, Leno did his comedy act at the city's Café Royal, his subjects ranging from General Motors ("Hey, what nationality is the name 'Goodwrench'?") to European food ("baked face of leprechaun with the sheep's-stomach pudding"). Like all the people before him who searched for the American Dream, however, Leno did not really locate it, the mythology as elusive as ever.[52]

Sharing the common denominators of success, fame, and wealth, the American Dream occasionally crossed paths with the cult of celebrity that arose in the 1980s. In 1986, for example, *Ladies' Home Journal* asked a number of celebrities what the Dream meant to them, their answers, not surprisingly, unusually upbeat. Trashing the American Dream would not have been very good for their public image, after all, the fact that all had, to varying degrees, "made it" another reason famous people (or their publicists) had quite a different take on the mythology than most social critics of the day. Public figures' responses are nonetheless interesting, devoid of the usual rhetoric, and, occasionally, refreshingly honest. "For me, the American Dream has been the chance to parlay a sense of humor and a love of people into a craft that has given others laughter and joy," wrote the seventy-five-year-old Lucille Ball, happy that her legacy was ensured. (She would die just three years later.) "My idea of the American Dream is a land where we don't have to let others talk us out of our dream," said Linda Evans, the actress currently starring in *Dynasty* thankful that she had not listened to people who told her she was too old to get into the business.

(Evans starting acting professionally on *The Adventures of Ozzie and Harriet* when she was eighteen, hardly long in the tooth.) Marie Osmond saw children ("the hope of a future that we are building today") as the heart of the American Dream, while Doris Day felt the phrase meant "a better world for all animals," specifically that everyone would become a vegetarian like herself. "What a land it would be if they were free!" Day exclaimed, speaking of "the lambs, the piggies, the cows, and the rest of the world's beautiful creatures."[53]

As expected, hard work and its rewards were often associated with the Dream by those individuals who had found great success in their field. "No matter where you were born, no matter what color you are or what background you come from, you can make it big if you work hard enough," wrote Ann Landers, the famous advice giver, who believed that "this is a land where effort, energy, hard work, dedication, integrity, honesty and performance count." Tennis player Martina Navratilova (who had become a US citizen five years earlier) felt similarly ("If you are capable, you may," went her brief contribution), with country singer Loretta Lynn chiming in, "It's the only county where anyone, no matter how educated or uneducated, can make anything happen—if they want it bad enough." Kenny Rogers also saw the Dream as an obstacle to overcome. "I always equate the American Dream with mountain climbing," the singer-songwriter and future chicken-restaurant owner said, this country one of the few "where the mountaintop is visible and accessible to all." Estée Lauder put a feminist spin on the to-the-victor-go-the-spoils view of the Dream. "For me, the American Dream means that if a woman pushes herself beyond the farthest place she thinks she can go, she can have it all—family, financial success, fun," the cosmetics queen told her sisters, just the kind of thing many readers of *Ladies' Home Journal* probably wanted to hear.[54]

Finally, the theme of freedom and equal opportunity frequently popped up in celebrities' definitions of the American Dream, these interpretations the truest to Adams's vision. "I think the American Dream is to have freedom to be who you want to be and where you want to be that person," Tom Brokaw proposed, distancing this idea from the mythology's more recent leanings toward financial success. "What I think is the richer dream is to choose a life that brings a deeper happiness spiritually, politically and culturally," the newsman continued. Chuck Yeager was in the same camp, thinking, "This is a land where one can take advantage of opportunities as they come along." "We are a country that says yes to adventure," the test pilot extraordinaire added, a very nice advertising slogan should we ever need to recruit people from other, less interesting, places. Robert Schuller, the famous pastor, said much the same thing, stating, "The American Dream means that I have the opportunity to make choices," while superchef Julia Child maintained, "The American Dream says anything can happen here." Lee Iacocca thought the Statue of Liberty embodied it best, "the beautiful symbol of what it means to be free," a perfect expression of the Dream's values. There was a catch, however. "Freedom is just the ticket of admission, but if you want to survive and prosper, there's a price to pay," the Chrysler CEO advised, his experience with the struggling car company giving him firsthand knowledge of this bit of wisdom.[55]

Few celebrities had known the high cost of surviving and prospering better than Elvis Presley, whose mansion in Memphis stood as clear evidence of how far a poor boy from Tupelo, Mississippi, could come. Graceland was a constantly evolving "monument to the American Dream," according to Martie Zad of the *Washington Post*, the ten-year anniversary of the King's death in 1977 a prime opportunity to revisit the place that had by then taken on the epic proportions of Charles Foster Kane's fictional Xanadu. More than a half-million people a year made a pilgrimage to the estate that had opened to the public in 1982, the house and its grounds viewed by some as more than a museum or even a shrine. Graceland was nothing less than a fourteen-acre symbol of the nation's core mythology, the embodiment of the Dream's trappings of success, wealth, and, as often as not, excess. A tour of the Jungle Room, poolroom, TV room (there were fourteen sets in the house), dining and living rooms, "Hall of Gold" (records, not jewelry), and racquetball court was (and remains) concrete proof of how the Dream could go astray when that dreamer has a bit too much time on his hands and way too much money in his pockets. Presley's seventeen horses with their custom-made saddles were no longer there, but the stables were, as were his 1973 Stutz, Ferrari, three "supercycles," the pink jeep from *Blue Hawaii*, and the pink Cadillac he had given to his mother. Elvis's giant jet was also on the grounds, the stories surrounding it (he once flew from Memphis to Denver for peanut butter sandwiches that were served to him and his guests on a silver platter from a limousine on the runway) now part of American folklore. "The King lives," Zad observed, his anything but graceful life illustrating that dreams can both come true and, some would say, go wrong.[56]

The Stuff of Which the American Dream Is Made

Although the ability to fly halfway across the country in your own jet for peanut butter sandwiches was one man's interpretation of the American Dream, it was a lot more helpful to find how ordinary folks viewed it. A few months after the October 1987 stock market crash, *Ladies' Home Journal* did just that, focusing on four families of different income levels to see how they and their Dream were faring during these most recent uncertain economic times. "Owning your own home, providing for your children's education, achieving financial security, and believing in a better tomorrow—this is the stuff of which the American Dream is made," Michael J. Weiss wrote in the magazine, his mission to discover if that Dream had become an impossible one. That appeared to be the case of the Elliotts of New Orleans, who were working hard just to stay afloat. With a gross household income of $28,600, the Elliotts (a married couple with two kids, like the three other families) were just squeaking by, watching every penny to maintain a lifestyle somewhere between the poverty line and middle class. The American Dream was for the Elliotts all about financial security, their goal simply to "better our condition," as they aptly put it.[57]

Making $43,000 a year, the second family, the Graffs of Minneapolis, were squarely middle class, Weiss's article continued. To them, the American Dream meant "being able to afford everything you need—though not everything you want," thinking a $60,000 annual income would allow them to not have to make the kind of compromises—a remodeled home instead of a new home, a postponed Hawaiian vacation, wearing less than stylish clothing, always using coupons when they went grocery shopping—they were currently making. That is exactly what the third family, the Edwardsons of Fairfax, Virginia, brought home, enough to support an upper-middle-class lifestyle that included not just a four-bedroom home in one of the nicer suburbs of Washington, DC, but a twenty-five-foot cabin cruiser as well. Just as the Graffs thought a little more money would make their American Dream come true, the Edwardsons believed $100,000 a year would give them enough breathing room to not have to worry about overextending themselves. The final family featured in the magazine, the Kemps of Silicon Valley, were making even more than that, their $150,000 gross annual income (in the top 1 percent in the nation) allowing them to live the (very) good life complete with a vacation condo near Yosemite, a Mercedes, and a Porsche. "The American Dream means we can do whatever we want to do, and try to make as much money as we want," they explained, happy with their luxurious lifestyle but striving for much more. The Kemps saw $250,000 as the number that would allow them to have a less frantic work schedule. "Just as we meet the goals we have set for ourselves, the horizons of our ambition once again recede, keeping fresh the struggle to get ahead, reach higher, improve our lifestyle," Weiss wrote in summing up his findings, the perpetual longing for more and more (or chronic dissatisfaction with what one had) a key characteristic of the Dream.[58]

Chronic dissatisfaction with what one has was a perfect way to describe the tone of one of the hottest shows on television, *thirtysomething*. Following the mundane yet somehow complicated lives of seven friends in Philadelphia in their thirties (two married couples with children and three singles), *thirtysomething* was a major hit for ABC in the late eighties and early nineties. Although the show's plot points were often like watching paint dry (home remodeling was actually one of them), *thirtysomething* struck a nerve with viewers, especially among young urban professionals who related to the characters' "yuppie angst." Should we have a second child? Should I return to work after giving birth? Can this marriage be saved? How can I find the time to have lunch with my friends? Such weighty (and fluffy) questions were posed in the show, exactly the kinds of things that real-life baby boomers were going through as they tried to manage relationships and careers. "The show speaks with a clear and sometimes painful voice to a generation of 'thirtysomethings' that is struggling with feelings of uncertainty and alienation while pursuing visions of the American dream," noted Patricia Hersch in *Psychology Today*, so much so that therapists were asking their patients to watch it before coming to a session. While *thirtysomething* was often trite and just plain annoying (I found it difficult to watch when I was a thirtysomething), the issues raised in the show—how to balance career, friends, and family; whether one was "selling out"; what it took to be an adult; and, most important, if it really was possible to have it all—were right on target, the nuts and bolts of the American Dream for a generation trying to make it happen.[59]

For at least one thirtysomething, Thomas Cangelosi of the *New York Times*, it was precisely yuppie angst that was wrong with the American Dream. Cangelosi painfully confessed he had recently come very close to buying a condominium, happy his offer had been rejected and that he had successfully skirted the responsibilities of home ownership. With no wife, no child, and no mortgage, Cangelosi felt he was living a more authentic American Dream than most of his fellow baby boomers living the traditional one that *thirtysomething* captured so well. Cangelosi had "the freedom to pursue the unlimited possibilities without and develop the unknown dimension within," he wrote, a perspective quite true to Adams's original vision. Almost all his friends, however, had "herded up the path of least resistance," retreating to suburban houses as an escape from uncertainty and risk. It was the antithesis of the American Dream, Cangelosi thought, seeing marriage as another way his peers were embracing complacency in order to avoid the emotional roller coaster of passion. In many respects, he felt baby boomers had returned to the world of their parents, an act of contrition perhaps for rebelling against it so vehemently in the 1960s. Having learned that idealism was impractical, intellectualism boring, and emotionalism self-destructive, his generation had decided to swallow a pill delivering a heavy dose of conservatism and simplicity. "Take this pill daily till all creative symptoms disappear, all uncertainty evaporates, all possible alternatives are eliminated and life is refined to a point—the period at the end of the American Dream," as Cangelosi described the prescription, something he saw as less the pursuit of happiness than "a warranty for manufactured happiness."[60]

Given that the United States may have no longer been the exclusive home to the American Dream, all this haranguing over whose version was more real was perhaps largely irrelevant. By the end of the 1980s, the

American Dream was thriving, rather ironically, in parts of Europe, much more so in fact than in the good old USA. The popular image of Europe after the war—poor, bombed out, and devoid of consumer goods—was simply no longer true, with clear signs that the members of the middle class in some countries were living better than their Yankee counterparts. Unlike most Americans, for example, people like Guy Joanny (a sales executive) and his wife, Colette (a gymnastics instructor), of Dijon, France, were not worrying about the cost of education, health care, and retirement, knowing their country's social programs would cover most of it. The Joannys took more than six weeks of vacation each year (the legal minimum was five in France), this idea too something generally unheard of in the United States. It was true that taxes were relatively high, but the French government had pensions for retirees just like in America, with many calling it quits at age sixty. Should the American Dream, some reasonably wondered, be renamed the European Dream?[61]

That many Europeans were enjoying a lifestyle closely resembling the standard American Dream while many of this country's citizens were not was a telling sign of the times. While "the eighties" are popularly remembered as a glorious decade of capitalism with Wall Street paper entrepreneurs praising the value of greed, the Dream remained out of the grasp for many if not most Americans. With the nation led by a president well versed in the art of illusion, the American Dream became more privatized over the course of the decade, mirroring the concentration of wealth and increasing divide between the "haves" and "have-nots." The myth was as powerful as ever but the reality much different, especially among the middle class for whom the Dream meant so much. The nation was about to turn another corner, however, a new century a prime opportunity to yet again rethink and re-create the American Dream.

5

The Anxious Society

What's that I smell in the air? The American dream.
Sweet as a new millionaire, The American Dream.
—"The American Dream," in the Broadway play *Miss Saigon*

ON FEBRUARY 10, 1999, a revival of Arthur Miller's *Death of a Salesman* opened on Broadway, running for 274 performances and winning a number of Tony Awards. (Previous Broadway revivals were in 1975, with George C. Scott playing Willy Loman, and in 1984, with Dustin Hoffman in the starring role.) Brian Dennehy played Willy in this latest production, doing justice to the character a half century after the play was first staged with Lee J. Cobb in the lead role. Although much of the world had changed in fifty years, Miller's classic seemed as relevant as ever, with many audience members no doubt squirming in their seats as they watched Loman's desperate longing for success and popularity. The American Dream was the real star of *Death of a Salesman*, with the boom times of the end of the twentieth century creating a cultural climate in which the pressure to "make it" was equal to or perhaps even greater than it was in any other period in the nation's history. Although it was an illusion, a product of our collective imagination, the Dream was still our guiding mythology in everyday life.[1]

The Dream seemed to be everywhere in the late 1990s, with everyone from Donald Trump to Sean "Puffy" Combs proud spokespeople for our way of life where, if you tried hard enough and caught a lucky break or two, anything was possible. Best of all, with an apparently limitless supply of bling to be had and McMansions to be built, the Dream was potentially infinite, a constantly expanding balloon offering endless spoils to the victors. It had only been the past couple of years that the American Dream experienced its renaissance, however, with the earlier part of the decade looking and feeling a lot like other periods when the Dream seemed nowhere to be found. Like always, the American Dream was proving to be an elusive, slippery thing, coming and going like a thief in the night.

Creativity, Compassion, and Connection

As soon as we started writing "1990" on our checks, in fact, one could sense something different in the air. Although "the eighties" effectively ended with the stock market crash of October 1987, the official turning of the decade's page was more reason to observe there had been a sea change in American culture. The "Gimme Decade," with its every-man-or-woman-for-himself-or-herself ethos, was over, those people who expressed it best (or worst)—people such as Leona Helmsley, Ivan Boesky, and Jeffrey Levitt—doing time for their transgressions. Consistent with the "kinder, gentler nation" that President George H. W. Bush envisioned in his acceptance speech for the nomination for presidency at the 1988 GOP convention, values like altruism and personal fulfillment were beginning to replace the values of avarice and materialistic indulgence, social critics were reporting, if true posing major implications to the dynamics of the American Dream. "Creativity, compassion and connection are going to be the hallmarks of the '90s," Douglas LaBier, a DC-area psychoanalyst, told the *Washington Post*, thinking the rat race led by yuppies was slowing to a crawl. LaBier's thesis was that, as they approached middle age, baby boomers were finally reaching adulthood, a reasonable assumption given their existential growing pains. A lot of successful boomers were laying down for a spell on the shrink's couch, complaining that there was not much more to show for their lives except an admittedly sweet Mercedes and an awesome cappuccino maker.[2]

LaBier was hardly the only one thinking the nation and its guiding mythology were changing skins. *Fortune*, that loud voice of capitalism, posed the question "Is Greed Dead?" as the title of a recent article, noting how words like *save, nurture,* and *share* were increasingly popping up in ordinary conversation. "The conspicuous consumption, cold careerism,

and self-centered spirit that made up so much of business as usual in the
'80s now come across as a bit tacky at best, ruinous at worst," the writer
of the article observed, where all this would go not exactly clear. "People
are looking for a way to go deeper inside themselves to find out what they
really value," suggested Jacqueline McMakin, coauthor of *Working from
the Heart*, another book about the cultural shift. Was some kind of mil-
lennialism afoot, some wondered, a spiritual renaissance that would usher
in a new age of enlightenment? Probably not (*Lifestyles of the Rich and
Famous* was still on television, after all), but there was little doubt that
America and its Dream were morphing into something quite different
from what they had recently been.[3]

People hoping that a new decade would usher in prosperity and
abundance for all were certainly disappointed when the 1990s began
with a resounding economic thud. The early nineties looked a lot like
the late 1980s, economically speaking, a lingering recession making it
appear that the Dream was, at best, in hibernation, at worst dead as a
doornail. Much more than any economic data, however, it was a film
that made this abundantly clear. In fact, no film before (and perhaps
since) Michael Moore's 1990 *Roger and Me* captured the implosion of
the American Dream so compellingly, the documentary a scathing take
on, as Henry Allen of the *Washington Post* put it, "Rust Belt despairs and
capitalism's betrayals of the worker." Moore was somehow able to take a
humorous approach to the serious problem of high unemployment in his
(and General Motors') hometown of Flint, Michigan, the conceit of the
film his attempt to meet and chat with Roger Smith, the CEO of GM.
(Moore was carrying on a proud family tradition of rabble-rousing; his
uncle took part in the legendary 1937 strike in Flint that led to the founding of the United Auto Workers.) "We are not talking about enlightened
snickering at ironies, we're talking lotsa laughs at the ongoing slapstick of
the American dream as dreamed and then awakened from in the light of
the world according to Roger Smith," Allen wrote, the film really more
social commentary than documentary.[4]

Underlying the humor in *Roger and Me* was, of course, a serious message (Moore toyed with the idea of calling the film *The Dance Band on
the "Titanic"*), the revelation that the country was not a classless land of

opportunity a painful one for thousands of autoworkers in Flint and many thousands of others having similar experiences. "It's about the dream," Moore said of his film, specifically the snatching away of something people were encouraged to believe in:

> The dream itself isn't good because it's a dream, it's not reality. Being able to own your home and own your car is not the reality of being in control of your own life, because they can snap it from you just like that. I don't want you to be angry about the dream being gone, I want you to be angry about the lie of the dream, the illusion that's created, the illusion that by having a few things of wealth that somehow you've made it and you're secure for the rest of your life.[5]

That the American Dream was a dream, an illusion that Americans had created for themselves, was becoming increasingly clearer. "Will the baby boomers be the first generation to give the lie to the American dream?" asked Peter Passell of the *New York Times* after reading a new report called "The Economic Future of American Families" written by Frank Levy and Richard Michel, economists at the University of Maryland. Levy and Michel were less than optimistic about the prospects for boomers, predicting business productivity would be relatively flat over the next few decades when adjusted for inflation. The thirtysomethings of the early 1990s would be less well off than their parents when they retired, the report argued, this fact being the "lie to the American dream" Passell felt was possibly looming. A majority of Americans themselves "saw the American dream of a good life slipping out of reach," another study issued just a month later revealed, as the *Times* also reported. Three-quarters of the people polled were concerned that their hopes and dreams for the future would never come true, the study conducted by Grey Advertising showed, the recession of the past few years obviously taking a toll. "Americans no longer believe life will simply get better and better, and they have become very cautious and uncertain about the future," said Grey's Barbara Feigin in summarizing the findings, with consumers' optimism much lower than in the go-go 1980s.[6]

Needless to say, the revelation that upward mobility was difficult if not impossible for a big chunk of Americans was a devastating blow to belief in the American Dream. A good many blue-collar Americans, seeing their factory jobs go up in smoke, were returning to school to learn new trades better suited to the "knowledge economy." (Computer technician was a popular choice.) Economists were predicting the recession would be over soon, but that forecast was cold comfort to people having trouble putting food on their table. While the intellectual and cultural elite seemed to be weathering the storm (and often actually benefiting from the opening up of global markets), at least half of the country's workforce was hitting the ceiling in their careers, assuming they still had one. The brighter future that was believed to be their national birthright had, by most measures, vanished, the concept of "downward mobility" a bitter pill to swallow.[7]

Although Americans had brushed up against "downward mobility" before, notably during the Great Depression and the deep recession of the early 1970s, the socioeconomic skid of the early nineties was a decidedly rude awakening. "It has been a powerful and enduring conviction that every generation of Americans would move beyond the social and economic station of its predecessor," wrote Barbara Vobejda in the *Washington Post* in late 1991, noting that "the notion of upward mobility has been shaken of late." If the bad news was that a new pessimism was sweeping across the land, the worse news was that it was, economically speaking, perfectly justified. The feeling of doom and gloom could be detected beyond the numbers, however, with a variety of developments—young people living with Mom and Dad longer than they previously had and putting off marriage and having kids, couples needing two jobs to maintain their lifestyle, and new mothers deciding to go back to work, to name a few—evidence that the American standard of living was in decline. "Taken together," continued Vobejda, "these changes reflect a fundamental rethinking about what American families can afford, how far they can expect to climb, and what dreams they can hold for their children," tough times once again interrupting individuals' best-laid plans.[8]

On a grander level, the best-laid plans of the nation itself had been interrupted, Robert J. Samuelson proposed in a 1992 cover story for *Newsweek* titled "How Our American Dream Unraveled." The "Good Society" of the 1950s had at some point morphed into "The Age of Entitlement," he argued, the (false) belief that prosperity was inevitably leading us down the rocky road we were now on. "The result is a deep crisis of spirit that fuels Americans' self-doubts, cynicism with politics and confusion about our global role," he wrote, despite the fact that "quality of life" had unarguably improved in many ways over the past few decades. As the Age of Entitlement wound down along with our crusade against communism, Samuelson explained, the country was no longer sure who it was and what it should be, this loss of identity the single most important issue of the day. "Our new era lacks a name, but its central challenge is clear: to restore the American Dream," he concluded, the reconciliation of ideals with realities a good way to start the process.[9]

The "deep crisis of spirit" that Samuelson believed was sweeping the nation had, it appeared, taken root over the past decade. In polls conducted at the beginning of the Reagan era, two out of three Americans said they believed that their standard of living would be higher than their parents'. In a 1992 Roper Poll, however, almost three of every four people reported that the American Dream was "harder to attain" than it was a generation ago, this apples-to-apples comparison a good way to measure the historical shift and, perhaps, predict the future.[10] "For many Americans, the future seems about as secure as a dandelion puff," the *Wall Street Journal* bemoaned in 1992, with job security having gone the way of the BetaMax in this new age of "downwardly mobile professionals" (or, almost inevitably, "dumpies").[11]

America's Best-Kept Secret

As the country voted in a new president, William Jefferson Clinton, promising "hope" and "change," a host of writers weighed in on the erosion of the American Dream and what to do about it. A rising standard of living had been a consistent theme in the history of the country, but the trend had reversed over the past twenty years, no one seemingly equipped to deal with or accept the unfamiliar territory of "negative growth." As growth slowed or went backward, other countries were catching up to the United States in standard of living, the standard perks of the Dream more likely to be found in France or Sweden.[12] Just the title of Katherine Newman's *Declining Fortunes: The Withering of the American Dream* spoke volumes, the shrinking job market, rising housing costs, high taxes, and growing cost of living expenses squeezing the middle class like a vise over the past couple of decades.[13] Edmund N. Luttwak's *Endangered American Dream* focused on our colossal national deficit, the Reagan-Bush administrations flagrantly violating the Economics 101 principle to not spend more than one earns.[14] And Wallace C. Peterson's *Silent Depression: The Fate of the American Dream* argued that even an apparently healthy economy hid the hardships that less well-off people had to endure.[15] Did the American Dream, one had to wonder, stand any chance of surviving?

Alice M. Rivlin, author of *Reviving the American Dream*, certainly believed so, as long as Americans themselves believed it. "Americans, long noted for their 'can-do' spirit, for self-assurance often bordering on cockiness, have become mired in pessimism," she wrote in 1992, thinking it had become "fashionable" to be bearish on the nation's economy. Rivlin, a senior fellow in the Brookings Economic Studies program, was puzzled and disturbed by this sort of populist defeatism, the nation's economic future actually very encouraging if one looked at the big picture. The country's tremendous resources, both natural and human, had not disappeared, after all, our productivity and standard of living still the highest in the world. In fact, the United States had survived far greater economic challenges in the past, and many other countries were going through much tougher difficulties. Rivlin's solution to reviving the Dream was for the government to do what many American businesses were doing to be more competitive: improving their products and services, offering better customer service, and getting the most from their employees. By focusing on its core "business," in other words, the federal government could do a lot to help Americans restore their faith in the future of the country and in its central mythology.[16]

Other conservatives claimed that the death of the American Dream was greatly exaggerated, more media hype than anything else. "The news media provide the despair-mongers with an ever-ready megaphone, continually dashing the American Dream by presenting economic hardship news through a magnifying glass, by dramatizing the downside so relentlessly, that people imagine things to be far worse than they really are," William A. Schreyer, the CEO of Merrill Lynch, told the Economic Club of Washington in 1992. For him, like Rivlin, the problem was not that the

Dream was dead but that many believed it was, the resulting hopeless-
ness and despair doing the real damage to the country. Schreyer actually
argued that the Dream was more alive than ever, the spread of consumer
capitalism proof of such. "It built America, and now it's attracting the
whole world," he insisted, adding that "the way this century is concluding,
it could well be called 'The Century of the American Dream.'"[17]

Schreyer's company was so interested in the current health and future
prospects of the American Dream, in fact, that Merrill Lynch sponsored
one of the most in-depth studies ever done on the topic. Combining data
from economic analyses, results from public opinion polls, and findings
from focus groups, its 1994 study uncovered two major challenges to the
Dream (defined as "a quintessentially American ideal that each generation will do better than the one before"), both involving baby boomers.
The first threat consisted of the astounding amount of money the government had committed to pay in the future, these Social Security benefits,
Medicare payments, pensions, and other outlays to potentially crash the
system as boomers retired. The second threat to the American Dream was
that baby boomers simply did not save enough, their standard of living to
decline significantly in retirement even if the government delivered on all
its promises. Big changes had to be made by both boomers and the government if the Dream was to be saved, the study warned, some of those
changes not surprisingly involving the kind of investment and financial
planning services that companies like Merrill Lynch offered.[18]

There was no doubt that most Americans were depending heavily on
government to help them realize the American Dream now and in the
future. About half of the people asked "What institution has the primary
responsibility for creating jobs and economic improvement?" in a 1994
Wall Street Journal/NBC poll replied, "The government," in fact, a shocking finding to people of a conservative bent. "Far too many Americans
have come to believe that the 'American Dream' is dead and that it's up to
Washington to resurrect it," complained Errol Smith, a Los Angeles radio
talk show host, blaming "liberal politicians" for propagating this bad idea.
The tremendous growth of government over the past few decades had led
to a "pampered generation," he thought, with the American traditions of
self-help and free enterprise now largely a thing of the past. For Smith

and others of his political ilk, the proper answer to the poll's question was private individuals, their desire to make more money by starting or expanding their business the key to resurrecting the Dream. "The American Dream is alive and well—this is perhaps America's best kept secret—but it requires 'American Dreamers,'" he urged, seeing the government as more the problem than the solution.[19]

Another conservative, Representative J. C. Watts Jr., a Republican congressman from Oklahoma, had his chance to tell voters what the American Dream was really about at the 1996 Republican National Convention. Watts distinguished the Republican idea of the Dream from the Democrats' version, the opportunity to climb the ladder of success much truer to its ideals than supposedly "compassionate" government handouts. "The American Dream is about becoming the best you can be," he said in his speech in San Diego at which Bob Dole was nominated as the party's candidate, not temporary fixes like welfare or subsidized public housing. Watts, the fifth of six children born to poor parents in rural Oklahoma, was especially careful to ground the Republican Dream in opportunity versus wealth. Rather than being about "your bank account, the kind of car you drive, or the brand of clothes you wear," he made clear, the Dream was about "using your gifts and abilities to be all that God meant for you to be," his rise to congressman a lesson in how it could come true for others.[20]

The Road Home

Conservatives may have thought the dashing of the American Dream was part of the liberal agenda, but some television shows of the early 1990s reinforced the idea that it would require extreme measures to make it come true. Escape from the hellish city to an Eden-like world was the only route to the Dream in two short-lived, mostly forgotten shows, ABC's *Byrds of Paradise* and CBS's *Road Home*. In the former, which ran for just the 1993–94 season, Sam Byrd (Timothy Busfield) moved with his three kids (two of them played by Jennifer Love Hewitt and Seth Green) to Hawaii after his wife was killed in a robbery in New Haven, the former Yale professor landing a plum job as a headmaster in a private school. Some locals resented the outsiders, but the family's beautiful home complete with two servants seemed like more than fair compensation. In *The Road Home,* which lasted just five episodes, paradise was the North Carolina coast, where Alison and Jack Matson and their four kids decided to settle after realizing the magic of the place. (One part of the magic was, ironically, that the kids stopped watching TV.) "Blue-collar" sitcoms like ABC's *Roseanne* and CBS's *Tom* had a much harder edge, the Dream nowhere to be found. "Remember when we used to have hopes for our own kids?" Roseanne asked her husband, Dan (John Goodman), in one show from 1994, the funny line also loaded with some detectable pain. And in an episode of *Tom*, starring Roseanne Barr's real-life (and soon-to-be-divorced) husband, Tom Arnold, the title character was skeptical of his wife's desire to go to college. "Just takes you four years longer to get to the same dead-end job," he quipped, this line too charged with a heavy dose of anger and bitterness. That Tom's dream house turned out to be located within spitting distance of the city dump was pouring salt in the wound, a metaphor perhaps for viewers' own, very real, disappointments.[21]

While Tom Arnold's televisual experience was certainly extraordinary, his dream of the perfect house in the perfect neighborhood was not at all. Despite often being impractical and even more often unaffordable, the American Dream of the single-family house in the suburbs (ideally with a two-car garage and big backyard) was an astonishingly persistent one. Eighty percent of Americans said it was "the ideal place to live," according to a 1992 national survey conducted for Fannie Mae, in fact, with nothing able to knock the Great American House off its foundation.[22] Other forms of housing were typically considered a compromise or temporary situation, the industry itself encouraging this kind of thinking through terms like *cooperative apartment* or *starter home*. Americans had inherited their love of the freestanding house from Europe, of course, where landownership conveyed status, security, and wealth. Whether it was a castle, manor house, villa, or just a cottage, the European country house was considered sacred, sometimes even deemed independent from the long arms of the church and state. The bucolic surroundings were a big part of this idea, naturally, the absence of the city's poverty, crime, overcrowding, and bad hygiene understandably making the house in the country seem like utopia. The suburban colonial, ranch, or Cape Cod was the

Americanized version of this utopian domicile, the fact that one did not have to be wealthy or royalty to live in one making it no less desirable.[23]

The financial benefits of owning one's home made the Dream that much more dreamy. "For many years," Benny L. Kass, a DC-area lawyer, wrote in the *Washington Post* in 1991, "homeownership has been the American dream," with tax laws encouraging people who could afford it to be the king or queen of one's castle. Not only had houses almost certainly appreciated in value over the years, but home owners could deduct mortgage interest and real estate taxes, the government in effect subsidizing the domestic articulation of the Dream. As well, when one sold a house and bought another principal residence within two years, he or she was able to "roll over" any profits without paying taxes on the gain, another way Congress was promoting home ownership. Having a literal stake in one's community was a way the government had Americans invest themselves in local, regional, and national interests, it could be argued, a win-win situation that kept everybody happy (except renters, perhaps).[24]

The real estate bust of the late eighties following the market crash had a profound effect on the way people viewed their homes, however, and, because it represented so much a part of it, the American Dream. "During the past two decades, owning a home has been only the first half of the American dream," stated Gary Blonston of Knight-Ridder, adding that "the second half has been selling it and making a killing." The steadily rising prices of homes across the country through the 1970s and 1980s were not going to continue in the 1990s, many experts thought, the windfall that came with selling a house possibly a thing of the past. The upside, of course, was that houses would be more affordable, allowing many unable to share in "the first half of the American dream" to finally do so. The numbers bore this notion out; median housing prices in most metropolitan areas were rising slower than the inflation rate (about 5 percent), reversing the trend of the past few years. That one's house was not an investment was going to take some getting used to, everyone agreed, the idea that it was just a (very expensive) consumer good quite a different way of thinking.[25]

Until something better came along, however, the urge to be the king or queen of one's own castle would be passed down from generation to generation of Americans. As middle-aged boomers traded up to bigger houses in the early nineties, baby "busters" were gobbling up these starter homes, finding them perfect for smaller families just as their parents had. It was, in the long view, a significant development, marking the end perhaps of the decades-long stretch in which most of the middle class was unable to become home owners and, correlatively, owners of the American Dream. "Now, as the 20th century draws to a close, a new generation of American homebuyers are dreaming new dreams," *American Demographics* beamed in 1993, the recent bursting of the housing bubble enabling Generation Xers to get their piece of the pie along with the financial and psychological security that came with it. The domestic Dream was also expanding in a more literal sense. The average square footage of a new single-family home hit the magic number of two thousand in 1989 and was continuing to grow, with two-story dwellings, garages, multiple bathrooms, central air-conditioning, and fireplaces now considered standard features. Media rooms and playrooms for the kids were also often popping up in new homes (even though families were smaller than in the postwar years), with supersized "McMansions" becoming a common sight in the suburbs.[26] By 1995 the typical American home was 40 percent bigger than it was in 1970, loaded of course with a lot more electronic goodies. The American Dream may have been in serious jeopardy, but there was no chance it was going to get smaller.[27]

The Opportunity

The unabated desire to achieve the American Dream and reap all of its rewards could be seen in a new and different brand of entrepreneurialism making its way across the landscape of consumerism. The best example had to be Provo, Utah–based Nu Skin International, which claimed it was now world heavyweight champion of the Dream. Like other successful network or "multilevel" marketing companies like Amway, Mary Kay, Shaklee, Herbalife, and A. L. Williams, Nu Skin's independent distributors recruited other distributors and so on, each "sponsor" taking a cut of the profits of the distributors in their "downlines." But unlike these other companies, a typical Nu Skin pitch came with a heavy dose of positive thinking, the promise of personal growth at least as important as glowing skin and shiny hair. Nu Skin's one hundred thousand distributors were supposedly selling something much more meaningful than the line of sixty cosmetic, hair care, and nutritional products, in other words the company's evangelical philosophy part and parcel of each transaction. A bit flaky, so to speak, but with sales of $230 million in 1990, it was hard to dismiss Nu Skin as a bunch of kooks, especially when people like Bill Cosby and Ronald Reagan were showing up at the company's annual conventions to inspire the troops.[28]

The "New Age Amway," as it was sometimes known, was getting a lot of unwanted attention, however. Attorney generals in at least six states were investigating the company, as was, it was believed, the Federal Trade Commission. Nu Skin was not much more than a pyramid scheme, some government officials argued, with selling distributorships more important than selling products. ABC's *Nightline*, *USA Today*, and *Newsweek* all had done exposés on the company, which vigorously defended itself as a perfectly legit operation. (Similar attacks had been made on Amway with some success.) Nu Skinners were, meanwhile, pursuing "The Opportunity," as they called it, trying to get rich while subscribing to the company's twelve-step-like program. (Weekly "Opportunity Meetings" and a belief in a "Higher Power" were essential parts of the Nu Skin philosophy.) Many Nu Skinners had yet to realize financial or spiritual fulfillment, however, the opportunity that looked so good on paper much less rewarding in real life because of the difficulty in recruiting other distributors.[29]

As usual, it seemed that good old hard work, rather than a clever organizational structure or devout faith in what one was doing, was a more likely path to realize the American Dream. People like Shahbaz Hussain of Washington, DC, had done just that, the immigrant from Pakistan (who had a master's degree in economics) and former taxi driver now the owner of five cab companies bringing in more than five million dollars a year. "This is the stuff American dreams are made of," thought Mohammed Hanif of the *Washington Post*, Hussain's classic rags-to-riches story exactly why people from the four corners of the earth kept arriving on our shores. Although remarkable in that it could happen at all, the story's arc was rather predictable, following four distinct stages. First was the dream itself, of course, the foreigner coming to America with grand ambitions and the willingness to do whatever it took to make them come true. Next came the tough part, the eighteen-hours-a-day, seven-days-a-week workload while typically coping with wretched living conditions, all the time putting away as much money as possible for the proverbial rainy day. Then, rather suddenly, that day would arrive, the immigrant realizing that he or she had indeed "made it." Hussain credited his success not just to hard work but also to his education, however, thinking the latter was what separated him from all the other taxi drivers trying to realize the same Dream.[30]

Shahbaz Hussain's American Dream was just the kind of success story featured in *The First Universal Nation*, a documentary that aired on PBS in 1992. Written by Ben J. Wattenberg, a senior fellow at the conservative think tank the American Enterprise Institute, the show focused on the nation's "melting pot," which was, he argued, "alive, flourishing, [and] expanding." A million new immigrants were jumping into the pot, for one thing, about the same number as at the turn of the twentieth century, but only 15 percent of them were now coming from Europe. Wattenberg found students from forty-one different countries at a school in Maryland, in fact, that they all seemed to be getting along evidence that our multicultural pot was not bubbling over, as the media often claimed. Marriage between people of different ethnicities and religions too was up, the show emphasized, another sign that America was indeed "the first universal nation" despite the more sensational reports of racial tension. Even more so than our melting pot, however, it was the exportation of our popular culture that illustrated the vitality of the American Dream. Through our movies, television shows, and Disney parks, values such as individualism and upward mobility were being spread around the world, Wattenberg proudly maintained, the underlying message being that "in America everything is possible."[31]

Whether it was an immigrant or native-born citizen who followed in Horatio Alger's footsteps to achieve the American Dream, his or her success was often held up as an example of what made this country great and different from all others. Nothing perhaps demonstrated this thought better than the Horatio Alger Award, a prestigious prize given by the Horatio Alger Association, a nonprofit created in 1947 to motivate young, disadvantaged Americans to overcome adversity. (The association also awarded three hundred thousand dollars in grants every year to deserving high school seniors.) Among the ten winners in 1992 were Clarence Thomas, Henry Kissinger, and Maya Angelou, each of their journeys "providing living proof that our free-enterprise system still offers opportunity to all," as James Moffett, chair of the award dinner, expressed it. It would indeed be difficult to come up with three more deserving candidates for the award. Thomas had risen from a poor childhood in the rural South to the Supreme Court of the United States, while Kissinger had fled Nazi Germany with his family at age fifteen and worked at a shaving-brush factory to put himself through night school before becoming the secretary of state for Presidents Nixon and Ford. Angelou, meanwhile, had lost the ability to speak when she was seven, overcame the disability, completed high school at age fifteen, and found a way to support herself and her son while she went to college on the way to becoming a best-selling author. Although they were more the exception than the rule, such real stories did a lot to counter the mountain of rhetoric that the American Dream was over, keeping the mythology a vibrant one for others to believe in.[32]

Others sought paths to the American Dream that did not require putting away loose change into a jar over many years or overcoming incredible adversity. A steady stream of Dreamers were heading to Bradenton, Florida, hoping they or their children would, with Nick Bollettieri's help, become the next Andre Agassi or Monica Seles. Bollettieri's tennis academy was the country's best-known school in the sport, the destination of choice for those parents thinking their prodigy could perhaps be turned into a champion. The great success of thirteen-year-old Jennifer Capriati was obviously having a ripple effect, making a good many parents of pre-teens believe that, when it came to hitting a ball over a net, one could never start too young. Other schools such as Harry Hopman/Saddlebrook near Tampa, which Capriati (who was already a millionaire) had attended, were also seeing a surge in applications, with children as young as seven from all over the world accepted into the program. (The youth movement in tennis was said to have started in 1989 when two seventeen-year-olds, Arantxa Sanchez Vicario and Michael Chang, won professional tournaments.) Women's tennis was especially youth oriented, with age sixteen or seventeen considered the make-or-break point. Even at this level, the pressure to win was tremendous, making Bollettieri think that just one in ten thousand kids should even consider going to his school, which for an annual tuition of twenty thousand dollars combined tennis with academics. For a select few, however, the rewards would likely be great, this thought enough to keep one's child whacking balls on a tennis court for four or five hours a day.[33]

The willingness to do almost anything—join a quasi-religious organization selling shampoo and vitamins, drive a cab for eighteen hours a day, or send one's child thousands of miles away—revealed the degree to which the American Dream had become about making money, preferably a lot of it. "Good lives well lived and still greater opportunities for [one's] children" was the original concept of the American Dream, John Steele Gordon made clear in 1990, but "unbounded wealth" had at some point stolen the show. "The 'American Dream' has come to mean an ideal not of liberty but of prosperity," Michael Ventura agreed, believing in fact that we now equated liberty with prosperity. Writing for *Psychology Today* in 1995, Ventura had come to this grand conclusion after spending some time in Las Vegas to get a better understanding of the psychology of money in America. Knowing they would probably lose, people came to Vegas to rebel against the fact that money controlled their lives, he proposed, with gambling serving as a kind of cathartic, emotionally fulfilling release from the almighty dollar. After literally paying penance, however, visitors to Sin City happily returned to their regular lives, their quest for the primary symbol of the American Dream—bread, dough, bones, clams, greenbacks, moola, scratch, simoleons, smackers, dead presidents—greater than ever.[34]

The Distance to the Moon

With precious few jackpots to be hit, most Americans would have to find the Dream in other, more imaginary, places. As in previous eras when the nation was struggling, its Dream on the rocks, many looked to heroes of the past for comfort and strength and as a reminder of its ideals. One such hero was Mickey Mantle, the Yankee great sixty-three years old in 1995 and recovering from a liver transplant. Mantle received thousands of letters, get-well cards, and telegrams at his hospital in Dallas, each one offering hope, inspiration, and thanks for the memories. Besides its sheer volume, the correspondence came from people of all ages and backgrounds, a clear sign that the motives for writing went beyond the slugger's exploits on the field. (In addition to hitting 536 home runs from both sides of the plate, Mantle often if not always played hurt, no doubt adding to his larger-than-life image.) Arriving in New York from the boonies of Oklahoma, Mantle had some mighty big shoes to fill—Joe DiMaggio's—but that he did for the next generation of fans. Mantle's Ruthian extracurricular activities and complicated personal life made him seem somehow relatable to ordinary folks, thus separating him from other great players of his time. Those individuals who had beaten the odds to achieve their Dream were especially attracted to Mantle's persona, the man's grit and determination serving as a prime example for others to dig down deep and refuse to quit. "Hillary and I were so sorry to learn of your health problems," went one letter, the writer telling Mantle that he held "a special place in the hearts of Americans across the country." The letter was signed by Bill Clinton, even the president of the United States looking to "the Mick" as a symbol of the American Dream. Mantle would die just a couple of months after the liver transplant, but his legacy in the pantheon of American Dreamers was ensured (the copyrighted slogan of Mantle's website is, in fact, "The American Dream Comes to Life").[35]

That Mantle, like Babe Ruth and other past baseball greats, was considered a quintessential archetype of the American Dream was no mere coincidence. Baseball and the Dream had often been paired as kindred spirits, with pundits of all stripes grabbing any opportunity to wax poetic on the commonalities between the sport and the mythology. A three-day conference called "Jackie Robinson: Race, Sports, and the American Dream" was held in 1997 at Long Island University, for example, where scholars, former baseball stars, and others discussed the man's legacy fifty years after he became the first black player in the Major Leagues. And every June since 1988, roughly a hundred scholars have gathered in Cooperstown, New York, home to baseball's Hall of Fame, to muse over the meaning of the game and, in particular, its relationship to the American Dream. At the three-day 1998 symposium, for example, one attendee talked about how baseball was "a mirror of the rise and assimilation of ethnic groups," the sport nicely tracking with immigrants' pursuit of the Dream (the Irish, decades ago, and recently Latin Americans and Asians). Another discussed the geographic similarities between the sport and the Dream, each literally grounded in the beauty of nature. "It creates an immense green field, a gorgeous vista invoking the pastoral, the agricultural, even the peaceable kingdom, but it hints that the lush green garden may also be a vale of tears," proposed George Grella, an English professor at the University of Rochester, both baseball and the American Dream picturesque visions that could, potentially, become sad ones.[36]

Even greater than the Dream's emotional bond with baseball was the one it shared with movies. *Hollywoodism*, a documentary that aired on A&E in 1998, wonderfully captured the intimate relationship between movies and the American Dream, showing how much DNA they had in common. Based on Neal Gabler's 1988 book *An Empire of Their Own: How the Jews Invented Hollywood*, the show focused on six producers— Carl Laemmle of Universal Pictures, Jack Warner of Warner Brothers, Louis B. Mayer of MGM, William Fox of Fox Film, Adolph Zukor of Paramount, and independent Sam Goldwyn—whose Jewish backgrounds fed directly into the kind of movies they made. All of these moguls' families had fled the pogroms in Eastern Europe, this shared experience shaping everything from westerns' good-guys-versus-bad-guys to the over-the-top escapist fantasies of 1930s musicals. As outsiders, "they envisioned an America that would welcome them, as the real America did not, and projected on screen a mythical country of picket fences, strong families, upward mobility and well-placed optimism, a country where the little guy makes good," wrote Caryn James of the *New York Times* in her review, the irony being that this view was embraced by the mainstream. Whether it was through Judy Garland singing "Over the Rainbow" in black-and-white Kansas, Fred Astaire in white tie and tails dancing to songs penned by Irving Berlin (who also wrote "God Bless America" and "White Christmas"), or even Frankenstein, the ultimate social outcast, Hollywood's Jews expressed the Dream's longing for happiness, success, and acceptance.[37]

If baseball, the movies, and the single-family house in the suburbs were the clearest expressions of the American Dream (next to cold, hard cash), the automobile would likely be next on the list. It was cars that went into that house's two-car garage, for one thing, but it was when they were speeding down the road that they most viscerally represented the Dream's fundamental dimension of freedom. James Morgan captured this idea in his 1999 book *The Distance to the Moon: A Road Trip into the American Dream*, the title taken from John Updike's calculation that the average American male drove the equivalent of the distance from the earth to the moon (about 239,000 miles) every seventeen years. Morgan went part of that distance over the course of seven weeks in a Porsche Boxster to get the material for the book, his round-trip cross-country trip from Miami to Portland (with a few side trips) a study in Americans' love of (and hatred for) the automobile. (The cross-country trip itself had much to do with the American Dream, of course, with Morgan following in the peripatetic tracks of everyone from Tocqueville to Lewis and Clark to Jack Kerouac.) Americans' obsession with cars was about "our bone-deep need for clean breaks and fresh beginnings, for self-reinvention, for fleeing the numbing grind of everyday existence," a good description of the restlessness associated with the Dream. In his review of the book for the *New York Times*, Bruce McCall, quite the car lover himself, explained why he thought automobiles were such a big part of the nation's folklore. "The automobile is the handiest tool ever devised for the pursuit of that unholy, unwholesome, all-American trinity of sex, speed and status," he proposed, describing an alternative set of building blocks of the American Dream.[38]

The mythological power that baseball, the movies, and the automobile wielded had much to do with the improbability of locating the American Dream in the workplace. With the American job market less than jumping, the chance that one could achieve the Dream by working in another country, something that had gained momentum during the 1980s, took off in the 1990s. Corporate America may have been downsizing, but a lot of companies and governments overseas were upsizing, with skilled workers from other countries in much demand. The spread of capitalism and the global economy had much to do with the transnationalism of the Dream, which was confirmed by tax forms filed by expatriates and by executive search firms. Russia was a popular destination, a bit ironically, as was eastern Europe, the Mideast, and Latin America. Middle-aged men laid off from their jobs were especially open to opportunities abroad after futilely looking for another one in the United States. Speaking the local language was a big plus, of course, as was an openness to cultural differences. Many naturally viewed the migration of hundreds of thousands of Yanks to distant lands to find opportunities unavailable in their own country as another nail in the coffin of the American Dream, with better business climates and more affordable homes the principal draws. Adventure too was part of the lure, exactly what had stirred many restless Europeans to come to America a century or two ago.[39]

The possibility that the Dream had moved overseas or resided exclusively within popular culture only seemed to make those persons looking for it in real Americans' lives look that much harder. Like others before her, Linda Schaffer, a filmmaker, went in search of the Dream, her year-plus journey documented in a ninety-minute television special that aired on TNT in 1996. Judging by the number of celebrities who appeared in her *American Dreams*—Michael Jordan, Mel Brooks, Gloria Steinem, and Maya Angelou, among them—one would think that she found it, or at least one of its dimensions. What Schaffer found instead was that "nobody really feels that they've made it yet," the Dream still at arm's length even for the rich and famous. Disillusionment was common among the ordinary folks Schaffer interviewed, although some maintained their belief that this country was a land of opportunity where dreams could and did come true. Again wealth and fame frequently popped up as the criteria for having made it among those individuals who had neither, as did the *Leave It to Beaver* scenario, especially among young people. Interestingly, one of the most optimistic people interviewed, a refugee from Vietnam, was newest to the country, while one of the most pessimistic was a Native American ("If this is the American dream, then I'm in the wrong place," the Coloradoan told Schaffer). Schaffer also uncovered a kind of "trading up" mentality when it came to the American Dream, those persons whose parents had achieved a Cleaveresque lifestyle wanting two homes, a luxury import rather than a Chevy or Ford, and vacations to the Caribbean instead of Disneyland. "The more you have, the more you aspire to," explained one person Schaffer interviewed, Mario Cuomo, the now former governor of New York still having a keen read on the past, present, and future of the Dream.[40]

A couple years later, another documentary crew set out to find the Dream, their end product airing on the Discovery Channel. With its five hour-long segments (centered around the Depression, World War II, the civil rights movement, the Vietnam War, and the "Reagan era"), *American Stories: The American Dream* was an ambitious effort, not surprising since the producers spent three years interviewing seventeen thousand people before selecting ten to feature in the series. By tracking the evolution of these ten individuals and their families over the course of three generations ("The American dream is about rise and fall and evolution," said the executive producer, Anthony Geffen, a Brit), the documentary strove to reveal "the yearnings and expectations, the achievements and the disappointments that have shaped the national psyche," as Kathryn Shattuck of the *New York Times* wrote in her review. The interviewees who told their stories included Dick Manoff, the son of poor Russian immigrants who became an advertising executive; John Gage, who went from Vietnam War protester to Internet pioneer; Jewell Blankenship, who moved to California during the Dust Bowl much like the Joads in John Steinbeck's *Grapes of Wrath*; Joe Mifsud, who came to this country from Malta in 1927 and worked on Ford's assembly line; General Baker, a black man from the South who made the "Great Migration" and worked alongside Mifsud in Detroit; and Endicott (Chub) Peabody II, a former governor of Massachusetts who was the epitome of the WASP establishment. "These stories take us to the heart and soul of the American dream," narrator Peter Fonda told viewers, the quest for betterment and to "move up" the common thread among the diverse collection of people featured in the series.[41]

The Good Life and Its Discontents

For Robert J. Samuelson, much of the heart and much of the soul of the American Dream had been missing in action for some time. Four years after his seminal 1992 article for *Newsweek*, Samuelson published what was probably the most thorough examination of the Dream since the term was coined by Adams. In his *The Good Life and Its Discontents: The American Dream in the Age of Entitlement, 1945–95*, Samuelson flushed out the central theme of "How Our American Dream Unraveled," that is, the contradiction between our current angst and the progress we had made over the past half century. "People sense something fundamental has ended, and they're fearful of an unseen future," he wrote, the fact that America was a much better place in 1995 than 1945 offering little consolation. That the "Good Society" of the 1950s and "Great Society" of the 1960s (as well as the counterculture, it could be said) never fulfilled their full promises—continually rising incomes, stable jobs, and the end of poverty, racism, and crime—was disappointing if not traumatic to the nation, Samuelson argued, exposing the American Dream as a fantasy. "It was too perfect to happen," he explained, the realization that an ideal, utopian society was purely a product of our collective imagination proving to be a crushing blow to the spirit of the nation and the source of our widespread disillusionment. Although most Americans were actually quite content with their personal lives, they also lacked confidence in the future, this disconnect the inspiration for the book's title.[42]

Because Samuelson's book bit off such a big piece of American history, critics, especially other economists, tended to be either very impressed by or equally dismissive of it. Writing for the *National Review*, Alan Reynolds, a senior fellow and director of economic research at the Hudson Institute, was of the former persuasion. "This is an ambitious, important work by one of the nation's most thoughtful and rigorous economic journalists," wrote Reynolds, quibbling with some of the author's number crunching but finding the book "entertaining and illuminating." Another well-known writer covering the economic beat thought Samuelson had bitten off much more than he could chew. Paul Krugman, an economist at Stanford University in 1996, used the *Washington Monthly* as a platform to voice his concerns about the book. Krugman argued that *The Good Life and Its Discontents* was not even really about economics but was, rather, a long essay about politics and society. Krugman also found Samuelson's two scenarios for the future (an emerging "age of responsibility" and, alternatively, a much more powerful federal government) "dubious," amazed that the author essentially ignored what he felt was the elephant in the room of American society: the growing gap between the "haves" and the "have-nots."[43]

It was precisely this gap that W. Bradford Fay, vice president of Roper Starch, focused on in his analysis of the breakup of the postwar American

Dream. Writing in *Marketing Research*, a trade publication for that field, Fay cited three different studies that showed that the rich were getting richer and the poor getting poorer. Rather than sort Americans into "haves" and "have-nots," Fay preferred to make a distinction between "cans" (people who could thrive without relying on the government, big business, or unions) and "cannots" (people who could not). Because these institutions could no longer guarantee Americans the kind of financial security they once did, it was up to individuals themselves to make it on their own. Self-reliance was once again becoming a key marker of the American Dream, with "playing by the rules" believed to no longer be an effective strategy to reach it. "Individual initiative, personal responsibility, and talent are the new currencies—not because these are virtuous qualities, but because they are necessities," Fay maintained, the dynamics of the Dream coming full circle from its origins based in personal freedom.[44]

Unfortunately, self-reliance was not going to make the realization of the American Dream any easier. In fact, many Americans were simply reaching too high, the standards of "the good life" and consumers' expectations raised to a very high level over the past couple of decades. "Individuals are pursuing bigger dreams while living in a society they perceive as increasingly unlikely to fulfill those dreams, either materially or spiritually," said Frank Luntz, a Republican Party pollster, with many Americans setting themselves up for disappointment through their wishful thinking. Some were even more pessimistic. "The American Dream is in crisis," wrote Charles J. Whalen in the *Humanist* in 1996, the "affluent society" of the 1950s and 1960s replaced by the "anxious society" of the 1990s. Although it could not be argued that downsizing was up and purchasing power down, the discomfort that much of the middle class felt went beyond economic statistics. Whalen argued that key social institutions (jobs, welfare, and the budget, namely) were out of whack with the economic realities of the nineties, this point the underlying reason for the pervasive sense of insecurity and instability. The two-party system was not helping matters, he added, the middle class stuck between the rock of the Left and the hard place of the Right.[45]

Although politicians may have been getting in the way of the American Dream through their ideological squabbling, it did not prevent them from using it as a device to get elected. Both major presidential candidates were referencing the Dream in their campaign speeches for the 1996 election, each no doubt aware of how the phrase had helped candidates in the past running for the office. Democratic candidate and incumbent Bill Clinton intended to keep the Dream alive "for all who are willing to work for it," while Republican candidate Bob Dole pronounced that the nation's (legal) immigrants had "as much right to the American Dream as the direct descendants of the Founding Fathers." Both candidates were clearly trading on Martin Luther King's concept of the Dream, specifically his "The American Dream" speech made in 1961 at Lincoln University in Pennsylvania and his "I Have a Dream" speech made in 1963 on the steps of the Lincoln Memorial. As a fundamental part of his fight for blacks' civil rights, King had cleverly linked the most salient definition of the Dream—personal success—to the "self-evident" truths stated in the Declaration of Independence ("that all Men are created equal, that they are endowed by their Creator with certain unalienable Rights, that among these are Life, Liberty, and the Pursuit of Happiness"). Having studied their history, Clinton and Dole went to school on King's use of the Dream, knowing that its true power resided in the nation's founding principles.[46]

With journalists, politicians, economists, and market researchers batting the American Dream around like a ping-pong ball, the floor was open for seemingly anyone and everyone to tap into its rhetorical power. Colin Powell, who had flirted with the idea of running for president that election year, went on the record to say that he had lived the Dream "to the fullest," working his way up through the ranks of the military to become President Reagan's national security adviser and then chairman of the Joint Chiefs of Staff under both President George H. W. Bush and President Clinton. A son of immigrants, Powell explained that his parents had found "a compassionate land and a compassionate people" upon arriving in the United States, further (and quite liberally) defining his view of the American Dream as "a government that protect[s] their labor, educate[s] their children, and provide[s] help to those of their fellow creatures who [a]re in need." The Dream was percolating well beyond the political arena, however, being used as a selling point in both popular and consumer culture. An "American Dream Park" was just opening near Shanghai, for example, its promoters confident the Chinese would be drawn to Disn-eyesque lands like Main Street, Miami Beach, and the Wild West. Real estate developers in this country, meanwhile, were planning to build a huge mall and entertainment complex called the American Dream in Silver Spring, Maryland, making it crystal clear what shopping and recreation were really about. There was even an American Dream Company, one of its ads asking Internet users, "Is it Wealth? Or is it a home of your own, a nice car, a boat, nice clothes, or perhaps a 57.6 modem and 64 megs of RAM?" It was, at least in this ad, the latter, illustrating the degree to which the meaning of the phrase had fragmented by the end of the twentieth century.[47]

If a 57.6 modem and 64 megs of RAM did not settle the matter once and for all, a survey by Roper Starch that same year (probably the first real quantitative study ever done on the topic) confirmed that the Dream meant different things to different people. The research company asked baby boomers (people aged thirty-two to fifty) if the American Dream had "personal meaning" for them and, if so, what that meaning was. Fifty-four percent of the sample said it did have meaning to them, with 15 percent saying it had meaning to others but not themselves. Significantly, more than a quarter (27 percent) of boomers said the Dream had no real meaning to anybody, perhaps reflecting the widespread feeling among them that their generation had been born too late for the mythology to ever become real. Of those respondents who did say it meant something, the answers were, predictably, diverse, or what *Adweek* called a "human jumble of inner-directedness, spiritual longing and materialism" in reporting the results (which allowed multiple responses):

Being true to yourself and not selling out	97%
Feeling in control of life	96%
Finding satisfaction within self	96%
Making enough to ensure comfortable future	96%
A job that gives personal satisfaction	96%
Owning a home	95%
Being true to your own religious beliefs	93%
Having a happy marriage	91%

Having children	81%
Staying sexual throughout your life	77%
Looking attractive	65%
Starting your own business	53%
Being wealthy	42%
Having power and influence	36%[48]

That inner-directed values such as being true to and finding satisfaction with oneself topped the list and outer-directed measures like wealth, power, and influence were at the bottom was interesting, to say the least, contradicting the consensus that the American Dream now meant, more than anything else, personal prosperity. Were thirty—and fortysomething baby boomers reaching the top of Maslow's hierarchy, seeking self-actualization rather than the envy of others?

These Are the Good Old Days

Happily for baby boomers, self-actualization and the envy of others did not have to be mutually exclusive. Clinton's second term would prove to be a prosperous four years in America, the Dream once again on the radar of or already a reality for many. The flush times, driven by the dot-com bubble and a raging stock market, were cause enough to put them in historical perspective. Mark Baldassare had argued that the postwar American Dream came off the rails in 1970, but Louis Uchitelle of the *New York Times* designated 1973 as the year in which our great run had come to a screeching halt. A number of events that year, including the removal of the dollar from the gold standard, the oil embargo, and worldwide grain shortages, pushed the American economy into a brick wall, with inflation, flat wages, and weakened unions making a bad situation worse. Like 1870, the year in which the Gilded Age is commonly said to have begun, and 1929, the beginning of the Great Depression, 1973 was a major milestone in American economic history, marking the end of one era and the onset of another.[49]

A generation later, however, there were clear signs that some of the country's postwar swagger was returning, another generation-long golden age unlikely but, at the very least, a bountiful stretch. The economic climate of low inflation and unemployment combined with high corporate profits in the late 1990s looked very much like the atmosphere of the 1960s, and the nation's leadership in digital technology was comparable in some respects to our unsurpassed military strength of the 1950s. "These are the good old days," pronounced *Fortune* in 1997, with much of corporate America declaring victory over the "lost generation" between the early seventies and midnineties. A remake of *Ozzie and Harriet*, however, was not quite ready to appear on television. Fin de siècle America was a completely different place than the country at midcentury, particularly in the workplace. Except for technology executives becoming instant millionaires on paper as their companies went public, upward mobility was still a major struggle, with just holding on to one's job a victory of sorts for some. The global economy had also made many product categories much more competitive, with working longer hours required to keep up with the Ngs and the Singhs. The recession was over, in other words, but so was the kind of prosperity that Americans once enjoyed, our many more possessions a weak substitute for the most valuable possession, the time in which to use them.[50]

As the good old days continued to roll on as we plunged headlong into a new century and millennium, those people who wanted to rain on the sunny parade were quickly silenced. "The American Dream of a rising economic tide benefiting everyone, of each generation doing better than the previous one, of opportunity and upward mobility rewarding success, is in full force," *Business Week* gushed in 1998, delighted to hear Federal Reserve chairman Alan Greenspan describe the current national economy as a "virtuous cycle." Best of all, wages for the lowest-paid workers were rising fast, closing the gap somewhat between the incomes of the rich and poor. Many families were catching up to where they had been in terms of their standard of living, the American Dream once again in their sights.[51]

Actually, all one had to do to see if the American Dream existed was to flip on one's computer. For the geeky pioneers who created it, the Internet offered the same kind of things all dreamers of the Dream had wished for—freedom, success, prosperity—the heady feeling not unlike the one experienced by the California gold rushers of a century and a half earlier. Many ordinary users of the Internet also found this new world to be a place of limitless opportunity, however, one very true to Adams's vision. "Cyberspace has become the ultimate embodiment of the American dream," wrote Kenji Sato in 1997, the chance to be whomever one wanted in this parallel universe without borders a dream come true. That the Internet was so much an American invention made the Dream that much more relevant for people around the world, Sato, a citizen of Japan, felt, this new promised land incorporating the same values as the United States at its best.[52]

Some of the heady feeling Internet pioneers were experiencing also had to do with the stock options they were typically receiving. Stock options had become part of the business scene after World War II, awarded to some executives considered essential to the future of their companies. Options got swept up in the Wall Street whirlwind of the 1980s, taken by many top executives in lieu of salaries and often reaping huge windfalls. The technology boom of the late nineties took stock options to an entirely new level, however, now considered the fastest way to get rich short of robbing a bank. "Stock options have become part of the American Dream and the managerial weapon of choice for the savviest companies," noted Edward O. Welles in *Inc.* in 1998, a way for start-ups to attract and keep good employees without having to pay them fat salaries. At quite a few software firms in Silicon Valley, employees at all levels were becoming millionaires on paper as they became shareholders through options, the amazing thing being that their companies had yet to make Dollar One. Getting in before one's company went public, when prices of the stock were typically extremely low (often under a dollar a share), could potentially result in a payday exceeding the average amount of money one made in an entire lifetime. "Join the right company, hitch your wagon to the star of the next Jobs, Gates, or Dell, and the payoff is yours," Welles wrote, the process "not unlike waking up one morning to find yourself holding the right lottery ticket."[53]

While stock options could be a rocket to wealth, the average investor was also enjoying the ride. The performance of the market in the late nineties (it rose 30 percent each year between 1995 and 1998) was so phenomenal that it shifted the trajectory of the American Dream, making this period another historical moment. "The American dream has become a

handful of blue chips and some high-growth stocks instead of three bed-
rooms and a two-car garage," wrote Edward Wyatt for the *New York Times*
in 1998, noting that American households had more assets invested in
Wall Street than in their homes for the first time in thirty years. Stocks
now accounted for 28 percent of Americans' total assets, the most since
the end of World War II. Although this fact was unusual, Wall Street had
always been home to the American Dream, of course, the past decade
of "paper entrepreneurs"—corporate raiders, bond traders and salesmen,
investment bankers, and hedge-fund managers—the latest of a long line of
people shuffling assets around to get rich in the process. Nobody knew the
fast money to be made in the market better than day traders, however, this
new breed of entrepreneur taking full advantage of advancements in technology and changes in the brokerage business. Self-employed speculators
working at home were the most extreme of these "extreme investors," their
Dream often arriving in record speed (and, as it would turn out, disappear-
ing just as fast).[54]

With the capitalistic flag flying high, those individuals considered
generals in the army were awarded special status. If Malcolm Forbes best
symbolized the upside of laissez faire capitalism in the 1980s, it was Donald Trump who most ably represented it in the 1990s, the man's name virtually synonymous with the American Dream. By the end of the decade,
Trump had bounced back nicely from his brush with bankruptcy, the
planned title of his forthcoming book—*The World According to . . . Donald
Trump*—quite appropriate for the man's voluminous persona. (It was sub-
sequently changed to the much less boisterous *The America We Deserve.*)
The theme of his latest book was that he embodied the American Dream,
his Darwinian perspective, willingness to roll the dice, unshakable faith in
the future, and headline-catching lifestyle what this country was all about.
"I'm having fun making great deals, and I'm living the American Dream,"
the Donald said in 1999, doing whatever he could to make the world con-
form to his mission in life. Not only that, but the world's most successful
real estate developer (his claim, which actually might have been true)
wanted all Americans to have a giant chicken in their own pots. "I'm going
to do everything I can to see that regular Americans can fly as high as their
wings will take them," he vowed, with little reason to doubt his word.[55]

With or without Trump's help, regular Americans were indeed flying high as the countdown to the new millennium begun (fears of "Y2K" notwithstanding). Independence Day in 1999 was a particularly exuberant one as the boom of the past few years continued, the much-maligned American Dream now being giddily celebrated. "America is delivering on its promise of the American Dream," stated publishing giant and billionaire Mort Zuckerman in his magazine *U.S. News and World Report* a week after the holiday, the mythology "more than ever . . . a reality." Zuckerman traced the Dream to the founding fathers' demand for political freedom, this turning out to be the wellspring for something that exceeded the imagination of even these visionaries:

> Nobody quite realized what freedom for the individual would mean economically, least of all, perhaps, the man who wrote the Declaration of Independence we celebrate today. But our political freedom, rooted in that essential respect for the individual, and our open door to the world unleashed stupendous energies and creativity. Free to transcend our origins, however humble, free to make of ourselves whatever our talents permit, we created a new social type—the self-made man. That's why, in America, we ask a person not who he is or who his family is but what he does.

Zuckerman was, not surprisingly, gung ho on the nation's future, the new frontier of technology perfectly suited to Americans' famous individualism, openness, and adaptability. Multicultural, tolerant, and egalitarian, Generations X and Y were also in synch with where we were headed, he felt, ideally equipped to negotiate their way through our fluid and mobile society. "As broader and broader segments of our population have participated in America's expansion and growth, the American dream joins us all," Zuckerman preached, fully believing, "We are not just creating it, we are living it."[56] As the nation and world crossed over into a new century, however, the American Dream would take another major curve in its twisting, turning roller-coaster ride, the future a much different thing than Zuckerman or anyone else could foresee.

6

American Idol

So we beat on, boats against the current, borne back ceaselessly into
the past.

—F. Scott Fitzgerald, 1925

IN THE SUMMER OF 2001, a group of students at Boston College taking a class on the American Dream dug deep into the meaning of the
nation's core mythology. Alongside readings by John Winthrop, Abraham
Lincoln, John Locke, and Jean-Jacques Rousseau, those students attending
David McMenamin's course first offered their definitions of the Dream,
their versions as varied as the students themselves. One believed the American Dream was the modern equivalent to "40 acres and a mule" (which he
translated to "a car, a garage, 2.5 kids, equal opportunity for everyone . . .
[and] a house"), for example, while another thought it was about, idealisti-
cally at least, "liberation from oppression." The class traced the idea of the
Dream back to the Enlightenment, then to Plato, and, finally, to the birth
of civilization near the Tigris and Euphrates Rivers (quite the epic journey).
The "notion of the promised land is as old as humanity," McMenamin told
his students, the Puritans following in Moses's divinely ordained footsteps.[1]

At the Fenway School in Boston a few years later, students were especially excited to read F. Scott Fitzgerald's *The Great Gatsby* as part of their
class on the Dream. (Boston is apparently the world capital of American
Dream pedagogy.) "I think this American dream is an interpretation of a
white man's dream," said Nicole Done, a seventeen-year-old from the Do-
minican Republic, thinking it was about "working hard for something you
want" rather than the pursuit of money. "The American dream has a lot

to do with money," disagreed Harkeem Steed, also seventeen, likening Jay Gatsby to his (weirdly similarly named) hero, Jay-Z. Across town, a sophomore English class and an American literature class at the Boston Latin School were also reading the 1925 novel (as well as *The Adventures of Huckleberry Finn, The Joy Luck Club, Ethan Frome,* and *Their Eyes Were Watching God*) as part of their own class on the Dream, the diverse collection of students there too finding its themes of possibility and aspiration relevant to their own lives. "The American dream is not open to everyone," thought Shauna Deleon, a sixteen-year-old from Jamaica, believing "there are certain pathways, certain gateways." Jinzhao Wang, a fourteen-year-old who had come to this country from China two years earlier, was particularly inspired by the green light at the end of the dock that for Gatsby, the self-made millionaire from North Dakota, symbolized hope. "My green light is Harvard," Wang shared with her class, already understanding something that many adults never learned. "The journey to the dream is the most important thing," she said, quite sure that "effort is the real ideal of the American dream."[2]

Such amazing insights from young people, especially ones new to this country, suggested that, more than three-quarters of a century after James Truslow Adams coined the term, the power and relevance of the American Dream remained as strong as ever. Fitzgerald's *The Great Gatsby* is in fact required reading at half the high schools in the country, with teachers finding that the book resonates strongly with urban teens, many of them first- and second-generation immigrants. More than anyone else, after all, adolescents relate to the concepts of striving for something, to want to achieve a goal just out of reach, or the desire to become a different person, these ideas from the book the bedrock of the Dream. That *Gatsby* is a cautionary tale is especially useful, teachers report, offering a lesson in "you better be careful what you wish for" in today's materialist culture.[3] Over the course of the first decade of the twenty-first century, many Americans would come to believe that the American Dream itself could very well be a cautionary tale, the price to try to make it come true too dear.

Other People's Money

As Americans woke up in the new century, the digital apocalypse turning out to be much ado about nothing, however, things were generally looking up in the economy and in most people's lives. Employment was high, inflation was low, and the Dow was still chugging along, the bursting of the dot-com bubble not yet wreaking havoc on the American economy. And with the election of George W. Bush that year, it became vividly clear that the president would not only be an avid cheerleader for laissez faire capitalism but also play a major role in shaping the American Dream. "His personal history . . . and his policies both fit the revised American Dream of our turn-of-the-century, in which the right connections, the leveraging of other people's money and the receiving of stock options are way cooler than the old Horatio Alger rags-to-riches attributes of hard work and business-building," wrote Frank Rich of the *New York Times* on the eve of the election, thinking that the Dream was now more about deal making than anything else. "In 2000, the fool is the guy who works 24/7 and lets us see all the sweat," Rich continued, the wealthy elite still very much the gate-keepers to the American Dream.[4]

The nation as a whole had benefited from the late-1990s economic boom, the clearest sign being home ownership. By the end of 2001, more people than ever (68 percent of adults) had realized the Dream of owning a home, the highest percentage since the Census Bureau started keeping track.[5] Even with the economy blowing up in the early 2000s (much like it had in the early 1970s, 1980s, and 1990s), Americans were determined to keep their Dream alive. Not just McMansions but luxuries of all kinds—many of them not costing an arm and a leg—were a ubiquitous part of American life, the outlandish consumerism of the times rivaling the decadence of the late eighties and late nineties. A good chunk of America's ongoing shopping spree was being funded by easy home refinancing, with the dollars saved on the mortgage quickly spent at the mall. "The beginning of the 21st century is turning out to be yet another cavalcade of 'bling bling,'" observed John Schwartz of the *New York Times*, Americans reluctant to let the good times stop rolling.[6]

Stop they did, but many had a lot to show from the five-year-or-so binge, making sociologists turn their attention to a major dimension of the American Dream: class. On the surface, at least, it seemed that class had become less distinct and important, the lines of income groups blurred by what were often quite similar lifestyle and consumption patterns. Both the rich and the not at all rich went to Starbucks, drove Toyotas, shopped at the Gap, and watched the local sports teams on television, after all, making it difficult to tell who had a big bank account and who lived paycheck to paycheck. Sociologists warned not to be fooled by a common interest in and shared pursuit of the symbols of the good life, however, the issue of class a much different thing when viewed through an economics lens than through a cultural one. The great disparity in income (the average Joe made $36,000 in 1999, while the average salary of the nation's top one hundred CEOs was $37.5 million, a multiple of more than one thousand) still made us a two-class society, some argued, whether Joe and Mr. Big Shot both drank lattes and wore khakis or not. In fact, social mobility was harder than ever, some research showed, with one study making the case that 20 percent of Americans belonged to a "privileged" class and the other 80 percent a "new working class." President Bush's economic programs were only furthering the divisions between the haves and have-nots, many critics argued, the cards increasingly stacked in the favor of the rich and the ones on track to becoming so. "The American dream is being sorely tested," said Robert Perrucci, coauthor of the study *The New Class Society: Goodbye American Dream?*—a big mistake to think that class was now largely a thing of our past.[7]

The mounting pile of research exposing the nation's ever-widening class divisions was ammunition for critics to argue that it may be time to bid adieu to the American Dream. Up until the 1970s, most Americans at or near the bottom of the economic ladder were able to gradually work their way up into the middle class as they gained experience and made more money. Upward mobility slowed as the postwar boom ran out of steam, however, the emerging technology-based global economy of the 1980s making it even tougher on blue-collar workers. And while the good economy of the 1990s allowed many working-class Americans to go to college or buy a home, it was now the middle class who were frequently kicked off the ladder as part of corporate cost-saving measures. "The big finding in recent years is that the notion of America being a highly mobile society isn't as true as it used to be," said University of Chicago economics professor (and Nobel laureate) James J. Heckman in 2003 after looking at data from the Bureau of Labor Statistics and the Federal Reserve Bank.

In short, class rigidity was up, not down, over the past few decades, with fewer Americans moving up and the ones already at the top more likely to stay there.[8]

Others were quick to point out that, despite the increasing class polarity and decreasing economic mobility, the Dream was being tested less than it may have appeared. The authors of one study looking into the dynamics of class, for example, found that most Americans were not particularly bothered by the nation's pervasive economic inequality, believing that material success was earned and thus fair. Most Europeans, on the other hand, were deeply disturbed by class divisions in their countries, thinking both the wealthy and the poor were not necessarily deserving of their fate. What was the "X factor" that accounted for Americans' and Europeans' different points of view? The American Dream, one could reasonably argue, the possibility of social mobility making it appear at least that class was not a permanent immovable force but rather a more fluid thing that could be changed. While Americans had a firm faith in equality from a humanist perspective, they were perfectly willing to accept an immense and ever-widening gulf between the haves and have-nots, in other words the Dream smoothing out any contradictions in the murky realm of class.[9]

For those people operating in the world of numbers, however, facts trumped mythology. Americans' faith in the traditional Dream—that the United States was a special place with plenty of opportunity to get ahead for anyone willing to work hard—obscured the reality of the situation, economists with mounds of hard data continued to point out. Besides the fact that almost 20 percent of American had zero net worth or were in the red in 2005, getting into the black had become more difficult. "Income mobility has declined in the last 20 years," reported Bhashkar Mazumder, an economist at the Federal Reserve Bank of Chicago, the implication being that we had become more of a class-bound society and less of a meritocracy. Income mobility in the United States was now no better than what it was in France or the United Kingdom and actually lower than in Canada, something that most Americans simply refused to believe (in part because it was a reversal of the pervasive, very real class hopping between 1950 and 1980). The "average intergenerational experi-ence seems to be more frozen in place today," wrote David Francis of the *Christian Science Monitor,* something quite different from what Ameri-cans chose to believe.[10]

The paradoxical nature of class in America was cause enough for the *New York Times* to publish "Class Matters," a series of articles on the topic, in 2005. (The *Wall Street Journal* was running a parallel series, it too find-ing that class was at least as important in American society as it was a few decades ago.) Often difficult to see on the surface but impossible to miss if one dug down a little bit, class (viewed by the *Times* as a combination of relative income, education, wealth, and occupation) was as significant as ever, the key driver of social mobility and, thus, the American Dream. "Mobility is the promise that lies at the heart of the American Dream," wrote Janny Scott and David Leonhardt in the first article of the series, the opportunity to move up making the vast disparity in class somehow easier to accept. In fact, a poll conducted by the newspaper found that more than half of American families making less than thirty thousand dollars a year said they had achieved the Dream or would eventually do so, rather incredibly.[11]

The truth was, however, that both the advantages and the disadvan-tages of being born in the United States were greater than many other countries, the polarity of class here making social mobility more possible in parts of Europe, as previous studies had shown. Still, the mythology of the American Dream persisted, with a Bill Clinton or Bill Gates taken as incontrovertible proof that the country was a level playing field on which anyone could potentially rise to the top. This fundamental faith in the Dream was critical to the health of the country as a whole, many agreed, the prospect of a large share of the population feeling alienated and unhappy not at all in the nation's best interests. "Even the most privi-leged among us will suffer the consequences of people not believing in the American dream," said Anthony W. Marx, the president of Amherst College, his school one of a number admitting more lower-income stu-dents to grease the mobility wheels.[12] The American Dream may have been largely an illusion, but it was a very useful and valuable one.

Bait and Switch

While the 2000s may not have been a golden age for the American Dream, it definitely was for books about it. David G. Myers's *American Paradox: Spiritual Hunger in an Age of Plenty*, for example, proposed that as we have grown richer, so have we become less content, this point his titular paradox that was destroying the American Dream. It was true that our standard of living was the highest in history, but the country was simultaneously plagued by a host of social problems, including high rates of divorce, teen suicide, violent crime, prisoners, and depression. Making more money was a poor substitute for happiness, Myers argued, blaming rampant individualism and its sycophantic sidekick, materialism. "The free market may make us richer, but it costs us the intimacy, commitment, caring, fairness and loyalty that make us happy," agreed Barry Schwartz, a psychology professor at Swarthmore, in his review of the book for *Psychology Today*, thinking that the Dream's focus on wealth "fills our bellies, but leaves us spiritually hungry."[13]

Richard Florida, the author of *The Rise of the Creative Class: And How It's Transforming Work, Leisure, Community, and Everyday Life*, believed that Americans were already choosing happiness over money in their pursuit of the Dream, however. "The American Dream is no longer just about money," Florida wrote in an article for *Washington Monthly* in 2003, his research showing that a new American Dream was emerging with the shared goal to "maintain a reasonable living standard while doing work that we enjoy doing." As in his book, Florida argued that creativity (which he defined as "the ability to come up with and implement a new idea") was the centerpiece of this new kind of Dream, more than ever the prime source of economic growth and factor for success. It was not "the chance to get rich," as Lincoln (and, more than a century later, Ronald Reagan) described the promise of America but, rather, Jefferson's "pursuit of happiness" that best captured the essence of the Dream, Florida insisted. "The dream is to reap intrinsic rewards from our work rather than merely be 'compensated' for the time and effort we put in," he explained, the rise of what he called the "creative sector" transforming the American Dream in a big way. "The old American Dream was a job with which to feed your family," Florida summed up, while "the new Dream is a job you love, with which to feed your family."[14]

Choosing happiness over money and benefiting from that decision was nothing new for Europeans, as the title of Jeremy Rifkin's new book, *The European Dream: How Europe's Vision of the Future Is Quietly Eclipsing the American Dream*, suggested. The introduction of the euro in 2002 and expansion of the European Union in 2004 were more reason to view the Continent as an integrated whole rather than a collection of independent states, making comparisons between Europe and the United States that much clearer. Rifkin did just that, zeroing in on the popular idea that Americans "live to work," while Europeans "work to live." Rifkin, an economist at the Wharton School, provided evidence that the stereotype was basically true, with people across the pond healthier, better educated, and less likely to be poor because of their more humane approach to capitalism. Americans were overworked, overpaid, and stressed out, Rifkin (an American who had spent a lot of time in Europe) believed, their Dream not dead but certainly showing its age.[15] Americans' Dream was rooted in individual autonomy and the accumulation of wealth, while Europeans' was grounded in connectedness and quality of life, he pointed out, begging the question of who was better suited to meet the challenges of the twenty-first century. As well, Europeans' realistic outlook was at least as great an asset as Americans' tolerance for risk, Rifkin argued, the former's secularism and social democracy other traits that served them well.[16]

The mere concept of a "European Dream," and that such a thing was superior in many respects to our own, was a severe blow to Americans taught to believe they were the chosen people of the modern age. As previous writers had shown, however, many Europeans received paid vacations, maternity leave, free or cheap health care, housing assistance, and tuition reimbursement not from their employers but from their governments, this fact alone making one wonder if the American Dream was still worth dreaming about. The role of our government was primarily to preserve individuals' property rights and protect the nation from outside threats, reflecting the big difference between the two cultures. "Bigger, faster, more" may not be necessarily better, Rifkin insisted, our model of success and values (religious, patriotic, independent) not the only fish in the global sea.[17] Our tradition of isolationism, individualism, and self-sufficiency was not in synch with where the world was headed, he went further, with Europe's more communitarian approach better designed for the world of tomorrow.[18] Rather than being the Old World, Europe was very possibly the New, he suggested, the two world wars functioning as a clear break with the past that better prepared them for the future.[19] Europe was hardly a utopia, Rifkin made clear (most of its citizens seemed to still be pessimists despite their government perks and six weeks of annual vacation, for one thing), but offered a path to prosperity that would be the envy of many an American.[20] Last, Europeans were no better than us in living up to their principles, their Dream as much of an ideal as ours.[21]

Although his book did not go as far as Rifkin's, Bob Herbert's *Promises Betrayed: Waking Up from the American Dream* of 2005 was also less than gung ho about the nation's prospects for the future. The country was as powerful and prosperous as ever, Herbert, a *New York Times* columnist, admitted, but that fact did not mean we were not going downhill in many respects, especially basic human rights. Trouble brewed in our justice, economic, and political systems, he opined in this collection of essays, with race relations still a major problem despite our increasingly multicultural society. The Iraq War had been a key turning point in the nation's history, Herbert felt, a clear sign that our once lofty ideals had sunk like a rock in recent years.[22]

Also believing that promises had been betrayed was Barbara Ehrenreich, whose *Bait and Switch: The (Futile) Pursuit of the American Dream* followed the plight of unemployed white-collar workers (about 20 percent of the nation's jobless). Ehrenreich's previous book, *Nickel and Dimed*, which examined the predicament of low-wage workers, had been a huge hit, her aim now "to do for America's middle class what [that book] did for the working poor." Going undercover as she did in her last book, Ehrenreich spent almost a year vainly searching for a public relations job paying fifty thousand dollars a year with health insurance, finding instead a variety of sources eager to help her maintain a positive attitude during her "transition."[23] "What does corporate America want from these middle-class college graduates who were raised in a Protestant America that promised material comfort and security if they worked hard, which is what they did, doing 'everything right,' playing by the rules, all the way to the disappearance of their 'midlevel' jobs and 'midlevel' pensions, and then 'downward mobility'?" asked John Leonard in his review of the book for *Harper's*. For Ehrenreich, the answer was two jobs in the service sector and a lot of self-help, not a particularly fair exchange for these folks' American Dream.[24]

For Paul Stiles, however, it was the American Dream itself that was the problem, as the title of his 2005 book *Is the American Dream Killing You?* implied. Out-of-control capitalism, or what he called "the market," functioned like "a financial version of The Matrix," Stiles thought, all of us swept up in an infinite loop of work and consumerism. Be it road rage, divorce, weak sex drive, latchkey kids, and much more, all of it was the result of our relentless pursuit of the Dream, the former Wall Streeter alleged, backing up his claim with numbers that indicated rising levels of stress, depression, and debt. That financial rather than social interests were guiding our lives was the dark side of the American Dream, Stiles proposed, echoing the argument Thomas Frank had made in his own vitriolic treatise of 2000, *One Market under God*. Was the American Dream killing the people who dreamed it?[25]

On Paradise Drive

Definitely not, judging by the number of people who, once excluded from it, were now eagerly and seemingly happily dreaming the Dream. Although race obviously remained a contentious issue, there was little doubt that the country had made great strides in accepting its inherent pluralism over the past generation, having a direct effect on the DNA of the American Dream. In his 2002 *American Skin*, Leon E. Wynter tracked what he called "the browning of mainstream commercial culture," arguing that as old definitions of race eroded, we were becoming a "transracial" society. Through much of the nation's history, most of blacks' innovations were co-opted by whites (jazz and rock and roll the most obvious examples), their contributions repackaged as watered-down, more marketable genres. Since the late 1970s, however, high-profile black superstars, mixed-race celebrities, and many disparate elements of African American culture had entered the mainstream, the net effect being a radical shift in the dynamics of race and ethnicity. The American Dream had also become transracial over this period, Wynter made clear, our core mythology no longer the exclusive province of people of European descent. "Near revolutionary developments in advertising, media, marketing, technology and global trade have in the last two decades of the 20th century nearly obliterated walls that have stood for generations between nonwhites and the image of the American dream," he wrote, with blacks, Hispanics, and Asians now key ingredients in the nation's melting pot. Importantly, advertising for iconic brands like Coca-Cola and Chevrolet was part of the "browning," Wynter pointed out, some of the most recognized symbols of the American Dream now projected through a multicultural lens.[26]

Not everybody was happy to see the nation and the Dream take on a different color, however. In his book *Who Are We? The Challenges to America's National Identity*, leading political scientist Samuel Huntington charged that immigrants from Latin America, primarily Mexico, were posing a major threat to the country's identity and to the American Dream. Unlike earlier groups of immigrants, he claimed, Latinos were not particularly keen on assimilating, preferring to speak Spanish, live among themselves, and not take advantage of educational opportunities. Even worse, Latinos did not seem interested in climbing the ladder of success, lacking the drive to start businesses or work their way up through companies like other people new to this country had done. "There is no Americano dream," Huntington wrote, rather astonished that Mexican Americans were not buying into the mythology that was so central to who we were as a nation. Others pointed out that it was a lot more complicated than Huntington made it out to be, however; the diversity of the Latin American community made it unfair to make such generalizations. Besides that argument, as David Brooks pointed out, Huntington seemed to be ignoring the fact that the Dream did not always follow a straight line and that outsiders had just as great a chance of achieving it as insiders. "Progress does not come incrementally, but can be achieved in daring leaps," Brooks astutely proposed in 2004, Americans' "common conception of the future" the thing that bound us together rather than speaking the same language, living in the same neighborhoods, going to the same schools, or having the same kind of jobs.[27]

Brooks knew of which he spoke, having just toured the country to write his new book, *On Paradise Drive: How We Live Now (and Always Have) in the Future Tense*. In it Brooks argued that a wide swath of the American Dream was now located in the outer suburbs, these master planned communities a direct result of exurban sprawl. Unlike the first ring of suburbs, these communities were not tied to host cities and had no center or real borders, marking a distinct shift in the nation's geographic and cultural landscape. And unlike the stereotype of suburbia—bland, conformist, homogeneous, and contented—these communities were diverse and chock-full with people going after their particular version of the Dream. "The reality is that modern suburbia is merely the latest iteration of the American dream," Brooks wrote, "the products of the same religious longings and the same deep tensions that produced the American identity from the start." The new frontier was just like the old frontier, in other words the fervent desire to succeed at something simmering amid the standard big-box retailers, acres of soccer fields, and seen-one-seen-'em-all housing developments.[28]

Others contended, however, that the suburbs may indeed have once been the home of the American Dream, but that ship had sailed long ago. Like "an architectural version of *Invasion of the Body Snatchers*, our main streets and neighborhoods have been replaced by alien substitutes, similar but not the same," wrote Andres Duany, Elizabeth Plater-Zyberk, and Jeff Speck in their scathing *Suburban Nation: The Rise of Sprawl and the Decline of the American Dream*. The authors (all part of an architectural firm specializing in designing people-friendly neighborhoods and communities) argued that the nearly half century of unchecked suburban growth had created a soulless, balkanized monster, the net effect a lower quality of life and the erosion of fundamental social values like equality, citizenship, and safety. Suburbs were not only economically and environmentally nonsustainable but nonfunctional, they held, extending the ideas that Dolores Hayden and Mark Baldassare had laid out more than a decade earlier in their respective books *Redesigning the American Dream* and *Troubles in Paradise* (and, a couple decades before that, in Jane Jacobs's classic *The Life and Death of Great American Cities*). A new model was needed for the suburbs, the three authors insisted in their manifesto, one that created "places that are as valuable as the nature they displaced."[29]

And according to a new video soon making the rounds, the future of the suburbs was going to be a much different thing than paradise. In their *The End of Suburbia: Oil Depletion and the Collapse of the American Dream*, filmmakers Gregory Greene and Barry Silverthorn proposed that as the world ran out of cheap petrofuels over the next couple of decades, the suburbs were ultimately doomed, the cost of energy (90 percent of some areas' electricity was produced by oil and natural gas) too high to make them affordable places to live. Designed around the automobile and to maximize consumerism, the suburbs—a netherworld between the production-based countryside and the conservation-oriented city—would be an unsustainable way of life in the years ahead. "New urbanists" like James Kunstler agreed, his 1993 book *The Geography of Nowhere* and 1996 *Home from Nowhere* describing the crabgrass frontier and our addiction to fossil fuels as "a living arrangement that has no future." The American economy was effectively based on suburban sprawl, Kunstler believed, which was the reason movements like his were largely ignored. In an ironic twist, however, the suburbs would become the slums of the twenty-first century, he predicted, with apocalyptic scenarios ranging from violence at gas pumps to wars over oil waiting for us if we did not adopt a "smart growth" approach to where and how we lived. Whether we liked it or not, a "postcarbon age" was rapidly nearing, these Chicken Littles warned, the American Dream to literally run out of gas before we knew it.[30]

"New urbanists" were no doubt happy to hear the news that what they considered the scourge of the suburbs—the megahouse or McMansion—was falling out of favor. After more than three decades of continual upsizing, in fact, the average American house was finally topping out in square feet, the turnaround driven by younger buyers more interested in amenities than space. Higher costs for land and energy as well as rising interest rates were making those buyers who could afford a tennis court–size master bedroom to reconsider, with the growing number of empty nesters also contributing to the shrinking of the Great American House. In his *The New American Dream: Living Well in Small Homes*, James Gauer observed that "plywood palazzos" with their dreaded "loom factor" were now associated with greed and, in particular, the recent corporate scandals, not an image a new home owner wanted to project to one's neighbors. The green movement too seemed to be part of the shift, with many now attuned to how big of a "footprint" each of us made on the environment. Bells and whistles like subzero refrigerators, exotic hardwood floors, high ceilings, and radiant heat now defined the domestic American Dream more than having the biggest house on the block, a sign of the times that quality was trumping quantity as a desirable attribute. The linguistic inspiration for McMansions, McDonald's, had recently discontinued its "supersized" french fries and soft drinks, in fact, another indication that the country was beginning to believe that bigger did not necessarily mean better.[31]

This Thing of Ours

While the American Dream was living in smaller quarters, it was as big as ever in popular culture. The trend toward multimedia platforms was serving the Dream well, the subject easily adaptable from print to television and vice versa. Another trend—the rise of television news anchors to media superstars—also helped to popularize the Dream, as celebrity journalists leveraged their status as literal voices of authority by telling American stories in other media. The elevation of the Dream to media event had started in 1998 with Peter Jennings's book *The Century* (a companion volume to a multipart series on ABC News and the History Channel), which looked at the key events of the twentieth century through the lives of ordinary people, and Tom Brokaw's book *The Greatest Generation*, which honored that group of Americans who valiantly endured the Depression and World War II. After the latter proved to be a best seller, NBC News anchor Brokaw published *The Greatest Generation Speaks* the following year and, two years later, *An Album of Memories*, a sort of scrapbook filled with notes and photos from real folks. "We lived the American Dream," wrote a recent widow in one of the letters in the book, her husband severely wounded in the war but somehow able to recover and raise three children with her. In all three parts of his trilogy, it was our ideals that allowed these Americans to be the greatest generation, Brokaw made clear, the Dream woven through their individual and collective stories.[32]

Having fallen behind in the ratings, at least in terms of book publishing, Dan Rather produced *The American Dream: Stories from the Heart of Our Nation* in 2001, which was even more of an ode to our central mythology than his competitors' books. Over the past two years, Rather had included feature reports called "The American Dream" in *CBS Evening News* broadcasts as well as in his radio commentaries for the network. Still, the newsman had not solved the mystery that was the subject. "Trying to wrap your mind around this Big Idea of American thought and history can be a bit like trying to lasso the wind," he began his book, something anybody writing about the Dream could appreciate. Through interviews with actors, teachers, writers, politicians, stockbrokers, founders of nonprofits, chefs, and activists, Rather, the son of a ditch digger and a seamstress/waitress, chased after the meaning of the Dream like the investigative reporter he was. Not surprisingly, the sixty-nine-year-old Texan uncovered many of the same themes (immigration, work, family, money, fame, liberty, enterprise, pursuit of happiness, education, innovation, and "giving back") that those individuals who preceded him had. The familiar ingredients for success—hard work, dedication, and a vision of the future—ran through all the accounts of these self-made men and women. More so than others' expeditions, however, Rather seemed to find the American Dream wherever he looked, the country apparently filled with everyday heroes overcoming obstacles to achieve extraordinary things. The author could have legitimately interviewed himself for the book, having risen from humble beginnings, and a yearlong bout with rheumatic fever when he was fourteen, to sitting in one of the most prestigious seats in the world five nights a week. "My dream came true, and I've never stopped being grateful," he wrote.[33]

While news anchors used the American Dream to help build multimedia platforms, producers of shows recognized that the subject made very good television. Shows like *Who Wants to Be a Millionaire?* and *Survivor* dangled the big juicy carrot of one million dollars (still, despite years of inflation, the amount of money considered what it took to qualify as "rich," and, thus, to have realized the Dream). But it was *American Idol* (like the two above a British import, ironically) that most compellingly expressed the essence of the American Dream in the first decade of the twenty-first century. More than the possibility of realizing fame and fortune, *American Idol* offered contestants the chance to be recognized for doing something really well, a powerful draw in these times when talent is viewed as perhaps the most valuable form of social currency. "What this is really about is the American dream," Simon Cowell, its creator, said in his pitch to the networks in 2001, with Fox finally deciding a show about the audition process might work. From the time it first aired on June 10, 2002, *American Idol* was an instant hit, the show tapping into a cultural nerve that reflected many aspects of the Dream, including our unabashed worship of celebrities and that we all perhaps had the potential of becoming one.[34]

As the most popular television show of the past decade and most visible expression of our adoration of and desperate pursuit for fame, *American Idol* was ripe for parody. In the 2006 film *American Dreamz*, starring Hugh Grant as an even-nastier version of Simon Cowell, the show (and Bush presidency) was turned upside down, the corruption and dysfunction that often come with sudden celebrity and wealth on full display. "Every age creates its own variation on the American dream," Manohla Dargis wrote in her review of the film for the *Times*, concluding that, more than anything else, *American Idol* illustrated that we were a nation of malcontents. "We, the ultimate insiders, cling to the fiction that we are outsiders, struggling for a place in the sun we already have," with anything less than becoming an idol viewed as falling short of the Dream, rather pitifully.[35]

It was a much different kind of television show—*The Sopranos*—that revealed the sheer depth and range of the American Dream. As the fourth season (of what would be six) of *The Sopranos* kicked off in the fall of 2002, there were no fewer than five new books about the show, each one in some way an attempt to decode what it really meant. Approaches ranged from the psychiatric ("Viewers resonate with the existential dilemmas . . . so vividly showcased," thought Glen O. Gabbard in his *The Psychology of "The Sopranos"*) to the semiotic ("Fatness is a signifier with many overlapping and even contradictory signifieds," stated one contributor to *This Thing of Ours*, edited by David Lavery) to the feminist ("Nearly all of Tony's 'business' relationships . . . are characterized by a phallocentric, linear representation of self," wrote another in the same work). David R. Simon's *Tony Soprano's America: The Criminal Side of the American Dream* took a more sociological view, however, the author positing that the show was mostly about the pervasive wickedness of the United States. *The Sopranos* was "a symbol of our national pathologies," Simon believed, the lead character and the kind of work he did a metaphor for the greed, violence, cover-ups, and misuses of power that peppered the country's history over the past half century. No other television show had gone to the dark side of the Dream like *The Sopranos*, he suggested, the series palpably illustrating what could and did go down when ambition lost its moral footing.[36]

On a much lighter note was another HBO show, *Entourage*, about a group of young men from Queens living the very good life in Los Angeles. "It's the American dream in a lot of ways," said Adrian Grenier, who played the rising star in the show (based on producer Mark Wahlberg's real life), believing it catered to viewers' fantasies, especially fans who were, like the characters, in their twenties. It was not just that Grenier's character and his posse had power and money but that they were having loads of fun, fans of *Entourage* explained, with nobody having to drive a cab eighteen hours a day or scrimp and save for twenty or thirty years to get a piece of the Dream. The show was, not surprisingly, a staple on college campuses but, interestingly, also quite popular with baby boomers and even seniors, its premise that working toward the Dream while having a really good time a nearly universally appealing proposition.[37]

Popular music (especially hip-hop, with its adoration of money and the luxuries it could buy) also was a central repository of the American Dream in the media-crazed 2000s. Although rappers like Jay-Z and P. Diddy had arguably usurped his honorary appointment as musical king of the Dream, Bruce Springsteen was now being recognized as an authentic national treasure. Over the course of three decades, the Boss had created an oeuvre based heavily on stories of characters left out of the Dream. His response to 9/11, the 2002 album *The Rising*, solidified his role as what Jon Parales called "America's conscience, questioner and consoler." With such a label, it was not surprising that critics, historians, and a few psychiatrists were interested in writing about Springsteen, even after what appeared to be the definitive biographies of the man, Dave Marsh's 1979 *Born to Run* and his 1987 sequel, *Glory Days*, had been published, as well as a handful of other books about him. Unlike the spate of books about *The Sopranos* (or other musical legends like Elvis Presley and Bob Dylan), the "Bruce Bibliography" was extremely positive, the New Jersey-ian considered a virtual saint because he and his music were almost synonymous with the American Dream. Besides being a principal voice of the mythology, Springsteen, the son of a bus driver and a legal secretary, was himself a perfect example of it in action, a rich rock and roller with a strong moral conscience an almost unbeatable hand. Jimmy Guterman's *Runaway American Dream*, Robert Coles's *Bruce Springsteen's America*, and Jim Cullen's *Born in the U.S.A.* each expressed this point in different ways, canonizing Springsteen as the Boss not just of pop music but, for a whole generation, of the American Dream as well.[38]

While Bruce Springsteen continued to write and sing songs about the travails of the working class, many white-collar workers were also seeing their Dreams vanish as corporate America slashed staff to cut costs or for more urgent reasons. Knowing a good story when they read about one in the papers, producers in Hollywood green-lighted *Fun with Dick and Jane*, an absurd yet real-enough depiction of what could happen when upward mobility took a nosedive. "The flip side of the American dream is a nightmare but, you know, also kind of funny," wrote Manohla Dargis in her review of the 2005 film for the *New York Times*, considering it "the first post-Enron comedy." As a dual-employed, happily married couple with an adorable kid in a nice suburban house with all the trimmings and a luxury car in the driveway, Dick (Jim Carrey) and Jane (Tea Leoni) are living the very definition of the good life when the film begins. But Dick and Jane soon see their world fall apart when his company is exposed as an Enron-like fraud, the chances of Dick finding a similar-paying job unlikely at best. As inconveniences (like the utilities being turned off) soon turn into desperation for the Harpers, hilarity definitely ensues but not without a too-close-for-comfort feeling. Some of the only recently well-to-do were having their Dream snatched away in a remarkably similar way, and were not at all amused about it.[39]

The Mists of History

Real or fictional corporate scandal aside, that the American Dream could still be seen in television shows and movies and heard in pop music no doubt contributed to making people from other countries come to the United States in the hope that they could be part of it all. As for many native borns, one thing in particular defined the Dream for immigrants: owning one's own home. About half of the nation's thirty million immigrants owned homes versus 70 percent of the people born in the country, but the gap was closing as more of the former eventually became US citizens. That a home was an investment and offered tax advantages was certainly important for immigrants, but other factors—a greater sense of security, belonging to an established community, and leaving a legacy for their children, in particular—were why the foreign born considered home ownership their top priority. A cottage industry serving the immigrant housing market had not surprisingly sprung up, with feng shui consultants brought in to help design homes for Asian customers and real estate agents enrolling classes in cross-cultural marketing. Home Depot was putting more advertising dollars toward the Latino market, knowing that things like sponsoring the Mexican national soccer team and supporting the Hispanic Chamber of Commerce would help get Spanish-speaking customers into their stores.[40]

Besides fueling the economy, immigrants served as a reminder that the American Dream was not as complex a thing as pundits often made it out to be or as ambitious an idea as many native borns frequently considered it. Celebrating her ten-year anniversary of arriving in the United States from Hungary, Zsofia Varadi explained what the Dream meant to her in refreshingly easy-to-understand terms. "For now, my American Dream is simple," she told readers of the *Christian Science Monitor* in 2004, her college degree, great job, nice apartment, and loving husband everything she currently needed. "While this might not seem like a big deal, what is a big deal is the knowledge that America is still the land of opportunity—and that what becomes of my life in the next 10 years is up to me," she added, recognizing that scenario just was not possible in many parts of the world.[41]

Just two days before Varadi had her modest story published, a much more famous immigrant, Arnold Schwarzenegger, governor of California and former movie star, got the chance to explain what the American Dream meant to him. Schwarzenegger's speech at the Republican

National Convention in New York was in fact titled "The American Dream," leaving no doubt that he believed it was not just his adopted country that made his amazing success possible but his political party as well. Schwarzenegger first recalled his Austrian childhood during which Soviet tanks roamed the streets, finding hope for something better in American movies, especially the ones starring John Wayne. Arriving in this country in the midst of the 1968 presidential campaign, Schwarzenegger felt Democratic candidate Hubert Humphrey's rhetoric sounded a lot like the socialism he was used to, while the Republican candidate's speeches were "like a breath of fresh air." Learning what party Richard Nixon belonged to, the champion bodybuilder immediately declared himself a Republican, maintaining his loyalty ever since ("And trust me, in my wife's family, that's no small achievement," he quipped). "To my fellow immigrants listening tonight, I want you to know how welcome you are in this party," Schwarzenegger proclaimed, his political persuasion more aligned with the Dream's themes of individualism, ambition, free enterprise, and future possibilities. "America gave me opportunities, and my immigrant dreams came true," he told a national audience, believing reelecting George W. Bush was the best way for others who came to this country from elsewhere to get the same chances he had.[42]

Unfortunately, things were a lot tougher and more complicated for many immigrants than the Governator made them out to be, in large part because of the doings of Republican politicians. ("Political conventions bear about the same relationship to reality as Mr. Schwarzenegger's films do," noted the *Economist* a few months after his speech.) In fact, thousands of Irish who had come to New York in the 1980s and 1990s were currently heading back to the Emerald Isle, their American Dream extinguished due to the tough economy and the post-9/11 crackdown on illegal immigrants. The high cost of education and health care was also a factor in Irish using the return portion of their round-trip tickets, with hopes that the prosperity of their native country would offer an easier life than in the Big Apple. "It's the complete reversal of the American dream," said Adrian Flannelly, head of the Irish Radio Network, considering the mass exodus historically significant given the role his people played in building the city. It was difficult to know exactly how many Irish were leaving, but travel agencies, real estate offices, and moving companies confirmed the trend, as would a weekend night visit to the normally packed but now half-filled Irish pubs in Queens, the Bronx, and Yonkers. Irish in Boston and Philadelphia were also making their way back across the pond, a brogue sadly becoming a more rare thing to hear in America.[43]

Although they would never come to fruition, President Bush, back in office for four more years, had grand plans of how to keep the American Dream alive for both (legal) immigrants and the native born. An "ownership society" was the principal theme in the president's 2005 inaugural address, which was the justification for the big changes he wanted to make to Social Security and tax policies. Having workers put some of their payroll taxes into their own investment accounts to at least partially privatize Social Security was the boldest idea, with a host of other initiatives designed to encourage Americans to take more responsibility for their finances and, especially, retirement. "Everyone deserves a chance to live the American dream, to build up savings and wealth and to have a nest egg for retirement that no one can ever take away," said Vice President Dick Cheney in a speech at Catholic University a week before Bush's address, the Republicans' vision of an "ownership society" potentially as sweeping as FDR's New Deal and LBJ's Great Society. Critics, of course, had a much different view of the proposals, thinking they were just another way the administration was robbing the poor to give to the rich. And in their book, *Coming Up Short*, economists Alicia H. Munnell and Annika Sunden made a compelling case that Americans were less than diligent about putting money into their 401(k) plans, suggesting that they would be equally lax at building up their Social Security nest egg.[44]

An "ownership society" was a world apart from what plenty of blue-collar workers were actually experiencing in the mid-2000s, especially in Michigan. A decade and a half after Michael Moore's *Roger and Me*, General Motors was in even greater financial trouble, as were many who had worked for the company. For generations, GM had been the source of the Dream for thousands of families, but, after its decades-long slide, it appeared like it was the end of the road. "The G.M. that was once an unassailable symbol of the nation's industrial might is a shadow of its former self," noted Danny Hakim of the *New York Times*, thinking that "the post–World War II promise of blue-collar factory work being a secure path to the American dream had faded with it." For those workers still having a job with the company, the prospect of losing it or having to take a significant pay cut was devastating, particularly for the ones whose fathers, grandfathers, and sometimes great-grandfathers had benefited from high wages along with great medical and pension perks. GM and its competitors were largely responsible for forging the social contract between employers and workers that was a boon to the country's middle class, with unions of course playing a big role in the broad prosperity and safety nets that came out if it. Blue-collar workers in auto plants were actually living upper-middle-class lives, by most accounts, but that particular Dream was vanishing as consumers increasingly opted for more-bang-for-the-buck foreign models.[45]

Even that ardent cheerleader for the American Dream Mort Zuckerman was beginning to think that some promises had indeed been betrayed. "Americans remain optimistic that it is possible the American dream has not receded entirely into the mists of history," the media mogul wrote in his *U.S. News and World Report* in 2006, not a very confident way to describe the mood of the people and state of the nation. While being natural optimists, we still had faith in the Dream, but "the hard reality . . . is that it is no longer possible for more than a very small minority to start our poor, work hard, and become well off," he confessed, considering our equal-opportunity society as being held "hostage." Again it was the widening gap between the richest and poorest Americans that was dragging the Dream down, with the big bulge in the middle falling further behind the top 20 percent of income earners and doing everything they could to avoid becoming part of the bottom 20 percent. For Zuckerman and others, the comparisons to the Gilded Age were all too clear, the United States in the early twenty-first century looking a lot like the nation in the late nineteenth when it came to distribution of wealth. Fifteen percent of Americans now possessed 85 percent of the nation's wealth, in fact, with the bottom half accounting for just 2.5 percent of total household net worth. Tax policies favoring the rich, foreign competition, and the "knowledge economy" were the primary reasons for this stratification, according to Zuckerman, believing greater educational opportunities for the economically disadvantaged were the only real way to close the gap between the rungs on America's ladder of success.[46]

If Mort Zuckerman was disappointed that the Dream had evaporated for most Americans, CNN's Lou Dobbs was downright surly about it. In his *War on the Middle Class: How the Government, Big Business, and Special Interest Groups Are Waging War on the American Dream and How to Fight Back*, the "lifelong Republican and strong believer in free enterprise," as he described himself, blamed nearly anyone and everyone for squeezing the big bulge in the middle dry. Free-trade policies endorsed by both the Clinton and the Bush administrations had done no favors for Americans holding manufacturing jobs, his own party letting the federal deficit spiral out of control while its members obsessed over issues like gay marriage. Lobbyists, Congress, credit card companies, the banking industry, and the media were no better, according to Dobbs, the nation's eleven million illegal immigrants also culpable for the war that was being waged on the Dream.[47] How, Dobbs asked, could America's "working men and women" fight back? Voters changing their registration from Democrat or Republican to Independent would be a good start, he thought, as would public financing of elections, reforming the lobbying system, imposing ethical standards on Congress, and overhauling the way trade negotiations worked. Sealing our borders like a drum was not a bad idea either, he fervently felt, these folks from across the Rio Grande also stealing the rug out from under the American Dream.[48]

Although Lou Dobbs made waves with his decidedly isolationist views, most Americans by the late 2000s agreed that the country had split into two societies, according to a new study from the Pew Research Center. In 2007 Americans were almost twice as likely to say that the nation was divided into "haves" and "have-nots" than in 1988, the study showed, the implication being that our self-perception as a "land of equal opportunity" was precarious at best. Because Americans had traditionally viewed individuals as accountable for their own success or failure rather than society at large, the authors felt their findings were quite important, an indication that something big had changed in the zeitgeist.[49] A CBS poll among seventeen- to twenty-nine-year-olds completed that same year offered more evidence that the country's tectonic plates had shifted. Just a quarter of the young people said that their generation would be better off than their parents', with almost half believing they would be worse off. "It's a scam," said Adam Gandelman, a Boston bike messenger, speaking of the American Dream, thinking our national mythology had outlived its usefulness.[50]

John Zogby strongly disagreed, however, the notable political pollster summarizing years of public opinion research in his 2008 book *The Way We'll Be: The Zogby Report on the Transformation of the American Dream*. Like the Pew researchers, Zogby thought the nation had left one era behind and entered another, but Zogby's take was far more positive. A "New American Consensus" was emerging, he argued, one that challenged the "more is better" definition (or perversion, one could fairly say) of the Dream. "The American Century is over and the Whole Earth Century has begun," he wrote, with younger people leading this new kind of "good life" grounded in authenticity, diversity, looking inward, and limits on consumption rather than material prosperity.[51] "We are in the middle of a fundamental reorientation of the American character away from wanton consumption and toward a new global citizenry in an age of limited resources," Zogby firmly believed, this downsizing of the American Dream a good thing.[52] Everyone seemed to agree that something big had happened to the Dream, but no one could agree on exactly what it was, this borne out in a 2009 *Time* poll. Fifty-seven percent of the people surveyed believed that the American Dream would be harder to achieve, the magazine reported, while, interestingly, nearly the same percentage, 56 percent, felt that the nation's best days were still to come. "It's this distinctively American combination of realism and idealism, of hardheadedness and optimism, that guarantees the U.S. will emerge from our financial doldrums with new energy, new ideas and new purpose," wrote Richard Stengel, his positive spin on the findings a function of knowing that the country always eventually bounced back and then some after it appeared like there was no way out.[53]

Whether America was heading this way or that way, a handful of books written by or about men who had achieved a decidedly upsized American Dream hit the shelves in 2008, helping to keep a more traditional version of the mythology alive. The most anticipated of the lot was Alice Schroeder's book *The Snowball: Warren Buffett and the Business of Life*, the first authorized biography of the man who was probably the most well-known and successful investor in the world. (Buffett's secret to the Dream was "finding wet snow and a really long hill," hence the title.) Other new books about men who had done well for themselves was T. Boone Pickens's hit *The First Billion Is the Hardest: Reflections on a Life of Comebacks and America's Energy Future,* Ted Turner's *Call Me Ted,* and Richard Branson's *Business Stripped Bare: Adventures of a Global Entrepreneur,* each of these part memoir, part how-to.[54]

The most exciting of this mogul mania had to be, however, Steven Watts's *Mr. Playboy: Hugh Hefner and the American Dream* (the book included a centerfold of the eighty-six-year-old legend in robe and pajamas surrounded by his gal pals from *The Girls Next Door*). Watts, a historian, certainly knew his way around the American Dream, having previously written biographies of Henry Ford (*The People's Tycoon*) and Walt Disney (*The Magic Kingdom*). In his latest, Watts looked beyond Hefner the man, examining the major impact *Playboy* had on American culture. It was Hefner's own striving for self-fulfillment (and definition of the good life) that drove the man, his story following the standard Horatio Alger arc but with some very interesting side trips. "Where else but in America could a repressed Midwestern boy rise, and fall into so many sacks, while creating and brand-managing a multimedia empire?" asked the *Atlantic* in its review of the book, a reasonable question given Hef's wild ride.[55]

The Audacity of Hope

Someone else was experiencing quite a ride, someone who believed we were on the cusp of a new kind of American Dream and had every intention of making it happen. With Barack Obama's 2006 *The Audacity of Hope: Thoughts on Reclaiming the American Dream,* a new chapter in the history of our core mythology began, the book laying out not only the musings of the junior US senator from Illinois but also the principal themes of his emerging presidential campaign and administration. Committed to a "project of national renewal," greater "civic life," and the ideals of "the common good," Obama made it clear in his book that his political objectives were heavily steeped in a communitarian approach to the Dream, the fact that he was the embodiment of it helping his cause considerably.[56] Obama, whose previous book, *Dreams from My Father*, was a best seller, had another one on his hands with *The Audacity of Hope*. His populist, Clintonesque take on what was wrong with and how to improve the country played nicely against President Bush's dismal approval ratings. While critics generally liked the book, especially the parts about his personal life, some were less than impressed with his plan of action. "His muddled, uninspiring proposals bear the stamp of . . . compromises," thought *Publishers Weekly*, not exactly a ringing endorsement for the man and his ideas.[57]

Most Americans thought otherwise, of course, overwhelmingly giving Senator Obama the chance to help citizens reclaim their Dream. Shortly before he moved into the White House, however, hope became an even more audacious idea as a housing crisis of major proportions nearly crashed the global economy ("This sucker could go down," President Bush perceptively described the situation). For the first time since disco was all the rage, home ownership in the United States was dropping, a function of hundreds of thousands of defaulting borrowers. Home owners holding "subprime" mortgages (carrying higher fee and interest costs than regular or "prime" mortgages) were finding themselves unable to make their monthly payments as their adjustable-rate loans became unaffordable. (It was not unusual for a $2,000 payment to jump to $2,800 the following month.) "The American Dream Foreclosed" went a *New York Times* headline in October 2007, the number of home-foreclosure filings up sharply, especially among people with low incomes and bad credit. With people making $35,000 a year allowed (and often encouraged by predatory lenders) to buy $350,000 homes, access to the American Dream had been made too easy, one could reasonably say, the tumbling Dow crashing the retirement plans of millions more.[58]

Sadly, the backlash to the subprime disaster did additional long-term damage to the American Dream of owning a home, as mortgage lenders made it much more difficult to get a loan. Higher interest rates and tightened standards to qualify for a loan were making it almost impossible for many to get their foot in the door, especially those buyers whose credit ratings were less than great. Renting had become, at least for the moment, the only alternative to the Dream, both for many of those individuals who had lost their homes and for those who were planning to sign on the dotted line. Landlords of apartment buildings were naturally delighted with this unexpected development, realizing they were suddenly in the housing catbird's seat. For the people who had lost their homes, however, it was a much different story, the heart and soul of their American Dream gone with little hope of getting it back in the foreseeable future.[59]

The cataclysmic housing crisis led some critics to suggest that the American Dream itself was part of the problem. Richard Florida argued that it might be time for Americans to abandon their belief that home ownership symbolized achievement of the Dream, agreeing with earlier critics who pointed out that the single-family home just did not make economic sense for many people. Besides being inflexible and expensive, a home of one's own did not make people happier, a recent study found, one's so-called dream house often a major source of stress. Too many folks were "indentured servants to their homes," the University of Toronto professor wrote in 2009, proposing that the "house poor" and, especially, those home owners in risk of foreclosure "rent out the American Dream" rather than buy it. Could Americans give up this central tenet of the good life even if it was a financial albatross around their necks?[60]

Joel Lovell, a writer for GQ and lifelong renter, felt even more strongly that Americans needed to get over their conviction that the Dream relied on owning a money pit. The common wisdom that renting was throwing your money away, one was not really an adult until he or she owned a home, buying a house was the best path to financial security, and so on was pure garbage, Lovell argued, the disaster area that was the current real estate market only more reason he was right and the rest of us (except Richard Florida, perhaps) were wrong. "Once you start crunching the numbers, it turns out the American dream is a total sham," he wrote in the magazine in 2008, the home-as-nest-egg a big, fat lie. After doing the math, Lovell determined that should he buy a place (in Brooklyn, it needs be said, where the cost of an apartment was almost the same as one in Manhattan), it would take twenty-eight years to break even. Anything less than that, the down payment, thirty-year mortgage, property taxes, maintenance costs, homeowner's insurance, and other expenses made purchasing a home a bad deal, even if the dream house appreciated

5 ercent per year. In pure investment terms, at least, home ownership was a losing proposition, he informed readers, unless one was prepared to stay put for almost three decades. The psychological and moralistic overtones associated with owning a home, and the flip side that renting was somehow suspect, were doing a real disservice to a lot of Americans, Lovell concluded, hoping the popping of the real estate bubble would convince others similarly.[61]

Whether one was a die-hard renter like Lovell or owned a home, it was easy to feel like the Dream was a shadow of what it had only recently been. For most home owners, the nest egg that was one's house now had a pretty big crack in it, for one thing, its value likely to be significantly less than just a few years ago, and investment portfolios had also shrunk considerably as the Dow dropped like a rock. As well, food, gas, health insurance, college tuitions, and energy were costing more, rubbing salt in the economic wound and making many feel their standard of living was going backward. "Fewer Americans now than at any time in the last half-century believe they're moving forward in life," the Pew Research Center depressingly reported in 2008, with most feeling the prospects ahead were nothing to be ecstatic about either. Again, looking back helped to put things in historical perspective, but the news was not any cheerier. The recession of the late 2000s was the first time since World War II that the average American family was in worse shape at the end of an economic expansion than at its beginning, according to the Economic Policy Institute, with a spokesperson for the organization calling the latest dip "a uniquely disappointing cycle." The consumerist American lifestyle, only recently as big as a McMansion with a couple of SUVs in the driveway, was suddenly a lot smaller, with no real sign that it was going to bulk up again. That General Motors was considering selling its Hummer brand was a sign of the times, an apt metaphor for the incredible shrinking American Dream.[62]

His politics already steeped in the Dream, presidential candidate Barack Obama stepped up his campaign rhetoric that referenced the mythology, knowing it would play especially well in a tough economic environment. "While some have prospered beyond imagination in this global economy, middle-class Americans—as well as those working hard to become middle class—are seeing the American Dream slip further and further away," he had said back in November 2007, a theme he returned to over and over again on the campaign trail as the election drew nearer. Senator John McCain, the leading Republican candidate, meanwhile, also referenced the Dream but had a much more optimistic take on the nation's woes. "We've always believed our best days are ahead of us," he said in June 2008, contradicting what average Americans were actually saying in surveys when asked about their prospects for the future. The fact was that the best days were indeed likely ahead for wealthy Americans (including McCain, whose wife, Cindy, was loaded), with the top 10 percent accounting for half of all income generated in 2006, according to Emmanuel Saez, a Berkeley economist. The richest of the rich—the top 1 percent—were continuing to pull even further away from the pack, something that Obama often mentioned in his effort to reclaim the Dream for everyone else.[63]

The American Dream also was a prominent piece of president-elect Obama's speech in Chicago's Grant Park four days after the election. "If there is anyone out there who still doubts that America is a place where all things are possible; who still wonders if the dream of our founders is alive in our time; who still questions the power of our democracy, tonight is your answer," his victory alone proof that that the mythology could still be a reality. "This is our time—to put our people back to work and open doors of opportunity for our kids; to restore prosperity and promote the cause of peace; to reclaim the American Dream" went his closing words, laying out his admittedly ambitious agenda for the next four years.[64]

Fortunately, others believed there was still hope for the American Dream and planned to do something about it. Peter G. Peterson, the cofounder of the Blackstone Group, certainly thought so and, better yet, was putting his money where his mouth was. The son of a Greek immigrant who had realized his Dream by working nearly around the clock in his restaurant in Nebraska, Peterson became a billionaire in 2007 when his company went public. As a second-generation American Dreamer, Peterson decided to follow in his father's footsteps by enabling others to realize their own possibilities. Peterson had a lot more cash in his pocket than did his dad, however, setting aside a billion dollars for a new foundation to "explain the undeniable, unsustainable and yet politically untouchable long-term challenges we face." Those challenges were remarkably similar to the ones put forth by Merrill Lynch in 1994, specifically unfunded government promises for retiring baby boomers, insufficient savings (both on a national and an individual level), and the ballooning costs of health care. Through his foundation, Peterson intended to educate young people about those looming perils so that they could be better prepared to tackle them over the decades ahead. The business community and media were other audiences he wanted to reach, each of them notoriously more interested in today than tomorrow. "I cannot think of anything more important than trying in this way to preserve the possibilities of the American Dream for my children's and grandchildren's generations, and generations yet to come," Peterson wrote in *Newsweek* in 2008, his article fittingly titled "You Can't Take It with You."[65]

Peterson's noble vision was an ideal foundation to build or, perhaps, rebuild the American Dream at a key moment in the nation's history. That the president of the United States was deeply committed to enabling middle- and working-class Americans to reclaim the Dream also showed how much the mythology still mattered, and that it remained a key indicator of the nation's and individuals' well-being. The recent housing crisis in particular plainly revealed that the American Dream continued to be a source of passion, with owning a home considered an essential step toward realizing it. Although now three-quarters of a century old, the Dream appeared to be as fragile a thing as it was in 1931 when James Truslow Adams conceived it, sensitive to the constantly shifting winds of economic, political, and social change. The future of the Dream is, as always, uncertain, but there is little doubt that in the years ahead it will continue to represent an important story line in, as Adams expressed it, the epic of America.

Conclusion

WHAT TO MAKE OF THE AMERICAN DREAM? Was it ever real, or was it indeed just a dream, something we conjured up while we had our eyes closed to the harsh realities of the day? It is still difficult to say, frankly, this eighty-year excursion illuminating the subject but doing little to definitively answer the question of whether the American Dream was anything more than an especially elaborate hallucination. On the one hand, it is hard to argue with people who swear they have lived it, their "better and richer and fuller" lives clear evidence the mythology is real. On the other hand, having "made it" could have had nothing at all to do with any mythology, their success, however measured, a result of being in the right place at the right time. Which way one leans depends a lot on if one believes that there is in general some kind of grand design or order to the universe, I suppose, the Dream's cosmology resting on the bigger idea of whether life is more than a random series of events.

Either way, it is impossible to ignore the enormous impact the American Dream has had on Americans and the nation as a whole these past eighty years. Much like other powerful mythologies like religion, the Dream is entrenched in everyday life, shaping not just the view of the world for those individuals who choose to believe in it but also the decisions one makes and the actions one takes. America would have been a much different place without its Dream, it is safe to say, all of us probably affected in some way by it. One did not have to be actively pursuing the American Dream for it to play a role in one's life, in other words, the mythology in our cultural DNA.

It was this absorption of and immersion in the American Dream that have accounted for the tremendous value it has added to people's lives. As a utopian ideal, the Dream functioned as a beacon of hope, something to strive for and keep one's spirits up when times got tough. As a common denominator, it helped bring Americans together, one of the precious few things we could all relate to in an increasingly multicultural and, too often, divisive society. For people new to the country, the Dream was a user-friendly vehicle of assimilation, allowing one to express one's Americanness while still retaining one's ethnic identity. Accommodating and tolerant of difference, the American Dream was and is, perhaps, the nation at its best, not surprising given that its fundamental tenets were conceived by the founding fathers, refined by the likes of Emerson, Whitman, and Thoreau, and, finally, articulated by the most popular historian of his day. The American Dream is, quite simply, a masterpiece, a work of art whose ideological beauty can arguably never be surpassed. That many a politician, including Barack Obama, as well as Madison Avenue have embraced it should be expected, the thing an unequivocal "killer app" of salesmanship.

That said, like anything of great value, the Dream has proved to be a wellspring of considerable trouble for many who have invested themselves in it. Rather than view it as just an ideal, an imaginary concept that helped define the nation and keep it afloat in choppy waters, some took it as something all Americans were entitled to, like the opportunity to vote or Social Security benefits when we retired. When what these folks mistook as a promise was broken by some economic event—a recession, corporate cutbacks, outsourcing, or another unfortunate but quite normal "correction"—their trust in the system was often crushed. The sudden disappearance of the Dream, or, should I say, its maddening unreliability and undependability, was a source of great frustration for many more Americans who had not had it snatched from their grasp. Constantly coming and going, the American Dream seemed to almost always reside in the past or loom in the future, rarely ever existing in the here and now. Although frequently on the horizon, just around the next corner, it was more often viewed as having once thrived, its (and thus our) best days behind us. The Dream was commonly described as "fading," "withering," "shrinking," "sliding," "unraveling," "squeezed," "threatened," "broken," "going backward," "in reverse," and "dying," when it was not already "dead." Although nostalgia certainly played a role in this longing for yesterday, news of the ailing American Dream also served as a useful platform to plan for the future. How can we revive this thing on life support? many asked, their solution usually serving a particular agenda, as proposals for how to build a better tomorrow almost always carry.

The crashing and burning of the Dream beginning in the late sixties was, in retrospect, a predictable phenomenon as the postwar American Way of Life ran out of steam. Propelled by the GI Bill, three-hundred-dollars-down houses needing to be filled with consumer goods, and a military-industrial complex filled with layers of bureaucracy, the Greatest Generation surfed the American Dream like a wave, enjoying the ride of what turned out to be the longest economic boom in history. When the wave crashed, so did the Dream, our mythology to never be quite the same again. Even before this crash, the original meaning of the American Dream had begun to change, Adams's "opportunity for each according to ability or achievement" largely reduced to the pursuit of wealth. This perversion of the Dream had major consequences for the fate of the nation, I believe, the switch from existential goals, that is, the realization and expression of one's identity, to financial ones bad for individuals and the country. Because wealth is perceived as relative rather than absolute, many researchers have found, chasing dollars is ultimately a no-win game, the fact that someone somewhere has more than you do spoiling the whole thing.

Even the realization of the classic American Dream has not brought happiness to many, it need be said. "Over generations of prosperity and growth, the American Dream has become an American Expectation," wrote Lauren Sandler for *Psychology Today* in 2011, "a version of happiness achieved by entitlement and equation." For many, that equation was marriage, kids, and a nice house supported by two generous incomes, or what Sandler called "the formula for a satisfied adulthood." Polls have shown, however, that achieving this widely accepted interpretation of the American Dream has often not brought happiness. In fact, Americans are less happy than they used to be, according to some long-term research studies, even among those individuals who have "made it." Happiness is a much more elusive thing than having a family and economic security, any psychologist could tell you, the idealization of the traditional American Dream making its reality unsatisfying.[1]

Still, most of us want to reach our American Dream and believe doing so will make us happier people. Unfortunately, the offspring of the Greatest Generation may very well make the Dream impossible for their children and grandchildren. Besides baby boomers' notorious propensity to spend versus save, the government benefits due to them and coming health-care needs will place a heavy burden on society as the trickle of sexagenarians turns into a flood. The continually growing spread between the haves and have-nots is also troubling. The pulling away of the rich from the rest of the pack (and the superrich from them) is simply not conducive to a broad distribution of the American Dream. Rising inequality and falling real wages have exposed our other primary mythology, upward mobility, making many of us realize the United States is not the "opportunity society" we have always believed it was.[2]

Given these huge social and economic trends, one has to wonder if the "millennial" generation has even a shot at their Dream. Writing for *Time* in November 2010, Fareed Zakaria had his doubts, thinking the idea of the American Dream was more alive in his native country of India than in the United States. "Indians are brimming with hope and faith in the future . . . [while] in the U.S., the mood is sour," he observed after a recent trip to his homeland, concluding that "the can-do country is convinced that it can't." Recent statistics bear out Zakaria's concerns. Sixty-three percent of Americans said they did not think they would be able to maintain their current standard of living, a *Newsweek* poll conducted in September 2010 revealed, not a very good prognosis for the American Dream. In the same magazine a few months later, Zakaria remained concerned that the nation's best days were behind us. World rankings in a wide variety of areas—college graduation, infrastructure, life expectancy, and many others—show that the United States is no longer "Number 1" as it once was and as we like to believe it still is. Soon after, Zakaria hosted a special on CNN called *Restoring the American Dream*, in which he and other experts offered their views on how the country could "get back to #1."[3]

Not everyone, however, is as worried about the fate of America and its foremost story. "Don't bet against the United States," wrote David von Drehle, Zakaria's colleague at *Time,* pointing out that the country's reported decline has always been a frequent topic in the national conversation. Fretting about the state of America and its future prospects has been nothing short of a nation pastime, von Drehle reminded readers, despite the fact that we seem to weather all storms and continue to get bigger and stronger. "Fallen trees don't prove the forest is dying," he stated, urging us to keep in mind the big picture and the long view. Tom Brokaw saw things similarly in his latest book, *The Time of Our Lives: A Conversation about America, Who We Are, Where We've Been, and Where We Need to Go Now to Recapture the American Dream.* Although the country is by all accounts off-track economically and politically, he acknowledged, there is reason for hope. "We have the world's most robust democracy, most powerful economy, most dominant military power, and most ambitious values agenda," Brokaw wrote, an ideal environment for the American Dream to survive if not thrive.[4]

Even cautious optimists like Brokaw would likely agree that realizing one's American Dream today is a tremendous challenge for the average citizen because of the powers that be. The 2011 documentary *Heist: Who Stole the American Dream?* blamed our financial systems for what the filmmakers saw as the pilfering of the Dream. Four decades of deregulation, outsourcing of tens of millions of jobs, and tax policies favoring the wealthy were the principal culprits for the theft, topped off by the recent subprime mortgage fiasco. Large corporations, in large part via relentless lobbying, worked in concert with the political arena to create our "99 percent" versus "1 percent" society, the film argued. Conservative think thanks like the Heritage Foundation and the Cato Institute were abettors to the crime, the film also suggested, key players in the distribution of wealth from the bottom up. With the market "freed," a flood of imports from low-wage countries invaded the American marketplace, gutting blue-collar industry and ravaging labor unions. While the country's manufacturing sector was being dismantled, Wall Street was running amuck, free to pursue short-term profits through mergers and acquisitions, leveraged buyouts, junk bonds, hedge funds, and the exotic "derivatives" that nearly crashed the whole economy. Americans have to resist the takeover of the country by big business, *Heist* concluded, urging viewers to enlist in the growing cause to change the prevailing economic system in order to regain possession of the American Dream.[5]

Indeed, many are taking action via a budding American Dream movement that has sprung out of the Occupy Wall Street movement and civil protest at the Wisconsin Capitol in early 2011. In October 2011, a "Take Back the American Dream" conference was held in Washington, organized by activists who believed that it was up to citizens themselves to jump-start the nation's guiding narrative. The economy is certainly not providing a favorable climate for new opportunities, activists have justifiably concluded, nor is the country's political system. The progressive American Dream movement is analogous to the conservative Tea Party, another organization dedicated to reviving the Dream. Thousands of house parties have been held across the country as part of the movement, at which individuals drafted a "Contract for the American Dream," with an equivalent effort taking place online. Job growth, an improved infrastructure, investment in education, universal health care, protecting Social Security, and tax reform are all part of the movement's agenda. Ambitious initiatives indeed, but history has shown that it is such populist movements that offer the most promise for fundamental change.[6] Importantly, the desire to relaunch the American Dream is not limited to persons on either side of the political spectrum. A month after the "Take Back the American Dream" conference, AARP, the Ford Foundation, *Time*, and the United Way coconvened an "Opportunity Nation" summit in New York. The ongoing Opportunity Nation campaign is to "promote opportunity, social mobility, and access to the American Dream," states the group's website, with nearly two hundred businesses and institutions signing up.[7] An American Dream movement in the larger sense is clearly percolating, the crisis of the mythology apparently reaching critical mass.

Despite the grim economic climate, young adults are surprisingly optimistic about their future, according to a 2009 survey by the Pew Charitable Trust. Fifty-eight percent of Americans between eighteen and twenty-nine believed they would move more easily up the ladder than their parents had, showing a firm faith in standard upward mobility. Eighty-eight percent of this same group felt it was possible to improve one's financial situation even during a bad recession like the current one, a rather remarkable vote of confidence in the system (or just pure naïveté). Critics were bemoaning how the American Dream would remain elusive at best for millennials, but the generation itself appears gung ho to go out and pursue it. The Dream feeds on such youthful optimism, it can safely be said, a positive outlook among young people serving as a constantly renewable resource for the mythology.[8]

A look back at the remarkable cultural history of the American Dream suggests the millennial generation should not give up on the Dream despite the major challenges they face. Often diagnosed as in critical condition if not pronounced dead on the scene, the Dream always seems to recover, our mythology having many more lives than the proverbial cat. The continual flow of immigrants to this country has and will continue to serve as a breeding ground for the American Dream, for one thing, their enthusiasm and energy to achieve great things rubbing off on all of us. New immigrants in fact tend to believe in the mythology most fervently, and politicians at all levels continue to employ the American Dream as the centerpiece of their campaign strategies. And despite the current bad economy, 34 percent of Americans say they have achieved the American Dream, another sign of its profound resiliency. "Most of the time we do not realize that what we are dreaming is the American dream," Christopher Caldwell wrote in the New York Times in 2010, the idea now as natural to us as an unconscious reflex.[9]

There are other reasons to be bullish on the American Dream despite all of the major challenges the nation faces. The country's increasing diversity will help fuel the Dream, our different backgrounds, experiences, and perspectives beneficial toward identifying opportunities and bringing them to life. And although a cliché, Yankee ingenuity will still be a principal driver of the Dream, our hardwired urge to build a better mousetrap as alive as ever. Richard Florida's argument that creativity is the most important social and economic currency appears to be correct, the American Dream in some way living proof that using one's imagination to develop new and original ideas and things is the best recipe for success. If that is not enough, the core values of the nation have not really budged an inch despite the incredible changes in society since 1931, these values to continue to serve the interests of the Dream whether it be boom times or bust. Although one can make a decent case that the American Dream will survive and perhaps even flourish in the United States in the years ahead, it is clearer than ever that the Dream is no longer solely ours (if it ever was) and that we will have to share it with other countries. We may have "invented" and mastered the fine art of the American Dream, in other words, but our exclusive hold on it is no more. Brazil and Russia appear to be now experiencing their own interpretations of the Dream, hard evidence that the world is becoming, as Thomas Friedman described it, increasingly "flat." As we plunge further into the twenty-first century, the mythology is destined to become the world's oyster, the Global Dream something a historian of the future will have to take under consideration.

Notes

Selected Bibliography

Index

Notes

Introduction

1. Jim Cullen, *The American Dream: A Short History of an Idea That Shaped a Nation*; Cal Jillson, *Pursuing the American Dream: Opportunity and Exclusion over Four Centuries*.

2. Jennifer L. Hochschild, *Facing Up to the American Dream: Race, Class, and the Soul of the Nation*, xi; Robert Bellah, "Civil Religion in America," in *The Robert Bellah Reader*, edited by Robert N. Bellah and Steven M. Tipton, 225.

3. Lee Artz and Bren Ortega Murphy, *Cultural Hegemony in the United States*, 275; Jillson, *Pursuing the American Dream*, 1.

4. Cullen, *American Dream*, 136.

5. Robert Sklar, *Movie-Made America: A Cultural History of the American Movies*, 215, 195–97, 3.

6. David Kamp, "Rethinking the American Dream," *Vanity Fair*, Apr. 2009, 118+.

7. Christopher Lasch, *The Culture of Narcissism: American Life in an Age of Diminishing Expectations*, 52–66.

8. Kamp, "Rethinking the American Dream."

1. The Epic of America

1. "American Dream Village Comes to Life for Yuletide," *Los Angeles Times*, Dec. 19, 1938, 6.

2. James Truslow Adams, "America Faces 1933's Realities," *New York Times*, Jan. 1, 1933, SM1.

3. Adams, "America Faces 1933's Realities."

4. James Truslow Adams, "What of 'the American Dream'?," *New York Times*, May 14, 1933, SM1.

5. H. S. Commager, review of *The Epic of America*, by Adams, *Books*, Oct. 4, 1931, 1; Karl Schriftglesser, *Boston Transcript*, review of *The Epic of America*, by Adams, Oct. 10, 1931, 5.

6. Allen Sinclair Will, "America, Nation of Dreamers," *New York Times*, Oct. 4, 1931, 61.

7. Anthony Brandt, "The American Dream," *American Heritage* (Apr.–May 1981): 24–25.

8. "Says Pioneer Spirit Is America's Guide," *New York Times*, Nov. 6, 1932, 8.

9. "Znaniecki Fears Economic Tyranny," *New York Times*, July 16, 1933, N1.

10. Brooks Atkinson, "Fate of the Idealist," *New York Times*, Mar. 5, 1933, X1.

11. "Says Nation Fails in Human Relations," *New York Times*, June 20, 1932, 6.

12. "Miss Thompson Offers Plan to Fight Fascism," *Washington Post*, Feb. 6, 1936, 13.

13. David Behrens, "Monopoly Marks 50th Anniversary," *Los Angeles Times*, July 31, 1983, F2.

14. "Millikan Assails Trade Rule by U.S. as Threat to Freedom," *Chicago Daily Tribune*, Aug. 7, 1934, 5.

15. James Truslow Adams, "'Rugged Individualism' Analyzed," *New York Times*, Mar. 18, 1934, SM1.

16. Charles A. Beard, "The Myth of Rugged American Individualism," *Harper's Monthly Magazine*, Dec. 1931, 13–22.

17. Adams, "'Rugged Individualism' Analyzed."

18. Shelby Cullom Davis, "Toward the American Dream," *Current History*, Dec. 1939, 41–43.

19. "The American Dream," *Atlanta Constitution*, Nov. 26, 1938, 6.

20. "Stern Comment on American Freedom," *New York Times*, Mar. 24, 1940, 73.

21. "The Texts of Willkie's Campaign Addresses in Queens and at the World's Fair," *New York Times*, Oct. 27, 1940, 42.

22. "Check Roosevelt, Hoover Demands," *New York Times*, Nov. 2, 1940, 1.

23. "Mark Twain's Odyssey," *Hartford Courant*, Dec. 3, 1935, 10.

24. Paul Jordan-Smith, "New Books and Their Makers," *Los Angeles Times*, Aug. 23, 1936, C8.

25. Stanley Young, "A Wide-Sweeping Novel of American Generations," *New York Times*, June 27, 1937, 78.

26. Ralph Thompson, "Books of the Times," *New York Times*, June 18, 1937, 19.

27. Percy Hutchison, "The American Dream," *New York Times*, Oct. 4, 1936, BR9.

28. Ibid.

29. "London Times Weighs American Farm Ideal," *New York Times*, Feb. 23, 1937, 23.

30. R. L. Duffus, "The Story of the American Dream of a Better Life," *New York Times*, Feb. 19, 1939, 86.

31. Lewis Gannett, "Books and Things," *Washington Post*, Feb. 17, 1939, 9.

32. Duffus, "American Dream of a Better Life."

33. Rose Lee Martin, "Lone Star State Still Goes It Alone," *New York Times*, June 7, 1936, 111.

34. Rockwell D. Hunt, "The American Dream," *Los Angeles Times*, Dec. 18, 1937, A4.

35. William MacDonald, "Toward the American Dream," *New York Times*, Nov. 27, 1938, 114.

36. Katherine Woods, "Emigrants from Europe and the American Dream," *New York Times*, Oct. 20, 1940, 94.

37. "Voices from Many Lands Tell Americanism Views," *Los Angeles Times*, Oct. 27, 1940, C6.

38. Woods, "Emigrants from Europe and the American Dream."

39. Herschel Brickell, "Three Centuries of Utopian Settlements in America," *New York Times*, Apr. 13, 1941, BR11.

40. Eleanor Roosevelt, "My Day: How to Realize the American Dream," *Atlanta Constitution*, Jan. 7, 1941, 14.

41. "Library Book List Makes Up 'The American Dream,'" *Chicago Daily Tribune*, Jan. 8, 1941, 12.

42. James Truslow Adams, "Forces That Make Us the United States," *New York Times*, July 13, 1941, SM8.

43. Hal Borland, "Workshop of the American Dream," *New York Times*, June 29, 1941, SM5.

44. Ibid.

45. "New Deal's Analyst Heaps Praise on It," *Los Angeles Times*, Feb. 1, 1942, C6.

46. "Retention of the 'American Dream,'" *New York Times*, Jan. 25, 1942, BR3.

47. Dorothy Thompson, "The American Dream," *Ladies' Home Journal*, July 1943, 6.

48. Francis Brown, "American Evolution," *New York Times*, Sept. 26, 1943, BR7 (emphasis in the original).

49. T. S., "At the Rialto," *New York Times*, Jan. 14, 1943, 25.

50. D. W. Brogan, "Europe's Portrait of Uncle Sam," *New York Times*, Mar. 21, 1943, SM7.

51. "Topics of the Times," *New York Times*, July 3, 1943, 12.

52. Ibid.

53. Rupert B. Vance, "Tragic Dilemma: The Negro and the American Dream," *Virginia Quarterly Review* (July 1944): 435–45.

54. Ibid.

55. Malvina Lindsay, "The Gentler Sex," *Washington Post*, Aug. 3, 1944, 10.

56. Leo Cherne, "So You Want Your Own Business!," *Los Angeles Times*, Mar. 31, 1945, D4.

57. Dorothy Rosenman, "Home Sweet Home," *New York Times*, Jan. 16, 1944, SM22. Some have argued that the suburban version of the American Dream began at the 1939–40 New York World's Fair, with General Motors's "Futurama" exhibit playing a major role in preselling the single-family home in new, planned developments outside cities. Christopher B. Leinberger, "The Next Slum?," *Atlantic*, Mar. 2008, 70–75.

58. "Calls for Wise Use of Leisure," *New York Times*, June 12, 1944, 22.

2. The Status Seekers

1. Webster Gault, "Sales of New Cars Climb Sharply Here," *Hartford Courant*, Dec. 15, 1960, 31; Virginia M. Irwin, "The American Dream of Eternal Youth," *Hartford Courant*, Mar. 24, 1961, 16; Brock Brower, "America's Sleeping Sickness—Staying Awake," *New York Times*, Oct. 15, 1961, SM47; "New View of Golf Is Coloring the American Dream Green," *Hartford Courant*, Apr. 7, 1963, D10.

2. George Gallup, "Half of People Polled Believe Riches Possible," *Los Angeles Times*, June 4, 1947, 6.

3. Greer Williams, "The End of an American Dream," *Saturday Evening Post*, Feb. 26, 1949, 23+.

4. Harold Walsh, "Mar. of Finance," *Los Angeles Times*, June 15, 1947, 11.

5. "Eisenhower Sees Threat to Freedom," *Hartford Courant*, Oct. 25, 1949, 1.

6. Malvina Lindsay, "Professional Career Craze," *Washington Post*, Jan. 13, 1949, 8.

7. Malvina Lindsay, "Search for Safe Living," *Washington Post*, June 16, 1949, 16.

8. Jack Gould, "The News of Radio," *New York Times*, June 27, 1947, 40.

9. "This Is Ed Sullivan Speaking," *Chicago Daily Tribune*, July 26, 1952, 10.

10. Jack Zaiman, "Election Will Tell If Dream Still Lives, Says Ribicoff," *Hartford Courant*, Oct. 25, 1954, 2.

11. Ibid.

12. Irving M. Kravsow, "Ribicoff Defends Talk on 'American Dream,'" *Hartford Courant*, Oct. 30, 1954, 1. Ribicoff's Dream continued in the years ahead; the man went on to become secretary of health, education, and welfare in President Kennedy's cabinet and, after that, a US senator from his home state.

13. "Essentials for American Dream Cited," *Los Angeles Times*, July 8, 1956, A8.

14. "Educator Says Women Remain Victims of Bias," *Los Angeles Times*, Apr. 5, 1955, 23.

15. Wallace Terry, "Negro Called Hope for Preservation of Nation's Dream," *Washington Post and Times Herald*, June 25, 1962, B2.

16. Cullen, *American Dream*, 126–27.

17. Chester Bowles, "'The Most Powerful Idea in the World,'" *New York Times*, May 13, 1951, SM5.

18. Newbold Morris, "Human Endeavor," *Hartford Courant*, May 2, 1952, 16.

19. John Crosby, "Dash of Humor Suggested to Brighten TV 'Cavalcade,'" *Hartford Courant*, Jan. 12, 1953, 6.

20. Frank Klingberg, "American Dream," *Los Angeles Times*, Sept. 19, 1954, B5.

21. "History Pageant Opens Exhibition at Broadway," *Los Angeles Times*, May 17, 1956, A3; Marie Smith, "'Dream' Display on View," *Washington Post and Times Herald*, Nov. 6, 1956, D2.

22. Ralph G. Newman, "Revitalizing the Drama That Saved American Dream," *Chicago Daily Tribune*, Dec. 2, 1956, J36.

23. Carl Sandburg, "For 'All Men, in All Lands, Everywhere,'" *New York Times*, Feb. 8, 1959, SM11.

24. "Ruth, Dead 10 Years, Represented American Dream," *Washington Post and Times Herald*, Aug. 17, 1958, C4.

25. Janet M. Beroth, "The Path of Glory," *Hartford Courant*, Nov. 22, 1959, F14.

26. Henry J. Taylor, "Glenn's Flight Lifts the Nation's Spirit, Enlarges American Dream," *Los Angeles Times*, Feb. 28, 1962, A5.

27. http://www.hud.gov/offices/adm/about/admguide/history.cfm#1950.

28. "1954 Housing Law Held Boon to Homeowners," *Los Angeles Times*, Aug. 29, 1954, E11.

29. William Henry Chamberlin, "The American Idea," *Wall Street Journal*, July 3, 1956, 8.

30. Orville Prescott, "Books of the Times," *New York Times*, Apr. 29, 1959, 31.

31. John F. Bridge, "Reading for Pleasure," *Wall Street Journal*, May 21, 1959, 12.

32. "Essence of America," *New York Times*, Aug. 9, 1959, E8.

33. John K. Jessup, "National Purpose: Start of a Debate," *New York Times*, May 19, 1960, 34.

34. "American Dream Is Found Clouded," *New York Times*, May 30, 1960, 20.

35. Eleanor Roosevelt, "What Has Happened to the American Dream?," *Atlantic Monthly*, Apr. 1961, 46–50; Jessup, "National Purpose."

36. Walter Kerr, "Dreams Might Ring True but They're Not Real," *Washington Post*, Feb. 5, 1961, G3; Howard Taubman, "The Theatre: Albee's *The American Dream*," *New York Times*, Jan. 25, 1961, 28.

37. The Rev. Dr. Billy Graham, "National Purpose: Graham Diagnosis," *New York Times*, June 6, 1960, 26; Archibald MacLeish, "National Purpose: MacLeish 'Dream,'" *New York Times*, May 30, 1960, 14.

38. Joseph Nolan, "How to Make a Million," *New York Times*, July 10, 1955, SM13.

39. George Lawton, "When Should a Man Retire?," *New York Times*, Apr. 27, 1947, SM12.

40. John L. Springer, "What Is the Right Time to Retire?," *New York Times*, Feb. 15, 1959, SM13.

41. "Strange Twist to an Old Dream," *Wall Street Journal*, Apr. 10, 1959, 12.

42. Saul Pett, "Hidden Clinkers Shrink 'Fabulous' Quiz Earnings," *Hartford Courant*, Nov. 22, 1959, 10B2.

43. William M. Freeman, "An American Dream Examined," *New York Times*, Feb. 10, 1961, 37.

44. Hal Borland, "He Made the American Success Story a Success," *New York Times*, July 19, 1964, BR16.

45. Donald Kirk, "Junior Achievers Realize American Dream," *Chicago Daily Tribune*, Jan. 24, 1960, N1.

46. George Lill, "A Challenge to June Grads," *Chicago Daily Tribune*, May 22, 1960, G40 (emphasis in the original); Kittie Turmell, "Scaling the Social Ladder," *Los Angeles Times*, Dec. 4, 1960, 89.

47. Barbara Schulz, "Teens Set Sights on the Professions," *Chicago Daily Tribune*, Dec. 12, 1961, B9.

48. Ralph McGill, "Where Dreams Are Born," *Hartford Courant*, Oct. 31, 1963, 14.

49. Mary Ann Callan, "Says Pat Nixon," *Los Angeles Times*, July 27, 1960, A1; Earl Mazo, "American Dream Come True," *Los Angeles Times*, July 29, 1960, 2.

50. Glen Bower, "Voice of Youth: Students Tell Views," *Chicago Tribune*, May 17, 1964, G8.

51. "Martin in Step . . . Smarty Pants . . . LBJ and American Dream," *Washington Post and Times Herald*, May 11, 1964, A2.

52. Robert E. Thompson, "Better Things in Offing, Johnson Tells Graduates," *Los Angeles Times*, May 30, 1964, 4.

53. Philip Benjamin, "Kirk Tells 6,273 Graduates at Columbia That the American Dream Is Over," *New York Times*, June 3, 1964, 33.

3. The Anti-Paradise

1. Dolly Whitham, "Group Eyes American Dream Changes," *Hartford Courant*, Apr. 8, 1975, 22B.

2. J. R. Wiggins, "Enduring Vision: A More Perfect Life," *Washington Post and Times Herald*, Jan. 20, 1965, D1.

3. Conrad Knickerbocker, "A Man Desperate for a New life," *New York Times*, Mar. 14, 1965, BR1; Robert R. Kirsch, "The Book Report," *Los Angeles Times*, Apr. 5, 1965, D6; Paul R. Jackson, "An American Dream," *Chicago Tribune*, Mar. 14, 1965, J1; "Australia Adds 3 to Book Ban List," *Washington Post and Times Herald*, June 10, 1965, A6; Anatole Shub, "The German List of Best Sellers," *Washington Post and Times Herald*, Sept. 2, 1965, A20.

4. "The American Dream and the American Negro," *New York Times*, Mar. 7, 1965, SM32.

5. "Review 1—No Title," *New York Times*, Nov. 7, 1965, BR91.

6. "Lynd Asserts 'New Left' Is American Dream," *Hartford Courant*, May 3, 1966, C33; Lynn Lilliston, "Waking to Demands of American Dream," *Los Angeles Times*, Aug. 16, 1966, C1.

7. D. J. R. Bruckner, "Why the American Dream Exploded," *Los Angeles Times*, Aug. 7, 1966, J2.

8. William K. Shannon, "Negro Violence vs. the American Dream," *New York Times*, July 27, 1967, 34.

9. Stuart H. Loory, "Humphrey Converts Young Negro Militant," *Los Angeles Times*, May 4, 1968, 3.

10. "Romney Says American Way Faces Crisis," *Chicago Tribune*, Feb. 6, 1968, A5; Richard L. Lyons, "Nixon on Ghettos," *Washington Post and Times Herald*, Mar. 8, 1968, A1.

11. William K. Shannon, "The Kennedy Legend," *New York Times*, June 9, 1968, E; "Ecumenical Services Held for Kennedy; Pastor Asks for 'Vocation of Citizenship,'" *Hartford Courant*, June 10, 1968, 26B.

12. Frederic Morton, "Topics: The Nouveau-Avant," *New York Times*, Nov. 25, 1967, 38.

13. Ibid.

14. William McPherson, "Impoverished American Dream," *Washington Post and Times Herald*, Oct. 26, 1970, C1.

15. McPherson, "Impoverished American Dream."

16. William Raspberry, "American Dream Fades," *Washington Post and Times Herald*, July 16, 1971, A23.

17. James J. Kilpatrick, "Bid Farewell to the Great Dream of Free Enterprise," *Los Angeles Times*, Aug. 24, 1971, B7.

18. Peter Petersen, "The American Dream," *New York Times*, Jan. 31, 1972, 41.

19. Cecil Eby, "Anti-Paradise," *Chicago Tribune*, Mar. 19, 1972, K4; Gerald Emanuel Stearn, comp., *Broken Image: Foreign Critiques of America*.

20. Crawford Woods, "Fear and Loathing in Las Vegas," *New York Times*, July 23, 1972, BR17.

21. Fred M. Hechinger, "Crisis of the Spirit," *New York Times*, Oct. 16, 1972, 37.

22. "Cluster Housing, Answer to Future," *Hartford Courant*, Feb. 27, 1972, D13; Martha Patton, "To Keep the American Dream from Becoming a Nightmare," *Chicago Tribune*, Apr. 9, 1972, E13.

23. Richard Christiansen, "American Dream Alive, Well on TV Commercials," *Los Angeles Times*, July 23, 1972, F7.

24. Del Earisman, "Prophecy for the Class of '72," *Hartford Courant*, May 7, 1972, J6.

25. Marvin D. Rowen, "The Unmaking of the American Dream," *Los Angeles Times*, June 4, 1972, F1.

26. George E. Jones, "Equality: American Dream—or Nightmare?," *U.S. News and World Report*, Aug. 4, 1975, 26–31.

27. Judith Martin, "Dreams Still Come True for Inventors," *Los Angeles Times*, Apr. 13, 1972, C2.

28. Jacqueline Trescott, "Amway: Distributing the American Dream," *Washington Post*, June 9, 1975, B1.

29. Leonard J. Fein, "To Try to Dream Again," *New York Times*, Feb. 11, 1973, 217.

30. Allen Sloan, "Cadillac and the American Dream," *New York Times*, May 13, 1973, 153.

31. Ibid.

32. Charles Champlin, "Movie Review," *Los Angeles Times*, June 12, 1969, OC_C1; Jack Hiemenz, "John Wayne: I Know Most of You Feel the Same as I Do," *New York Times*, June 17, 1973, 130.

33. Daniel J. Leab, "The Blue Collar Ethic in Bicentennial America: *Rocky* (1976)," in *American History/American Film: Interpreting the Hollywood Image*, edited by John E. O'Connor and Martin A. Jackson, 258–59.

34. Steve Harvey, "Urge to Be No. 1: All-American Dream," *Los Angeles Times*, Sept. 2, 1973, D4.

35. Bob Walton, "'American Dream' Is Alive and Well," *Chicago Tribune*, Sept. 30, 1973, W_A5; Marjorie Hunter, "U.S. in Disarray, Dr. Mead Charges," *New York Times*, Sept. 26, 1973, 17; Bill Moyers, "This Ominous Sense," *New York Times*, Oct. 4, 1973, 45.

36. David H. Rhinelander, "'American Dream' at End, Doctors Told," *Hartford Courant*, Oct. 26, 1973, 10. Alvin Toffler's 1970s *Future Shock* was of course fully dedicated to the idea that individuals could no longer process the kind and level of social change the country was going through.

37. Vernon Jarrett, "Americans Need to Revise Dreams," *Chicago Tribune*, Jan. 13, 1974, A6; Art Buchwald, "Fuming over the American Dream," *Washington Post and Times Herald*, Dec. 9, 1973, E1.

38. George P. Elliott, "Waking from the American Dream," *Nation*, Nov. 16, 1974, 491–95.

39. Kevin P. Phillips, "American Dream about to End?," *Hartford Courant*, June 3, 1974, 26.

40. Ronald G. Shafer, "A Fading Dream," *Wall Street Journal*, Sept. 3, 1974, 1.

41. "The No-Frills American Dream," *Business Week*, June 16, 1975, 17; Colin Campbell, "Economic Reality: Intruder on the American Dream," *Psychology Today* (June 1975): 36–37.

42. Patricia A. Johnson, "Born Too Late for the American Dream," *Los Angeles Times*, Apr. 3, 1976, B5; Joann S. Lublin, "Homeowner Blues," *Wall Street Journal*, Aug. 2, 1976, 1.

43. Dick Turpin, "Home Occupants of Future: Bob, Carol, Ted, and Alice," *Los Angeles Times*, Jan. 26, 1977, E10.

44. Natalie Levy, "RVs: A Fun Cure for a National Case of Wanderlust," *Chicago Tribune*, May 11, 1977, D1; Ed Sylvester, "Mobile Homes: Low Cost Dream or Blight?," *Los Angeles Times*, Sept. 16, 1979, SD_A1.

45. Robert Lindsey, "Economy Mars Belief in the American Dream," *New York Times*, Oct. 26, 1975, 1.

46. Dr. John Raines, "American Dream Proves Elusive," *Hartford Courant*, Nov. 2, 1975, B3.

47. Robert Penn Warren, "History Serves the Interpreter of the American Dream," *Hartford Courant*, Jan. 19, 1975, A29.

48. Alan Merridew, "Blacks Finding Their 'Dream' in Suburbs," *Chicago Tribune*, Jan. 22, 1976, W1.

49. Andrew Greeley, "The American Dream Is True," *Chicago Tribune*, Nov. 6, 1975, A4.

50. Stanley Karnow, "American Dream Alive and Well," *Hartford Courant*, Jan. 4, 1979, 18.

51. Richard H. deLone, "Upward Mobility: The Most Illusionary American Dream," *Los Angeles Times*, Sept. 23, 1979, G3.

52. William Overend, "Updating and Redefining the American Dream," *Los Angeles Times*, Dec. 20, 1976, OC_A1.

53. Gary Deeb, "Tempo TV & Radio," *Chicago Tribune*, Sept. 19, 1978, A11.

54. Elaine Markoutsas, "Tempo TV," *Chicago Tribune*, Dec. 27, 1979, A13.

55. Michael Policastro, "'The American Dream': Can It Survive Awakening?," *New York Times*, Oct. 28, 1979, NJ30.

4. Born in the USA

1. George F. Will, "Singing the Big Blues over the Scrunching of the American Dream," *Los Angeles Times*, Apr. 12, 1984, H7.

2. "The Moments of Truth, 1980 . . . ," *Los Angeles Times*, Dec. 25, 1980, OC_B1.

3. Herbert I. London and Albert L. Weeks, "Strength from Our Myths," *Los Angeles Times*, Sept. 1, 1980, B5.

4. John Lahr, "Dreamers of the Day," *Harper's*, Jan. 1981, 74–76; Peter S. Prescott, "American Dreams: Lost and Found," *Newsweek*, Oct. 13, 1980, 114+.

5. Nancy Shiffrin, "Book Reviews," *Los Angeles Times*, Oct. 23, 1980, F28.

6. Connie Lauerman, "Tempo," *Chicago Tribune*, Dec. 15, 1981, B1.

7. Robert C. Yeager, "The Middle-Class Squeeze," *Chicago Tribune*, Apr. 6, 1981, A1.

8. Lewis Beale, "Tempo," *Chicago Tribune*, Jan. 4, 1983, D1; Yardena Arar, "Rock Singers Turn More Frequently to Messages of Hard Times, Despair," *Hartford Courant*, Dec. 26, 1982, EE4B.

9. Robert Hilburn, "Springsteen: Brooding over the American Dream," *Los Angeles Times*, Sept. 19, 1982, O61.

10. Stephen Holden, "Springsteen Scans the American Dream," *New York Times*, May 27, 1984, H19.

11. Ron Aldridge, "New ABC Series," *Chicago Tribune*, Jan. 25, 1981, H3.

12. Owen McNally, "Back-to-the-City, with Television Gloss," *Hartford Courant*, Apr. 24, 1981, B9.

13. Paul Weingarten, "Tempo," *Chicago Tribune*, Aug. 27, 1980, B1.

14. Sheila Benson, "Movie Review," *Los Angeles Times*, May 11, 1984, I1.

15. Jerome Charyn, *Movieland: Hollywood and the Great American Dream Culture*; David Ansen, "Baseball Diamonds Are Forever," *Newsweek*, Apr. 24, 1989, 72–73.

16. Robert Sklar, "Frozen Idyll," *New York Times*, July 16, 1989, BR17.

17. Lance Morrow, "Downsizing an American Dream," *Time*, Oct. 5, 1981, 95–96.

18. Thomas P. Murphy, "Giving Up on the American Dream," *Forbes*, Aug. 29, 1983, 166.

19. Ellen Goodman, "Is American Dream Today's Nightmare?," *Chicago Tribune*, May 3, 1984, D_A1.

20. Arlie Russell Hochschild, "The House as Homewrecker," *New York Times*, Mar. 25, 1984, BR13.

21. Peter T. Kilborn, "Average Price of New Home Tops $100,000 for First Time," *New York Times*, June 30, 1984, 1.

22. Matthew L. Wald, "The American Dream Is Changing," *New York Times*, Oct. 28, 1984, RER1.

23. Ronald Alsop, "Mobile-Home Dealers Roll Out Sophisticated Sales Techniques," *Wall Street Journal*, Dec. 20, 1984, 29.

24. Lisa Anderson, "The Man Who Created Suburbia," *Chicago Tribune*, Feb. 3, 1985, L1.

25. Dennis McLellan, "Suburbia Changing, but Still Part of the American Dream, Author Says," *Los Angeles Times*, July 6, 1986, OC_D1.

26. Joel Garreau, "Transcending Race Barriers and Living the American Dream," *Washington Post*, Nov. 29, 1987, A1.

27. Glenna Whitley, "Persistence Pays for Contest Junkies," *Los Angeles Times*, Aug. 18, 1983, D12.

28. Scott Kraft, "Betting Proving Boon to States' Coffers," *Hartford Courant*, July 30, 1984, A5A.

29. "Buying a Franchise Often Has Pitfalls," *Los Angeles Times*, Mar. 19, 1985, OC_C10.

30. Sylvia Porter, "Money Management," *Chicago Tribune*, Jan. 1, 1965, B3.

31. Sally Saville Hodge, "Franchising Gives Little Guy Chance to Grab Brass Ring," *Chicago Tribune*, Sept. 24, 1984, B1.

32. Elizabeth Kastor, "The Corporate Cheerleaders—Ta-da!," *Washington Post*, Apr. 9, 1988, C1.

33. Earl C. Gottschalk Jr., "The American Dream Is Alive and Well in Koreatown," *Wall Street Journal*, May 20, 1985, 106.

34. Ibid.

35. Ronald Alsop, "Firms Translate Sales Pitches to Appeal to Asian-Americans," *Wall Street Journal*, Apr. 10, 1986, 35.

36. Tony Schwartz, "Daisy Tsui," *New York Magazine*, Apr. 25, 1988, 115–17.

37. Philip Moffitt, "Does Anyone Know What Time It Is?," *Esquire*, Nov. 1984, 17–18.

38. "Does America Still Exist?," *Harper's*, Mar. 1984, 43–58.

39. Ibid.

40. Ibid.

41. Ibid.

42. Ibid.

43. Mario M. Cuomo, "The American Dream and the Politics of Inclusion," *Psychology Today* (July 1986): 54–56.

44. Paul Richter, "Madison Ave. Pushing Patriotism," *Los Angeles Times,* Sept. 9, 1985, D1.

45. Richard N. Goodwin, "Democracy Teeters on the Income Gap," *Los Angeles Times,* Oct. 24, 1985, B5.

46. Benjamin R. Barber, "Celluloid Vistas," *Harper's,* July 1985, 74–75.

47. Ibid.

48. Lou Cannon, "Emotional Plea Caps Reagan Tour," *Washington Post,* Nov. 4, 1986, A10.

49. Ibid.

50. Lou Cannon, "President Extols State of Nation," *Washington Post,* Jan. 26, 1988, A1.

51. Mel Elfin, "The Haves, the Have-Nots, and the Have-Somewhats," *New York Times,* Oct. 9, 1988, BR10.

52. "On the Road with Charles Kuralt," *Washington Post,* Oct. 13, 1985, BW10; Clifford Terry, "'American Dream': Mom, Cars, and Leno," *Chicago Tribune,* May 2, 1986, N5.

53. Sherry Suib Cohen, "The American Dream," *Ladies' Home Journal,* July 1986, 105+.

54. Ibid.

55. Ibid.

56. Martie Zad, "The King Lives at Graceland," *Washington Post,* Aug. 16, 1987, TV6.

57. Michael J. Weiss, "What Price the American Dream?," *Ladies' Home Journal,* Mar. 1988, 109+.

58. Ibid.

59. Patricia Hersch, "thirtysomething therapy," *Psychology Today* (Oct. 1988): 62+.

60. Thomas Cangelosi, "Has the Way to the American Dream Become a Rut?," *New York Times,* Dec. 11, 1988, CN44.

61. Edward Cody, "In Dijon, Living the Good Life," *Washington Post,* Oct. 30, 1988, 37.

5. The Anxious Society

1. Rafael Castillo, *"Death of a Salesman," New York Times,* Feb. 21, 1999, AR7.

2. Don Oldenburg, "New Path for the '90s," *Washington Post,* Feb. 20, 1990, C5.

3. Ibid.

4. Henry Allen, "Have Grin, Will Film Despair," *Washington Post*, Jan. 11, 1990, E1.

5. Ibid.

6. Peter Passell, "Keeping Chicken in Every Pot," *New York Times*, Feb. 6, 1991, D2; Kim Foltz, "Advertising," *New York Times*, Mar. 25, 1991, D9.

7. Susan Dentzer, "The Vanishing Dream," *U.S. News and World Report*, Apr. 22, 1991, 39.

8. Barbara Vobejda, "Economy Puts a Downside on the Belief in Upward Mobility," *Washington Post*, Dec. 19, 1991, A23.

9. Robert J. Samuelson, "How Our American Dream Unraveled," *Newsweek*, Mar. 3, 1992, 2.

10. Amy Bernstein, "Dream On," *U.S. News and World Report*, July 27, 1992, 11.

11. Clare Ansberry and Thomas F. O'Boyle, "Future Imperfect," *Wall Street Journal*, Aug. 11, 1992, A1.

12. Ibid.

13. Michiko Kakutani, "American Dream Shrinks to a Nap," *New York Times*, May 28, 1993, C30.

14. Christopher Lehmann-Haupt, "America's Dream on a Slide into the Third World," *New York Times*, Sept. 27, 1993, C14.

15. Louis Uchitelle, "Is Growth Moral?," *New York Times*, Mar. 27, 1994, 356.

16. Alice M. Rivlin, "Reviving the American Dream," *Brookings Review* (Summer 1992): 5.

17. William A. Schreyer, "The Century of the American Dream," *Vital Speeches of the Day* (Nov. 1, 1992): 49.

18. "Study Focuses on Saving the American Dream," *CPA Journal* (July 1994): 9.

19. Errol Smith, "The American Dream Needs 'American Dreamers,'" *National Minority Politics* (Nov. 1994): 23.

20. J. C. Watts, "Conservative Congressman Defines 'American Dream,'" *New York Amsterdam News*, Oct. 5, 1996, 12.

21. John J. O'Connor, "Critic's Notebook: After American Dream, Waking Up Cranky," *New York Times*, Mar. 24, 1994.

22. "A House with a Picket Fence Still Fits the American Dream," *New York Times*, June 2, 1992, A12.

23. Roger K. Lewis, "Designing an Affordable Housing Future," *Washington Post*, Nov. 23, 1991, E1.

24. Benny L. Kass, "Mortgage Deduction, Other Tax Benefits Are Keys to the American Dream," *Washington Post*, Jan. 19, 1991, F8.

25. Gary Blonston, "Era of Big Profits on Sales May Be Over," *Washington Post*, May 12, 1990, F1.

26. James W. Hughes and Todd Zimmerman, "The Dream Is Alive," *American Demographics* (Aug. 1993): 32.

27. Alan Reynolds, "The Origins of Grumpiness," *National Review*, July 1, 1996, 52–53.

28. Marjorie Williams, "The Selling of the American Dream," *Washington Post*, July 30, 1991, C1.

29. Ibid.

30. Mohammed Hanif, "Living the Dream in America," *Washington Post*, Oct. 14, 1991, 1. Hussain would run for governor of Texas in 2010 but be defeated in the primaries.

31. Walter Goodman, "Melting Pot? Simmering Nicely," *New York Times*, June 19, 1992, C26.

32. Marvine Howe, "Chronicle," *New York Times*, Jan. 16, 1992, B7.

33. Robin Finn, "American Dream of the 90's: My Child the Tennis Champ," *New York Times*, Aug. 6, 1990, A1.

34. John Steele Gordon, "Sowing the American Dream," *American Heritage* (Dec. 1990): 22; Michael Ventura, "The Psychology of Money," *Psychology Today* (Mar.–Apr. 1995): 50.

35. Ira Berkow, "Dear Mickey: Messages and Prayers for an American Hero," *New York Times*, June 25, 1995, S9.

36. "Conference Celebrates Legacy of Jackie Robinson," *Jet*, Apr. 21, 1997, 51; Edward A. Gargan, "Field for Philosophizing and Other Dreams," *New York Times*, June 27, 1998, B9.

37. Caryn James, "TV Weekend; Migrating to Movieland, Where Outsiders Fit In," *New York Times*, Mar. 20, 1998.

38. Bruce McCall, "King of the Road," *New York Times*, July 18, 1999, BR6.

39. Robert Bryce, "The American Dream Glitters Still—in Foreign Countries," *New York Times*, Aug. 6, 1995, F10.

40. Lena Williams, "Testing the Resonance of the American Dream," *New York Times*, June 23, 1996, 39.

41. Kathryn Shattuck, "Exploring the Dream and the Drive: To Move Up," *New York Times*, June 28, 1998, AR27.

42. Robert J. Samuelson, "Great Expectations," *Newsweek*, Jan. 8, 1996, 24.

43. Reynolds, "The Origins of Grumpiness," 52–53; Paul Krugman, "It's a Wonderful Life," *Washington Monthly*, Jan.–Feb. 1996, 48.

44. W. Bradord Fay, "The Fading Post-war Middle Class," *Marketing Research* (Fall 1996): 47–48.

45. David Whitman, "I'm OK, You're Not," *U.S. News and World Report*, Dec. 16, 1996, 24; Charles J. Whalen, "The Anxious Society," *Humanist* (Sept.– Oct. 1996): 18–19.

46. "Your American Dream?," *Christian Science Monitor*, Sept. 12, 1996, 20.

47. Ibid.

48. Mark Dolliver, "Giving Some Content to a National Cliché," *Adweek (Eastern Edition)* (Oct. 7, 1996): 31.

49. Louis Uchitelle, "That Was Then and This Is the 90's," *New York Times*, June 18, 1997, D1.

50. Ibid.

51. "Fanfare for the Common Man," *Business Week*, June 22, 1998, 218.

52. Kenji Sato, "Borderless," *New York Times*, June 8, 1997, SM64.

53. Edward O. Welles, "Motherhood, Apple Pie, and Stock Options," *Inc.*, Feb. 1998, 84.

54. Edward Wyatt, "On Paper, a New American Dream," *New York Times*, Feb. 15, 1998, WK2; Diana B. Henriques, "Surfing for Dollars," *New York Times*, Nov. 14, 1999, BR32.

55. Margaret Carlson, "He's the Dream, in Supersize," *Time*, Sept. 27, 1999, 47.

56. Mortimer B. Zuckerman, "Living the Dream," *U.S. News and World Report*, July 12, 1999, 68.

6. American Idol

1. Adam Cooke, "Students Probe the Promise of American Dreams," *Christian Science Monitor*, July 3, 2001, 14.

2. Sara Rimer, "Gatsby's Green Light Beckons a New Generation of Strivers," *New York Times*, Feb. 17, 2008, A1.

3. Ibid.

4. Frank Rich, "George W.'s America," *New York Times*, Nov. 4, 2000, A21.

5. Kathleen O'Brien, "Realizing the American Dream," *New York Times*, Apr. 14, 2002, 9.

6. John Schwartz, "Supersize American Dream: Expensive? I'll Take It," *New York Times*, Dec. 16, 2002, C8.

7. Felicia R. Lee, "Does Class Count in Today's Land of Opportunity?," *New York Times*, Jan. 18, 2003, B7.

8. Aaron Bernstein, "Waking Up from the American Dream," *Business Week*, Dec. 1, 2003, 54–58.

9. James Surowiecki, "People of Plenty," *Fast Company*, Mar. 2003, 31+.

10. David R. Francis, "The American Dream Gains a Harder Edge," *Christian Science Monitor*, May 23, 2005, 17.

11. "Class and the American Dream," *New York Times*, May 30, 2005, A14; Janny Scott and David Leonhardt, "Class in America: Shadowy Lines That Still Divide," *New York Times*, May 15, 2005, A1.

12. Scott and Leonhardt, "Class in America."

13. Barry Schwartz, "Waking Up from the American Dream," *Psychology Today* (July–Aug. 2000): 74.

14. Richard Florida, "The New American Dream," *Washington Monthly*, Mar. 2003, 26.

15. Michael Isikoff, "Periscope," *Newsweek International*, Sept. 6, 2004, 4.

16. "The European Dream: How Europe's Vision of the Future Is Quietly Eclipsing the American Dream," *Publishers Weekly*, Aug. 2004, 56+.

17. Katje Richstatter, "The European Dream: How Europe's Vision of the Future Is Quietly Eclipsing the American Dream," *Tikkun*, Jan.–Feb. 2005, 72+.

18. Jennifer Vogel, "America vs. Europe," *E*, Jan.–Feb. 2005, 59+.

19. Brendan Driscoll, "Rifkin, Jeremy. The European Dream: How Europe's Vision of the Future Is Quietly Eclipsing the American Dream," *Booklist*, Sept. 1, 2004, 30+.

20. Isikoff, "Periscope."

21. Pete Engardio, "Nice Dream If You Can Live It," *Business Week*, Sept. 13, 2004, 22.

22. Vanessa Bush, "Herbert, Bob. Promises Betrayed: Waking Up from the American Dream," *Booklist*, Apr. 15, 2005, 1418.

23. "Bait and Switch: The (Futile) Pursuit of the American Dream," *Publishers Weekly*, Sept. 2005, 72+.

24. John Leonard, "New Books," *Harper's*, Sept. 2005, 79+.

25. "Is the American Dream Killing You? How the Market Rules Our Life," *Publishers Weekly*, Oct. 2005, 62+.

26. Michiko Kakutani, "Pop Culture Conjures a Transracial American Dream," *New York Times*, Sept. 9, 2002, E6.

27. David Brooks, "The Americano Dream," *New York Times*, Feb. 24, 2004, A25.

28. David Brooks, "Our Sprawling, Supersize Utopia," *New York Times Magazine*, Apr. 4, 2004, 46.

29. "Suburban Nation: The Rise of Sprawl and the Decline of the American Dream," *Publisher's Weekly*, Mar. 2000, 88; Donna Seaman, "Suburban Nation: The Rise of Sprawl and the Decline of the American Dream," *Booklist*, Mar. 1, 2000, 1177.

30. Natalie Canover, "Running on Empty," *New York Times*, Mar. 13, 2005, LI1; Dennis Harvey, "The End of Suburbia: Oil Depletion and the Collapse of the American Dream," *Variety*, Oct. 24, 2005, 23.

31. Fred A. Bernstein, "Are McMansions Going Out of Style?," *New York Times*, Oct. 2, 2005, K1.

32. James Sullivan, "The American Dream: Stories from the Heart of Our Nation," *Book*, May 2001, 62.

33. Ibid.; Mary Carroll, "The American Dream: Stories from the Heart of Our Nation," *Booklist*, Apr. 1, 2001, 1427; Susan M. Colowick, "The American Dream: Stories from the Heart of Our Nation," *Library Journal*, May 15, 2001, 136; "The American Dream: Stories from the Heart of Our Nation," *Publishers Weekly*, Apr. 16, 2001, 52; Larkin Warren, "Dan Rather's Dream," *Good Housekeeping*, June 2001, 89.

34. Bill Carter, "How a Hit Almost Failed Its Own Audition," *New York Times*, Apr. 30, 2006, C1.

35. Manohla Dargis, "Paul Weitz's 'American Dreamz': An 'Idol' Clone with a Presidential Aura," *New York Times*, Apr. 21, 2006.

36. David Kelly, "Deconstruct This!," *New York Times*, Sept. 15, 2002, 8.

37. Gary Strauss, "Diverse Crowd Follows 'the American Dream,'" *USA Today*, Apr. 5, 2007, 2D.

38. Jon Parales, *"Bruce Almighty,"* *New York Times*, Apr. 24, 2005, B1; A. O. Scott, "The Boss Bibliography," *New York Times Book Review*, July 3, 2005, 10.

39. Manohla Dargis, "Stranded on the Flip Side of the American Dream," *New York Times*, Dec. 21, 2005, E1.

40. Sue Kirchoff, "Immigrants Chase American Dream," *USA Today*, Aug. 5, 2004, 1B.

41. Zsofia Varadi, "I Celebrate with Gratitude My Living of the American Dream," *Christian Science Monitor*, Sept. 2, 2004, 19.

42. Arnold Schwarzenegger, "The American Dream," *Vital Speeches of the Day* (Sept. 15, 2004): 721–23.

43. "Fixing the American Dream," *Economist*, Dec. 11, 2004, 34; Nina Bernstein, "Immigrants Reverse Their Trek as American Dreams Fade," *New York Times*, Nov. 10, 2004, B1.

44. David E. Rosenbaum, "Bush to Return to 'Ownership Society' in Push for Social Security Changes," *New York Times*, Jan. 16, 2005, A20.

45. Danny Hakim, "For a G.M. Family, the American Dream Vanishes," *New York Times*, Nov. 19, 2005, A1.

46. Mortimer B. Zuckerman, "Rich Man, Poor Man," *U.S. News and World Report*, June 12, 2006, 71–72.

47. "War on the Middle Class: How the Government, Big Business, and Special Interest Groups Are Waging War on the American Dream and How to Fight Back," *Publishers Weekly*, Oct. 2006, 46.

48. Mary Whaley, "War on the Middle Class: How the Government, Big Business, and Special Interest Groups Are Waging War on the American Dream and How to Fight Back," *Booklist*, Oct. 15, 2006, 22.

49. "Doubting the Dream," *Atlantic*, Dec. 2007, 27.

50. Peter Grier, "American Dream Update," *Christian Science Monitor*, July 3, 2007, 1–10.

51. "The Way We'll Be: The Zogby Report on the Transformation of the American Dream," *Publishers Weekly*, Aug. 2008, 45; Elizabeth L. Winter, "Zogby, John. The Way We'll Be: The Zogby Report on the Transformation of the American Dream," *Library Journal*, Aug. 2008, 90.

52. Susan Berfield, "The American Dream Downsized," *Business Week*, Sept. 8, 2008, 92.

53. Richard Stengel, "American Thrift," *Time*, Apr. 27, 2009, 2.

54. Hardy Green and Deborah Stead, "It's All about the Hot Shots," *Business Week*, Aug. 11, 2008, 17.

55. "Mr. Playboy: Hugh Hefner and the American Dream," *Publishers Weekly*, Oct. 2008, 59; "Mr. Playboy: Hugh Hefner and the American Dream," *Atlantic*, Apr. 2009, 96.

56. Gary Hart, "America Idol," *New York Times Book Review*, Dec. 24, 2006, 14.

57. "The Audacity of Hope: Thoughts on Reclaiming the American Dream," *Publishers Weekly*, Oct. 17, 2006, 52; Danna Bell-Russel, "Obama, Barack. The Audacity of Hope: Thoughts on Reclaiming the American Dream," *Library Journal*, Oct. 2006.

58. "The American Dream in Reverse," *New York Times*, Oct. 8, 2007, A18; Ford Fessenden, "The American Dream Foreclosed," *New York Times*, Oct. 14, 2007, LI1.

59. Noelle Knox, "Fading American Dream Fuels Rentals," *USA Today*, Aug. 30, 2007, 3B.

60. Richard Florida, "Rent Out the American Dream?," *USA Today*, Mar. 10, 2009, A11.

61. Joel Lovell, "The American Dream, No Money Down," *GQ—Gentlemen's Quarterly*, Feb. 2008, 78.

62. David J. Lynch, "Economy Squeezes American Dream," *USA Today*, June 9, 2008, 1A.

63. Ibid.

64. Barack Obama, "Reclaiming the American Dream," *Vital Speeches of the Day* (Jan. 2009): 2–4.

65. Peter Peterson, "You Can't Take It with You," *Newsweek*, Apr. 7, 2008, 56. See Peterson's autobiography, *The Education of an American Dreamer: How a Son of Greek Immigrants Learned His Way from a Nebraska Diner to Washington, Wall Street, and Beyond* (New York: Twelve, 2009), and, for more on concern about the nation's debt, David M. Walker's *Comeback America: Turning the Country Around and Restoring Fiscal Responsibility* (New York: Random House, 2010).

Conclusion

1. Lauren Sandler, "The American Nightmare," *Psychology Today* (Mar.–Apr. 2011): 70–77.

2. Rana Foroohar, "What Ever Happened to Upward Mobility?," *Time*, Nov. 14, 2011, 26–31, 34.

3. Fareed Zakaria, "Restoring the American Dream," *Time*, Nov. 1, 2010, 30–35; Fareed Zakaria, "Are America's Best Days Behind Us?," *Time*, Mar. 3, 2011, 28–33.

4. David von Drehle, "Don't Bet Against the United States," *Time*, Mar. 3, 2011, 34–35; Tom Brokaw, *The Time of Our Lives: A Conversation About America,*

Who We Are, Where We've Been, and Where We Need to Go Now to Recapture the American Dream (New York: Random House, 2011), 14.

5. http://www.heist-themovie.com/synopsis.html.

6. Robert L. Borosage and Katrina vanden Heuvel, "The American Dream: Can a Movement Save It?," *Nation*, Oct. 11, 2011, 11–15.

7. http://www.opportunitynation.org/pages/about-us/.

8. Joseph Lawler, "Millennials and Hope: Is the American Dream Still Alive?," *American Spectator* (Dec. 2010): 26+.

9. Christopher Caldwell, "Fantasy Points," *New York Times*, Nov. 7, 2010, 19–20.

Selected Bibliography

Adamic, Louis. *From Many Lands*. New York: Harper and Brothers, 1940.

Adams, James Truslow. *The American: The Making of a New Man*. New York: Charles Scribner's Sons, 1943.

———. *The Epic of America*. New York: Little, Brown, 1931.

Artz, Lee, and Bren Ortega Murphy. *Cultural Hegemony in the United States*. Thousand Oaks, CA: Sage, 2000.

Baldassare, Mark. *Troubles in Paradise*. New York: Columbia Univ. Press, 1986.

Barber, Benjamin R. *Strong Democracy: Participating Politics for a New Age*. Berkeley and Los Angeles: Univ. of California Press, 1985.

Bellah, Robert N., and Steven M. Tipton, eds. *The Robert Bellah Reader*. Durham, NC: Duke Univ. Press, 2006.

Boorstin, Daniel J. *The Image; or, What Happened to the American Dream?* New York: Atheneum, 1962.

Branson, Richard. *Business Stripped Bare: Adventures of a Global Entrepreneur*. London: Virgin Books, 2008.

Brokaw, Tom. *An Album of Memories: Personal Histories from the Greatest Generation*. New York: Random House, 2001.

———. *The Greatest Generation*. New York: Random House, 1998.

———. *The Greatest Generation Speaks: Letters and Reflections*. New York: Random House, 1999.

Brooks, David. *On Paradise Drive: How We Live Now (and Always Have) in the Future Tense*. New York: Simon and Schuster, 2004.

Bryant, Arthur. *The American Ideal*. London: Longmans, Green, 1936.

Calverton, V. F. *Where Angels Dared to Tread*. Indianapolis: Bobbs-Merrill, 1941.

Charyn, Jerome. *Movieland: Hollywood and the Great American Dream Culture*. New York: Putnam, 1989.

Cole, Robert. *Bruce Springsteen's America: The People Listening, a Poet Singing*. New York: Random House, 2005.

Cornuelle, Richard C. *Reclaiming the American Dream*. New York: Random House, 1965.

Coyle, David Cushman. *Roads to a New America*. New York: Little, Brown, 1938.

Cullen, Jim. *The American Dream: A Short History of an Idea That Shaped a Nation*. New York: Oxford Univ. Press, 2003.

———. *Born in the U.S.A.: Bruce Springsteen and the American Tradition*. Middletown, CT: Wesleyan Univ. Press, 2005.

Davis, Kenneth S. *The Hero: Charles A. Lindbergh and the American Dream*. New York: Doubleday, 1959.

de Botton, Alain. *Status Anxiety*. New York: Pantheon, 2004.

deLone, Richard H. *Small Futures: Children, Inequality, and the Limits of Liberal Reform*. New York: Harcourt, Brace, Jovanovich, 1979.

Dobbs, Lou. *War on the Middle Class: How the Government, Big Business, and Special Interest Groups Are Waging War on the American Dream and How to Fight Back*. New York: Viking, 2006.

Dotson, Bob. . . . *In Pursuit of the American Dream*. New York: Atheneum, 1985.

Duany, Andres, Elizabeth Plater-Zyberk, and Jeff Speck. *Suburban Nation: The Rise of Sprawl and the Decline of the American Dream*. New York: North Point Press, 2000.

Easterbrook, Gregg. *The Progress Paradox: How Life Gets Better While People Feel Worse*. New York: Random House, 2003.

Ehrenreich, Barbara. *Bait and Switch: The (Futile) Pursuit of the American Dream*. New York: Metropolitan Books, 2005.

———. *Nickel and Dimed: On (Not) Getting by in America*. New York: Metropolitan Books, 2001.

Embree, Edwin R. *Brown Americans: The Story of a Tenth of a Nation*. New York: Viking, 1943.

Evans, M. Stanton. *The Liberal Establishment: Who Runs America and How*. Old Greenwich, CT: Devin-Adair, 1965.

Florida, Richard. *The Rise of the Creative Class: And How It's Transforming Work, Leisure, Community, and Everyday Life*. New York: Basic Books, 2002.

Foster, Michael. *American Dream*. New York: William Morrow, 1937.

Frank, Thomas. *One Market under God: Extreme Capitalism, Market Populism, and the End of Economic Democracy*. New York: Doubleday, 2000.

Franklin, Jay. *Remaking America*. Boston: Houghton Mifflin, 1942.

Gabbard, Glen O. *The Psychology of "The Sopranos": Love, Death, and Betrayal in America's Favorite Gangster Family*. New York: Basic Books, 2002.

Gabler, Neal. *An Empire of Their Own: How the Jews Invented Hollywood.* New York: Crown, 1988.

Gardner, Ralph D. *Horatio Alger; or, The American Hero Era.* Vernon, BC: Wayside Press, 1964.

Gauer, James. *The New American Dream: Living Well in Small Homes.* New York: Monacelli, 2004.

Greenbie, Marjorie Berstow. *American Saga: The History and Literature of the American Dream of a Better Life.* New York: Whittlesey House/McGraw-Hill, 1939.

Guterman, Jimmy. *Runaway American Dream: Listening to Bruce Springsteen.* New York: Da Capo, 2005.

Harris, Marvin. *America Now: The Anthropology of a Changing Culture.* New York: Simon and Schuster, 1981.

Hayden, Dolores. *Redesigning the American Dream.* New York: W. W. Norton, 1984.

Herbert, Bob. *Promises Betrayed: Waking Up from the American Dream.* New York: Times Books, 2005.

Herskovits, Melville J. *The Myth of the Negro Past.* New York: Alfred A. Knopf, 1941.

Hochschild, Jennifer L. *Facing Up to the American Dream: Race, Class, and the Soul of the Nation.* Princeton: Princeton Univ. Press, 1995.

Huntington, Samuel. *Who Are We? The Challenges to America's National Identity.* New York: Simon and Schuster, 2004.

Jennings, Peter. *The Century.* New York: Doubleday, 1998.

Jillson, Cal. *Pursuing the American Dream: Opportunity and Exclusion over Four Centuries.* Lawrence: Univ. Press of Kansas, 2004.

Johnson, Charles S. *Patterns of Negro Segregation.* New York: Harper and Brothers, 1943.

Klineberg, Otto. *Characteristics of the American Negro.* New York: Harper and Brothers, 1944.

Kunstler, James. *The Geography of Nowhere: The Rise and Decline of America's Man-Made Landscape.* New York: Simon and Schuster, 1993.

———. *Home from Nowhere: Remaking Our Everyday World for the 21st Century.* New York: Simon and Schuster, 1996.

Kuralt, Charles. *On the Road with Charles Kuralt.* New York: Putnam, 1985.

La Farge, John. *The Race Question and the Negro: A Study of the Catholic Doctrine on Interracial Justice.* New York: Longmans, Green, 1943.

Lasch, Christopher. *The Culture of Narcissism: American Life in an Age of Diminishing Expectations.* New York: W. W. Norton, 1978.

Lavery, David, ed. *This Thing of Ours: Investigating "The Sopranos."* New York: Columbia Univ. Press, 2002.

Livesay, Harold. *American Made: Men Who Shaped the American Economy.* Boston: Little, Brown, 1979.

London, Herbert I., and Albert L. Weeks. *Myths That Rule America.* Washington, DC: Univ. Press of America, 1981.

Luttwak, Edmund N. *The Endangered American Dream: How to Stop the United States from Becoming a Third World Country and How to Win the Geo-economic Struggle for Industrial Supremacy.* New York: Simon and Schuster, 1993.

MacCleod, Celeste. *Horatio Alger, Farewell: The End of the American Dream.* New York: Seaview Books, 1980.

Mailer, Norman. *An American Dream.* New York: Dial Press, 1965.

McMakin, Jacqueline, and Sonya Dyer. *Working from the Heart: A Guide to Cultivating the Soul at Work.* New York: HarperCollins, 1994.

Morgan, James. *The Distance to the Moon: A Road Trip into the American Dream.* New York: Riverhead, 1999.

Munnell, Alicia H., and Annika Sunden. *Coming Up Short: The Challenge of 401(k) Plans.* Washington, DC: Brookings Institution Press, 2004.

Myers, David G. *The American Paradox: Spiritual Hunger in an Age of Plenty.* New Haven: Yale Univ. Press, 2000.

Myrdal, Gunnar. *An American Dilemma: The Negro Problem and Modern Democracy.* New York: Harper and Brothers, 1944.

Newman, Katherine. *Declining Fortunes: The Withering of the American Dream.* New York: Basic Books, 1993.

Obama, Barack. *The Audacity of Hope: Thoughts on Reclaiming the American Dream.* New York: Crown, 2006.

O'Connor, John E., and Martin A. Jackson, eds. *American History/American Film: Interpreting the Hollywood Image.* New York: Continuum, 1988.

Odum, Howard W. *Race and Rumors of Race.* Chapel Hill: Univ. of North Carolina Press, 1943.

Ottley, Roi. *New World a-Coming: Inside Black America.* New York: Houghton Mifflin, 1943.

Packard, Vance. *The Status Seekers.* New York: David McKay, 1959.

Peattie, Louise Redfield. *American Acres: The Story of Amie Honeywell.* New York: Dell, 1936.

Perrucci, Robert, and Earl Wysong. *The New Class Society: Goodbye American Dream?* Lanham, MD: Rowman and Littlefield, 1999.

Peterson, Wallace C. *Silent Depression: The Fate of the American Dream.* New York: W. W. Norton, 1994.

Pickens, T. Boone. *The First Billion Is the Hardest: Reflections on a Life of Comebacks and America's Energy Future.* New York: Crown Business, 2008.

Rather, Dan. *The American Dream: Stories from the Heart of Our Nation.* New York: William Morrow, 2001.

Reich, Charles A. *The Greening of America: How the Youth Revolution Is Trying to Make America Livable.* New York: Random House, 1970.

Riesman, David. *The Lonely Crowd.* New Haven: Yale Univ. Press, 1950.

Rifkin, Jeremy. *The European Dream: How Europe's Vision of the Future Is Quietly Eclipsing the American Dream.* New York: Tarcher, 2004.

Rivlin, Alice M. *Reviving the American Dream: The Economy, the States, and the Federal Government.* Washington, DC: Brookings Institution Press, 1994.

Roueche, Berton. *The Delectable Mountains and Other Narratives.* Boston: Little, Brown, 1959.

Samuelson, Robert J. *The Good Life and Its Discontents: The American Dream in the Age of Entitlement, 1945–95.* New York: Random House, 1995.

Schroeder, Alice. *The Snowball: Warren Buffett and the Business of Life.* New York: Bantam, 2008.

Simon, David R., with Tamar Love. *Tony Soprano's America: The Criminal Side of the American Dream.* Boulder, CO: Westview Press, 2002.

Sklar, Robert. *Movie-Made America: A Cultural History of the American Movies.* New York: Vintage Books, 1994.

Smart, Charles Allen. *Wild Geese and How to Chase Them.* New York: Random House, 1941.

Smyth, Nathan Ayer. *Lest Freedom Fail.* New York: Dodd Mead, 1940.

Stearn, Gerald Emanuel, comp. *Broken Image: Foreign Critiques of America.* New York: Random House, 1972.

Sterner, Richard. *The Negro's Share: A Study of Income, Consumption, Housing, and Public Assistance.* New York: Harper and Brothers, 1943.

Stiles, Paul. *Is the American Dream Killing You? How the "Market" Rules Our Lives.* New York: Harper Collins, 2005.

Tebbel, John. *From Rags to Riches: Horatio Alger Jr. and the American Dream.* New York: Macmillan, 1963.

Terkel, Studs. *American Dreams: Lost and Found.* New York: Pantheon, 1981.

———. *The Great Divide: Second Thoughts on the American Dream.* New York: Pantheon, 1988.

Thompson, Hunter S. *Fear and Loathing in Las Vegas: A Savage Journey to the Heart of the American Dream.* New York: Random House, 1972.

Trump, Donald. *The America We Deserve.* New York: Renaissance Books, 2000.

Turner, Ted. *Call Me Ted.* New York: Grand Central, 2008.

Tyler, Gus. *Scarcity: A Critique of the American Economy.* New York: Quadrangle/New York Times Book Company, 1976.

Watts, Steven. *Mr. Playboy: Hugh Hefner and the American Dream.* Hoboken, NJ: Wiley, 2008.

Whyte, William H. *The Organization Man.* New York: Simon and Schuster, 1956.

Wynter, Leon E. *American Skin: Pop Culture, Big Business, and the End of White America.* New York: Crown, 2002.

Yeager, Robert C. *Losing It: The Economic Fall of the Middle Class.* New York: McGraw-Hill, 1980.

Zogby, John. *The Way We'll Be: The Zogby Report on the Transformation of the American Dream.* New York: Random House, 2008.

Index

Adamic, Louis, 29–30
Adams, James Truslow: on American
 Dream as unifying force, 31–32; *The*
 American: The Making of a New
 Man, 35; on "better, deeper, richer
 life," 25, 42; as coiner of "American
 dream," 3, 167; concept of American
 Dream, 13–17; and "epic of Amer-
 ica," 195; as influenced by Adam
 Smith, 52; on "opportunity for each
 according to ability or achievement,"
 198; original vision of American
 Dream, 43, 85, 106, 125–26, 130,
 134, 163; on "rugged individualism,"
 19–20
Affirmative action, 85–86
Albee, Edward, 61
Alger, Horatio: attributes of hard work
 and business-building, 168; "epoch,"
 44; "feeling about the American
 Dream," 37; versus Allen Ginsberg,
 79; and Hefner, 190; Horatio Alger
 Award, 149–50; as iconic individual-
 ist, 127; Celeste MacCleod on, 106;
 "rags to riches" story, 58; as spokesperson for American Dream, 4;
 squandering of fortune, 65–66; and
 Thompson, 83; "vulgarity" of, 93
"Allentown," 108
All in the Family, 101

"American Century," 74, 189
American Dilemma, An, 38, 46
American Dream: and advertising,
 8, 84, 120, 125, 197; and African
 Americans, 37–38, 47, 49–50, 74–75,
 76–77, 91, 99, 115–16, 118–19, 159,
 175–76; and art, 25; and automobile,
 153–54; and communism, 8, 43,
 50–51, 52, 82, 123, 141; and conservatism, 75, 77–78, 126, 142–44; and
 creativity, 172–73, 202; and education, 5, 14, 51, 67–68, 98, 100, 120–
 21, 132, 135, 145, 149, 169, 187–88;
 and entrepreneurialism, 3, 5, 26,
 39–40, 65, 66, 86–88, 117, 119–20,
 125, 147, 164; and equal opportunity,
 3, 6, 34, 37, 47–48, 58, 85–86, 92,
 100, 127, 130, 166, 187, 188; and
 free enterprise, 8, 22, 52, 66–67, 81,
 83, 87, 93, 143, 150, 185, 188; and
 "the good life," 1, 17, 56–57, 63, 74,
 79, 156–57, 158, 169, 182, 183, 189,
 190, 192–93; and home ownership, 6,
 26, 40–41, 56–57, 83–84, 94–96, 98,
 99, 101, 103, 110, 111–16, 132, 134,
 145–47, 153, 168, 169, 184, 191–92,
 195; and Irish Americans, 153,
 185–86; and Japanese Americans, 38,
 119; and Jewish Americans, 29, 32,
 47–48, 119, 121, 153; and keeping up

235